Juan Facundo Riaño

The industrial arts in Spain

Juan Facundo Riaño

The industrial arts in Spain

ISBN/EAN: 9783337229030

Printed in Europe, USA, Canada, Australia, Japan

Cover: Foto ©Thomas Meinert / pixelio.de

More available books at **www.hansebooks.com**

SOUTH KENSINGTON MUSEUM ART HANDBOOKS.

SPANISH INDUSTRIAL ARTS.

This Volume, forming one of the Series of Art Handbooks issued under the authority of the Lords of the Committee of Council on Education, has been prepared by SEÑOR JUAN F. RIAÑO, *of Madrid, whose Catalogue of Art Objects of Spanish production in the South Kensington Museum, issued in* 1872, *has proved of great value and interest.*

April, 1879.

THE INDUSTRIAL ARTS
IN SPAIN.

BY

JUAN F. RIAÑO.

WITH NUMEROUS WOODCUTS.

Published for the Committee of Council on Education,

BY

CHAPMAN AND HALL, LIMITED,
LONDON.
1890.

RICHARD CLAY AND SONS, LIMITED,
LONDON AND BUNGAY.

CONTENTS.

ILLUSTRATIONS.

The Department of Science and Art is indebted to MR. JOHN MURRAY *for the use of the Woodcuts Nos. 19, 20, 30, and 31. No. 50 is from a Spanish Woodcut.*

SPANISH INDUSTRIAL ART.

GOLD AND SILVER WORK.

THE Greek and Latin authors who have described the Spanish Peninsula, state that the quantity of gold and silver ore found there was very great, and that hence the district became an important centre of commercial activity of Phœnicians, Carthaginians, Greeks, and Romans. Some authors have gone so far as to assert that the Phœnicians made the anchors of their ships of gold and silver, and that the Carthaginians were astonished to find in Andalusia, that the mangers and vases for holding wine and oil were made of the same materials. These references have been constantly mentioned in ancient Spanish authors. Ambrosio de Morales, in his "Antiguedades de España," Alcala 1577, enters into every detail on this subject.

I have seen a specimen of this period, a bowl of an earlier and different style to Roman silversmiths' work, which belongs to a collector in the province of Cordova. This bowl is of a conical shape : it is perfectly plain, and has an inscription in Iberian characters engraved on one of its sides : there are signs outside and at the bottom which indicate that this bowl was made on the wheel. Velazquez in his "Ensayo sobre las letras desconocidas," Madrid, 1752, describes a silver bowl of a similar kind, which was found in Andalusia in 1618 full of Iberian coins : this bowl

B

weighed ten ounces. Several ornaments, chiefly consisting of necklaces and earrings, may be studied at the Academy of History, and private collections, in Madrid; they have been classified by antiquarians as belonging to this uncertain period, and are similar in style to others which have been frequently found in England and the north of Europe. The most interesting objects of this kind which I have seen in Spain, are gold ornaments proceeding from Galicia; they were found there by Sr. Villaamil, who gave a description of them in the "Museo Español de Antiguedades," vol. iii. p. 545.

The information and remains which have reached us illustrating silver and gold work of the Roman domination are more important; we find, however, in this and similar artistic industries that, as a general rule, the Romans imposed their style and system on the inhabitants of the countries which they conquered, and it is not easy to point out any one example which can be given as an exception to this general rule. It is, undoubtedly, a fact that objects of all kinds in gold and silver were used in Spain to a very great extent—for, notwithstanding the destruction of ages, we still possess inscriptions which allude to silver statues, and a large number of objects in the precious metals exist in museums and private collections. See "Inscrip. Hisp. lat.," by Dr. Emile Hübner, Berlin, 1869. Of these it will be sufficient to mention one of the most important. It is known in the province of Santander by the name of the dish of Otañez; and belongs to a gentleman who lives in that locality. It was found at Otañez at the end of the last century, buried in a stone quarry. This dish is made of silver, it weighs thirty-three ounces, and is covered with an ornamentation of figures in relief, some of which are gilt, representing an allegorical subject of the source of medicinal waters. In the upper part is a nymph who pours water from an urn over rocks; a youth collects it in a vessel; another gives a cup of it to a sick man; another fills with it a barrel which is placed in a four-wheeled car to which are yoked two mules. On each side of the fountain are altars on which sacrifices and libations are offered. Round it is the inscription : SALVS. VMERITANA, and at the back is engraved, in confused characters, the words : L. P. CORNELIANI. PIII. . . . .

Another very interesting silver dish may be seen at the Academia de la Historia, Madrid. Although not of Spanish manufacture, it deserves special notice in a description of works of this style. This dish was found in 1847, buried in a field at Almendralejo, province of Estremadura : it is 28⅝ English inches in diameter, and weighs 533 ounces. It is ornamented with fine figures in relief, representing the Emperor Theodosius appointing a magistrate. The emperor is seated on his throne in the centre, at the sides are his sons Arcadius and Honorius, with four soldiers of the guard, and the magistrate, who receives the volume. In the lower part there is an allegorical representation of a nymph holding the horn of abundance, winged angels, and ears of wheat, probably alluding to the abundance and plenty of the empire. Round the rim is the following inscription :—

D. N. THEODOSIVS PERPET.
AVG OB DIEM FELI CISSIMVM.

At the back, in points, are the following Greek words.

ΠΟC ΤΝ ΜΕΤ.

We can form a very good idea of the jewel work of the Visigothic period from the discovery of the treasure of Guarrazar. These jewels were found in 1858 at the village of this name, six miles from Toledo, on the spot where, in the Visigothic period, a Christian sanctuary had existed. The objects found, which may be seen at the Museum of Cluny, Paris, and Armeria Real, Madrid, constitute the most important collection in Europe of the jewel work of that period. No less than eleven votive crowns, some of extraordinary magnificence; two crosses with inscriptions, and a large number of fragments of all kinds, of gold and precious stones, were found at Guarrazar. Unfortunately a great part of the treasure has been lost, for the labourers, who were the first to find it, sold several objects to the silversmiths at Toledo, who melted and destroyed specimens of the highest artistic interest. Those that remain in Spain are—

At the Royal Armoury of Madrid : A gold crown of Swinthila in'aid with precious stones, with pendent cross, and inscriptions of letters hanging from it : SVINTHILANVS REX . OFFERET. See woodcut on p. 7. A similar crown of Theodosius, with the inscription: OFFERET MVNVSCVLVM . SCO STEFANO ETHODOSIVS . ABBA. The cross of Lucetius with the following inscription : + IN NOMINE DNI. IN NOMINE SCI OFFERET LVCETIVS : E. Fragments of another crown and of large crosses : several stones and fragments, and an emerald, on which is engraved *en creux* the Annunciation of the Virgin.

At the Archæological Museum, and in several private collections in Spain, may be seen a large number of stones and pearls which were found at Guarrazar.

Among the objects at the Archæological Museum at Madrid, a small section, which proceed from a different locality, have also been classified as Visigothic. They consist of necklaces, earrings, and rings, and are less important in workmanship than those found at Guarrazar. The student will find further details in "Museo Español de Antiguedades," vol. vi., p. 137.

The objects forming part of the treasure of Guarrazar now in the Museum of Cluny, Paris are : Crown of Recesvinthus, with pendent cross and inscription : + RECESVINTHVS REX OFFERET. A similar crown, without inscription. Four crowns formed to imitate basket work, with crosses hanging from the centres. Three crowns, the rims of which are formed of *repoussé* work, only one of which is ornamented with precious stones, and without pendent crosses. The cross of Sonnicus with the follow ing inscription : ✠ IN DI NOMINE OFFERET SONNICA SCE MARIE IN SORBACES.

Swinthila reigned from 624 to 631, A.D. ; Recesvinthus from 650 to 672 A.D. ; hence these crowns belong to the 7th century, and the remaining objects are certainly of the same period.

Much has been written on these Visigothic jewels by French and Spanish authors, the most interesting and valuable studies are :—" Descrip. du Trésor de Guarrazar, par M. Lasteyrie. Paris, 1860." " El arte Latino Bizantino en España y las Coronas de Guarrazar," by Señor Rios, Madrid, 1861. Consult also his article in "Monumentos Arq. de España." "Coronas de Guarrazar que se conservan en la Armeria Real de Madrid," by Señor Rada. Museo Español, vol. iii. Madrid, 1874.

The importance of this goldsmith's work has led these authors to discuss several archæological and artistic points which deserve attention. I will also give my opinions on this subject, which in some respects differ from those hitherto advanced. In the Middle Ages the name of crown was equally applied to those worn on the head, to the votive crowns hung before altars, and to the pendent lamps which were also of this circular form. The "Etimologies" of San Isidoro help us, unfortunately, but little on this subject ; but Du Cange, in his "Glossarium Mediæ et infimæ Latinitatis" gives us sufficient details to understand the differences between them. I refer the student to two works on this subject, which treat especially of crowns of light, which none of the authors who have written on Guarrazar have consulted : "Tratado de la Sagrada Luminaria," by Gonzalez Villar, Madrid, 1798. "De Lucernis Pensilibus," by Fanceulli, Maceratae, 1802.

The crowns found at Guarrazar were undoubtedly votive offerings, for they all have chains by which they were suspended in the sanctuary in which they were found. Their size and the structure of their rims lead us to suppose that they may have been worn on the head. The same observation applies to a similar crown at the Cluny Museum; if so, the chains, cross, and pendent letters were added when the crown was offered to the sanctuary.

Although details which appear in the handwork of these jewels betray a certain rudeness, not uncommon in the time they were made, their beauty and richness are truly surprising. These crowns are decorated round their rims with rosettes of pearls and sapphires, and a delicate ornamentation of *cloisonné* work, which encloses a substance resembling red glass. From the upper part are attached four chains formed of leaves *percées à jour*, these are united to a double gold rosette with pendent sapphires, in the centre of which is set a piece of rock crystal. In the cross of Recesvinthus the pendant is in the form of a capital, and from it hangs a small cross of the same style of work: from the lower rim of the crown are suspended the letters, which are ornamented with the same vitreous paste, *cloisonné*, and from each hang large single pearls and sapphires.

The border of some of these crowns is formed of a net-work of small gold massive balustrades, having between them square spaces in which pearls and sapphires are set. Others are made simply of *repoussé* gold, their chief interest consisting in the ornamentation which has been so artistically carried out. Some of them have inscriptions and a few stones set at intervals. The pendants from these crowns are inferior in richness to the others already described. The pendent crosses are ornamented in the same style, either with *cloisonné* work or *repoussé* inscriptions.

One of the most interesting results produced by the study of the treasure of Guarrazar has been to show us the immense luxury which it represents, if we remember the period of decay and poverty of the Visigothic monarchy. We find this magnificence frequently alluded to by ancient writers. The Arabs when they took possession of Toledo in the 8th century, mention in different works the immense quantity of jewels of all kinds

VOTIVE CROWN OF KING SWINTHILA, MADRID.

which they found and carried away. The gold and silversmith's work of this period was everywhere in a very high state of development. We find it constantly alluded to in the works of Paul Silentiarium and other writers of the time of Justinian, and in the inventories and references given by Du Sommerard of the jewel work anterior to the Carlovingian period in Italy and France. The Visigothic kings, who copied from the Eastern emperors even their legal forms, followed this rule to a great extent in everything which bore relation to their daily life.

The most important question is to determine the origin and locality where these jewels were made. M. de Lasteyrie considers that jewellery ornamented with red glass *cloisonné* work was only made by nations of the Germanic race. To prove this he presents, among other arguments, the comparison of a fragment of the ornamentation which appears on the crown of Recesvinthus, with a similar one on the Evangelistiarium of Theodolinda in the treasure of Monza, which he considers to be of German workmanship. These theories are untenable. Sr. Rios is of a different opinion, and considers these jewels to have been made in Spain, owing to the similarity of ornamentation with different specimens which occur in Spain in architectural remains of the Roman and Visigothic periods.

Both these writers give in my opinion the decorative elements of the crowns of Guarrazar an importance which they do not possess. The ornamentation which most frequently occurs consists of a combination of circles, imbrication, and palms of such an elementary kind that it would be difficult to ascertain its origin; it appears equally in mosaic work of the later Roman period, in vases and other objects of the best times of Greek art, and in Asiatic and archaic works. It may be affirmed that the ornamentation of the goldsmith's work of the north and south of Europe are derived from a common origin; from the oriental civilization which in the first centuries of the Middle Ages penetrated into Europe; it may also be affirmed that its manufacture and technical proceedings are precisely similar. Later on, the ornamentation and manufacture of these jewels received from the western nations some slight modifications; but this artistic industry by no means proceeded from them.

One example will be enough to prove this. Setting apart the famous *cloisonné pectorale* at the Boulac Museum, Cairo, and other jewels of the queen, Aah-Hotep, 17th century B.C.; the hawk of a similar period, Louvre Museum (Paris), and a number of analogous objects in the British Museum, we have enough specimens of this kind to show that *cloisonné* work was known in the east from the very earliest period. I will draw especial attention to the *plaque* in the Museum of Wiesbaden, found at Wolfsheim in 1870. It is formed of gold, with a circular and triangular ornamentation and squares, *découpés à jour*, set with jacinths, or red glass paste. At the back may be read an inscription in Persian characters, which gives the name of a Sassanide king, Artachshaber, of the 3rd century of our era. (See A. von Cohausen, "Roemischer Schmelzenschmuck," Wiesbaden, 1873). I know no more ancient specimen in the north of Europe of these jewels with coloured stones, nor can I give a better example of their oriental origin. Those who may wish to make a more profound study on this subject, can also examine the interesting jewels with stones found at Petrossa, Wallachia, in 1835, now in the Museum of Bucharest. They are attributed to the Visigothic King Athanaric, who lived towards the middle of the 4th century of our era, and are considered in the present day of undoubted Sassanide origin.

The artistic and technical origin of the jewels of Guarrazar must be looked for in the East; their manufacture was most probably Spanish. On part of these jewels, inscriptions of the names of the *donatarios* appear, and it is highly improbable that they were made in another country. We cannot imagine the extraordinary magnificence of the Visigothic court, so similar to that of Constantinople and other contemporary ones, without the presence at each of a group of artists whose task was to satisfy these demands.

The Visigothic style continued to be followed in Spain at the court of the Christian kings, until the 11th century, notwithstanding the Moorish invasion, and the poverty of the kingdom. The specimens at the treasury of the cathedral of Oviedo, and others which will be described farther on, will give a good idea of the manufacture of jewels of this period. Among the relics which are kept in the shrine called the *Camara Santa*, at Oviedo, are two most interesting gold processional crosses studded with stones, which are known by the names of *Cruz de los Angeles*, and *Cruz de la Victoria* or *de Pelayo*. The *Cruz de los Angeles* is 16½ inches high, by 16 inches wide, it is covered at the back with an ornamentation in fine filigree work, set with different stones. In the front are five medallions, and an inscription in the vacant spaces. Among the gems there is a good cameo, and seven engraved stones in the Gnostic style. (Consult "Monumentos Arquitectonicos de España, Camara Santa "). The inscription on this cross shows us that it was made, A.D. 808.

> " Susceptum placide maneat hoc in honore Dei
> Offeret Adefonsus humilis servus Xpi
> Hoc signo tuetur pius
> Hoc signo vincitur inimicus
> Quisquis auferre presumpserit mihi
> Fulmine divino intereat ipse
> Nisi libens ubi voluntas dederit mea
> Hoc opus perfectum est iu Era DCCCXLVI.'

The cross of Victory is supposed to have been the same wooden one borne by Don Pelayo when he began, early in the 8th century, his struggles against the Mahomedan invasion, it was decorated in the next century with gold platings and precious stones. It is 36 inches high by 28½ inches wide ; the ornamentation is similar to the former one, and in the vacant spaces at the back appears the following inscription, by which we learn it was made at the Castle of Gauzon, Asturias, A.D. 828.

> " Susceptum placide maneat hoc in honore Dei, quod offerent
> Famuli Christi Adefonsus princeps et Scemæna Regina
> Quisquis auferre hoc donoria nostra presumpserit
> Fulmine divino intereat ipse
> Hoc opus perfectum et concessum est
> Santo Salvatori Oventense sedis
> Hoc signo tuetur pius, hoc vincitur inimicus
> Et opera us est in castello Gauzon anno regni nostri.
> XLII. discurrente Era DCCCLXVI."

Another most interesting object at this shrine is Don Fruela's casket, which is ornamented with agates set in gold, and is similar in style. The inscription, which appears outside, gives the date A.D. 910.

> " Operatum est Era DCCCCXLVIII."

A diptych which belongs to the same shrine may also be mentioned. It was given by Bishop Don Gonzalo, who was bishop of Oviedo from A.D. 1162 to 1175. Round it are the words— *Gundisalvus Episcopus me jussit fieri.* This diptych is 5 inches long by 7 wide: it is ornamented with ivory figures, stones, crystals and engraved gems. Although I do not consider it to be of Spanish workmanship, it is necessary to mention the splendid *Arca Santa,* in which it is believed many of the relics were taken to Oviedo. It is covered with silver plates, with *repoussé* and chiselled work representing different religious subjects : the Crucifixion, Our Lord surrounded by the attributes of the Evangelists, saints, apostles, angels, and a fine ornamental border with letters, imitating Cufic inscriptions. This splendid casket is 3 feet 9½ inches long, by 3 and 3½ wide, and 28½ inches high, and appears to have been made between the 10th and 12th centuries. The figures are similar in style to the paintings and sculpture of this period, and it is highly probable that it may have been the work of Italian artists. The Cufic inscription is illegible, and is interrupted in the angles by the symbols of the

Evangelists.   This style of simulated inscriptions was frequently
used by Italian artists.

A cross of the same style as those already described exists at
the cathedral of Santiago.   It is made of wood covered with
gold platings and precious stones ; some of these are old intagli,
which are set in delicate filigree work.   Round it runs a long
inscription, from which it appears that it was a present from
Adefonsus Princeps cum conjuge Scemena Regina, and that it was
made in Era DCCCCA.   Duodecima ; A.D. 874.   The number of
gems which have reached us, after so many centuries of ruin, the
similarity of the different specimens, and the statement which
appears on the cross of King Pelayo, that it was made at the
castle of Gauzon, prove that the goldsmith's industry had attained
great importance in Spain during this period.

By studying the different objects of silver and gold work which
still exist in Spanish churches, we can form a good idea of the
historical progress of this industry in the following centuries of
the Middle Ages ; but before we do so, it is well to make some
observations upon objects of *orfevrerie*, the work of the Moors.
There is a constant connection between these objects and those
made of ivory : the same characteristics exist which I shall here-
after point out as appearing in Moorish ivory carvings.   The art
of ivory carving was imported from the East, the subjects are
much alike in ivory and metal when men and animals are represented, and the inscriptions and bands of ornamentation are
similar in style.   The main variations consist in the different
systems employed in metal work, by which the work differs according to the proceedings adopted of *repoussé* or chiselling, filigree,
niellos or enamels.

A fine Casket belongs to this kind of oriental work which still
may be seen on the high altar of the cathedral of Gerona, Spain.
This casket is 15 inches long by 9 wide and 10½ high.   It is
made in the usual manner of wood covered with silver gilt
platings with a heavy *repoussé* ornamentation of leaves enclosed

within circles of pearls. Round the rim of the cover runs the
following Cufic inscription :

بـم الله بركة من الله وبمن وسعادة وسرور دايم لعبـد الله الحكم امير المومنين
المستنصر بالله مما امر بعمله لابى الوليد هشام ولى عهد المسلمين تم على يدى
خوذن بن بثله

" In the name of God. The blessing of God and happiness and
prosperity and permanent joy for the servant of God, Alhakem
Emir Amumenin Almostanser Billah, because he ordered this
casket to be made for Abdul walid Hischem, heir to the throne
of the Muslims. It was finished by the hands of Hudzen Ibn
Bothla."

Alhakem reigned in Spain from A.D. 961 to 976, in which year
he was succeeded by his son Hischem II. This casket belongs,
therefore, to this period, and is especially interesting as giving the
artist's name. Two other silver Arabian caskets may be seen at
the Archæological Museum, Madrid, which were formerly at the
shrine of San Isidoro of Leon, but they possess less artistic
interest than the casket at Gerona. One of these is elliptical in
form ; it is ornamented with a good design of leaves and tendrils,
and Cufic inscription ; the whole of the casket is enamelled in
black. The ornamentation belongs to the 12th century. The
inscription only mentions the owner's name, Abdo Shakir. The
other casket is silver-gilt, square in form, and rather poorly ornamented. The two Cufic inscriptions which surround it are
laudatory. At the cathedral of Oviedo there is another silver
casket with a laudatory inscription and medallions with figures,
in which from very early times, the remains of Sᵗᵃ· Eulalia have
been kept. I suspect that this casket and the former one are not
of Spanish Arab workmanship, for besides the circumstance that
their inscriptions can be applied to any owner, their ornamentation is unlike others of the same kind. In the first casket it is
insignificant, but on the shrine of Sᵗᵃ Eulalia the background of

the medallions is covered with an imbricated pattern which I have never seen repeated on any Arab or Moorish example in Spain. It is highly probable that they were productions of Oriental industry and were imported commercially.

Several specimens of the 14th and 15th centuries, the last period of the Moorish domination, exist in Spain. They consist of jewels and sword handles. The most interesting trinkets are a bracelet and fragments of a necklace and earrings which are at the Archæological Museum, Madrid. They are made of gold, covered with a geometrical *repoussé* ornamentation, and a delicate filigree pattern. There are specimens also at the Kensington Museum, Nos. 1455 to 1447, 70, consisting of a bracelet, silver-gilt, formed of seven alternate oval and rectangular plaques, with impressed pattern and applied filigree and bossed ornament, and earrings made of gold, formed of clusters of united circles and lozenges with filigree bosses. Other jewels of less importance are known to exist, consisting of bracelets, amulets, earrings, and rings, mostly made of silver niello-work, these are ornamented with geometrical patterns and inscriptions of little importance.

Moorish arms are most artistic; they are fully described in the article Arms. The most important specimens are in the Royal Armoury, and noble house of Villaseca, Madrid; another fine example of a similar style is at the Generalife of Granada. The hilt and settings of the sheath are of solid silver, gilt, and covered with geometrical patterns ornamented in high relief, parts of which are filled with translucid *cloisonné* enamel. In some instances the hilt is made of ivory. It is impossible (see plate on p. 85) to find anything more beautiful than the ornamentation of these swords, or greater perfection in every detail. It is evident, therefore, that this industry had reached a very high grade of perfection at Granada in the second part of the 15th century. The sword now in the possession of the Villaseca family belonged to Boabdil, the last Moorish king; the one at Granada to one of Boabdil's nearest relations.

In continuing our description of Christian silver-work in the 11th and 12th centuries, we meet with two historical chalices of the highest interest. One was made by the order of Saint Domingo de Silos [A.D. 1045–1074] when abbot of this church. This chalice still exists there, with the following inscription :—

In nomine Domini ob honorem Sci Sebastiani Dominico abbas fecit.

It is ornamented with fine filigree work, forming zones and horse-shoe arches, in a similar style to that of the silversmiths' work of Asturias, which has never been completely abandoned in Spain. The author of the life of this saint, Fr. Juan de Castro, Madrid 1688, says, p. 297, that he does not consider it was ever used for the sacrifice of the mass, owing to its great height [13 inches]. The other chalice might have been seen until very lately at San Isidoro, Leon ; it has been temporarily concealed owing to political disturbances. The cup and foot are of agate, probably specimens of the classic period ; the mounting, which dates from the time of D^{na}. Urraca, is studded with a profusion of precious stones and pastes. Some of the gems of the chalice and paten are antiques.[*] In the centre of the paten is set a splendid flat onyx. Round the lower part runs the following inscription :—

+ *In nomine Dñi Urraca Frediñadi.*

Dona Urraca, who was a sister of Alfonso VI., and was gene-rally called *Urraca Fernandez*, bestowed many important gifts on the church of San Isidoro. She died A.D. 1101. Another interest-ing chalice of the same period, although not of the same importance as those just named, belongs to Cardinal Moreno, archbishop of Toledo. Round the stem are represented the emblems of the Evangelists, and the inscription : *Pelagius abbas me fecit ;* this

[*] For further details of this interesting work of art, see " Monumentos Arquitectonicos de España," in which a good reproduction is given.

formula appears so frequently that it must be understood in the sense of *fecit fieri*, ordered to be made.

The Santo Caliz at Valencia has been traditionally held as the cup used by Our Saviour at the Last Supper. This chalice consists of a circular cup hollowed out from a fine brown sardonyx which is tastefully moulded round the lip. The base is formed of another inverted sardonyx. These are united by straps of pure gold. The stem is flanked by handles, which are inlaid with delicate arabesque in black enamel. Oriental pearls are set round the base and stem, which alternate with rubies, sapphires and emeralds. This chalice is a work of the Roman imperial epoch, and the mounts are of a later date. Other specimens of jewellers' work of the Roman period might be mentioned which exist in Spain, but I do not find sufficient evidence to justify the opinion that they were made in that country. I consider those that I have described to be of Spanish origin, for they keep to the same technical modes of workmanship as the jewel work of Asturias, and the inscriptions which appear on them refer to historical personages. It would be difficult, considering all things, to suppose they were imported.

We can mention in the thirteenth century a specimen of Spanish silversmiths' work which illustrates the transition to the new style, and the progress in the design of the figures owing to the Italian Renaissance—I refer to the interesting triptych at the Cathedral of Seville, known as the "Tablas Alfonsinas," made by the order of Don Alfonso el Sabio for holding relics. It is of wood, covered inside and out with silver-gilt plates; it is 22 inches high by 39 wide when its three leaves are open (the woodcut opposite represents the outside of left leaf), and is divided inside into fifteen compartments full of minute ornamentation, among which are set a large number of capsules covered with rock crystal containing relics, each one with an inscription of enamelled gold, *cloisonné.* Several good cameos with sacred subjects appear near the edge of the side leaves. The outside of this triptych is deco-

ONE LEAF OF TRIPTYCH IN CATHEDRAL OF SEVILLE.

rated with twelve medallions containing the arms of Castile and
Aragon, and forty-eight others in which are repeated alternately the

c

subjects of the Adoration of the Magi and Annunciation of the Virgin, which are also *repoussé.* In the centres are eagles, which S^r. Rios supposes to allude to Don Alonso's claim to be crowned Emperor, in which case it was made in the year 1274. (See Mus. esp. de Antig., vol. ii. p. 83.) The ornamentation which surrounds the panels belongs to the 16th century. S^r. Rios suggests that the possible or probable author of this interesting object of silversmith work was Maestro Jorge, a silversmith of Toledo, who is praised by Don Alonso in his Cantigas—he also mentions the names of Don Lorenzo and Don Niculas as silver-smiths of Seville who worked in this period.

The most important example of Spanish silversmith's work of the 14th century is the Retablo and Baldaquino of the cathedral of Gerona. Mr. Street, in his Gothic Arch. in Spain, p. 326, describes this work of art in the following manner: " The Retablo is of wood entirely covered with silver plates, and divided vertically into three series of niches and canopies : each division has a subject, and a good deal of enamelling is introduced in various parts of the canopies and grounds of the panels. Each panel has a cinque-foiled arch with a crocketed gablet and pinnacles on either side. The straight line of the top is broken by three niches, which rise in the centre and at either end. In the centre is the Blessed Virgin with our Lord ; on the right San Narcisso ; and on the left St. Filia. The three tiers of subjects contain figures of saints, subjects from the life of the Blessed Virgin, and subjects from the life of our Lord."

At the base of this Retablo may be read the words—*Pere Bernec me feu*—Peter Bernec made me. Bernec was a silver-smith of Valencia, and in another document he was called Barners. It has been supposed that two other contemporary silversmiths, whose names appear in papers of the cathedral, worked also at the Retablo. Their names were Raimundo Andreu, and Master Bartolomé. Formerly in front of this altar there was a magnificent silver and gold frontal studded with stones, a fine work of the 11th century—which was unfortunately carried off by the French in their invasion of the Peninsula early in the present century, and was probably with other innumerable priceless treasures melted by them. See further details in " Viage Literario de Villanueva," vol. xii. p. 180.

In the Sala Capitular of the Cathedral of Gerona there are three splendid processional crosses belonging to the 15th and 16th centuries; one of them is of enamelled gold, and is undoubtedly one of the most artistic works of the kind in Spain.

Among Spanish art treasures of the 15th century of a historical style must be mentioned the splendid silver throne of king Don Martin de Aragon, d. 1410, still existing in the cathedral of Barcelona; it is covered with chiselled ornamentation, and a band of velvet embroidered with gold and completely studded with precious stones. This throne is carried in the procession of Corpus Christi. The monstrance, a splendid work of art in the Gothic style, ornamented with delicate pinnacles and jewel work, is placed on a fine silver foot and carried on this day in front of this throne. This monstrance is covered also with jewels of great value which almost conceal it, the gifts of royal personages. The fine Gothic silver-gilt cross must also be mentioned, known at Toledo by the name of *Guion de Mendoza ;* it was borne before the great Cardinal Mendoza, and was the first cross placed on the highest point of the Alhambra Torre de la Vela on the day of the conquest, 2nd January, 1492.

The following woodcut represents a processional cross of Spanish work of the beginning of the 15th century, in the South Kensington Museum, No. 514-'73. It is of wood covered with plates of silver-gilt *repoussé* work. On one side is a rood with the Virgin and St. John. Over the figure of Christ is the word Inri. At the extremities angels in high relief bear the emblems of the Passion. On each side of the figure of Christ are plaques of translucent enamel representing the penitent and impenitent thief, at the foot of the cross the Resurrection and

SPANISH PROCESSIONAL CROSS.   SOUTH KENSINGTON MUSEUM.

Adoration of the Magi, and above the figure of Christ the Nativity.

At the back there is a figure in high relief of the Almighty; in the four extremities the emblems of the Evangelists in high relief and enamelled plaques representing the Annunciation, Flight into Egypt, Christ's descent into Hades.

This cross, which is three feet in height, is marked in several places with the name of

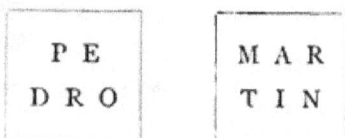

P E D R O	M A R T I N

A large number of images exist in Spain belonging to this period, and even to an earlier date, chiefly consisting of images of the Blessed Virgin ; their garments are formed of silver platings, chiselled and *repoussé* in the traditional Byzantine style. Among the most remarkable may be mentioned those preserved in the cathedrals of Seville, Pamplona and Astorga. The following document undoubtedly alludes to one of these figures. It is dated 12th May, 1367 :—

" I Sancho Martinez Orebse, silversmith, native of Seville, inform you, the dean and chapter of the church of Seville, that it was agreed I should make an image of Saint Mary with its tabernacle, that it should be finished at a given time, and that you were to give me the silver and stones required to make it."

Notwithstanding the poverty of the Spanish monarchs, their personal ornaments were rich and splendid. We find in " Memorials of Henry the VIIth," edited by Gairdner, an interesting description by Machado, the herald or king-of-arms of Henry VII., of the embassy sent to Spain in 1489, to ask for the hand of the Princess Catharine for the Prince of Wales. The account he gives us of the jewels worn by Queen Isabel la Catolica is most interesting. They varied at every interview.

In one of these she wore "a line of trimming composed of oblong bosses, of gold, each decorated with fine and valuable jewels, so rich that no one has ever seen the like. She wore round her waist a girdle of leather made in a man's style; the pouch was decorated with a large balass ruby, the size of a tennis ball, between five rich diamonds and other stones, the size of a bean. The rest of the girdle was decorated with other precious stones. Round her neck she wore a rich gold necklace composed of white and red roses, adorned with jewels. Two ribbons were suspended from her breast adorned with diamonds, balass and other rubies, pearls, and other jewels of great value to the number of a hundred or more" (p. 341.)

"After the King came the Queen, mounted on a fine mule, and all the harness of the said mule was adorned with pearls and other precious stones. She was dressed in a robe of a rich woven cloth of gold made in the fashion of the kingdom, and over that a mantilla all spangled with lozenges of crimson and black velvet, and on each lozenge was a large pearl. And with each of these pearls was a rich balass ruby the size of a beech nut, the richest thing that could be seen, no man ever saw anything equal to it. She had on her neck a large necklace, adorned with large diamonds, balass rubies, carbuncles, large pearls, and a great number of other rich precious stones. She had upon her head-dress two balass rubies as pendants, the size of a pigeon's egg, and at the end of the said rubies a large pearl, which jewel was supposed to be worth 12,000 crowns" (p. 348.)

In the specimens described belonging to the Visigothic period, and many others to which we might refer, we find constant similarity in form with silversmith's work of other European countries. It is true that we occasionally meet with Moorish *orfevrerie*, and some details, such as filigree work, due to oriental influence; but in general Byzantine, Roman, and Gothic styles were adopted and copied in Spain; and the technical details were the same with those followed in other countries, with the exception of *champlevé* enamel, which appears to have been almost exclusively used at Limoges in the middle ages. It is interesting, however, and worthy of remark, that important objects are also found in Spain decorated with *champlevé* enamel, such as the splendid altars of San Miguel in Excelsis (Navarre). and Santo Domingo de Silos (Rioja), and the image of the Virgin de la Vega at San Esteban (Salamanca), three specimens of the greatest importance.

In the Renaissance period, Spanish *orfevrerie* enters into its most brilliant epoch, not only on account of the beauty of the form of the objects produced, but also owing to its great rich-ness. Among objects of this period the most important are the *Custodias* or monstrances of the cathedrals; these are exclusively peculiar to Spanish art. The almost incalculable quantity of silver-work produced at this period is accounted for by the reconquest of the Peninsula from the Moors, the discovery and possession of America, and other circumstances which in-creased the power and wealth of Spain, and elevated the country to great importance.

We find frequent mention at this time of silversmiths, many of whom came from Germany, France, or Italy, attracted by the large number of works ordered. Many settled in Spain, such as Enrique de Arphe, Jacome Trezzo, Mateo Aleman, Hans Belta, and others. The Spaniards who joined them were greater in number, and not inferior in merit. Silversmiths were already at that time divided into different groups, according to the technical proceedings which each one adopted : *plateros de la plata*, workers in silver, was the name given to those who worked exclusively in *repoussé* and chiselled work, and imitated sculpture and architec-tural models; goldsmiths, those who worked jewels with stones, enamels, and niello-work. Even within these groups were workers in filigree, and those who decorated different objects with painted or mosaic work, *atauxia*, in the Moorish style. Almost all the most important Spanish towns were large centres of these industries. Leon, Burgos, Valladolid, Cuenca, Toledo, Cordova, and Seville rivalled each other in the number and quality of their productions The Venetian ambassador, Navagiero, who visited Valladolid in 1527, says, " Sono in Valladolid assai artefici di ogni sorte, e se vi lavora benissimo di tutti le arti, e sopra tutto d' argenti, e vi son tanti argenteri quanti non sono in due altri terre, le prime di Spagna " (" Il Viaggio di Spagna," Vinegia, 1563, p. 35.)

In order to complete the study of this subject, it is necessary, besides, to give some notice of the legal dispositions contained in the Municipal Ordinances and in other laws of a more general character.

In Capmany's " Memorias," vol. i., part 3, p. 88, are to be found several statutes concerning the silversmiths of Barcelona from the 14th century, proving the importance of this guild in 1301. At this period three of its members formed part of the town Council. The introduction of a statute of 1489 proves the excellence of the works which they made. " Experience having shown us in past times, and proof existing at the present time, that such clever silversmiths have existed and exist at Barcelona that their works are highly reputed by kings and great people, and held in great honour and estimation in the town itself." The Silversmiths' guild still preserve the folio volumes full of drawings, and the description of the different objects which they presented for the approbation of the jury, during the 16th and 17th centuries. The designs contained in these volumes constitute a most interesting collection of jewels, giving a good idea of the great height of this industry in Barcelona.

Baron C. H. Davillier is about to publish a volume on Spanish silversmiths, in which etchings of several of these designs will be reproduced. In the list of artists which follows I give the names of the most remarkable of those who worked at Barcelona.

In the Municipal Ordinances of Toledo of the year 1494,

some laws relating to silversmiths appeared; they are, however, uninteresting. The same thing occurs with the Ordinances of Seville, which were re-compiled in 1526. The guild of silver-smiths of Toledo must have been most important, for in 1423 they already formed a brotherhood or guild under the protection of St. Eloy, in which they agreed to help the members of the guild in every way. See " Documentos Ineditos," published by Zarco del Valle, p. 166. The Ordinances of Granada enter more into details concerning the technical proceedings of silversmith's work. These Ordinances appeared in 1538; the work in the Moorish style is described in full detail; it appears to have been preserved in this locality more than elsewhere.

We can judge of the enormous quantities of objects which were made by those still to be seen in Spanish cathedrals and churches, having survived the French invasion of the present century. For full details of the barbarous treatment of these works of art during the French invasion, see Ford's " Handbook of Spain." The expropriations of the Spanish government during the civil wars of 1833 to 1840, and the injudicious law of expropriations of 1869 for the purpose of collecting artistic objects, have brought about the destruction and disappearance of numberless works of art in order not to give them up to the government.

The same splendour and abundance of silver objects of every kind existed in the royal palaces and houses of the grandees. Madame d'Aunoy in her "Voyage en Espagne, Lyon, 1643," p. 109, says: " L'on ne se sert point de vaisselle d'étain, celle d'argent ou de terre sont les seules' qui soient en usage. Le duc d'Albur-querque est mort, il y a déjà quelque tems ; l'on m'a dit que l'on avoit employé six semaines à écrire sa vaisselle d'or et d'argent. Il y avoit 1400 douzaines d'assiettes, 500 grands plats, et 700 petits, tout le reste à proportion, et 40 échelles d'argent pour monter au haut de son buffet, qui étoit par gradins comme un autel placé dans une grande salle." The splendid silver table belonging to the Marquis of Villaseca at Madrid gives a good

idea of the furniture of this time. In the Inventories, a great
number of which exist, we find numerous details of silver objects
of every kind. In one which was drawn up in 1574, of the
effects of Princess Da Juana (MS. folio, Acad. de la Historia),
the sister of Philip II., we find mention, without counting the
jewels, of a silver balustrade, weighing 121 pounds, to be placed
round the bed. The greater part of the kitchen utensils were
also made of silver.

Among the most important objects of Spanish silversmith work
are undoubtedly, as I have said before, the custodias.

The name of custodia is given in Spain, not only to the monstrance or ostensoir where the Blessed Sacrament is exposed, but
also to a sort of temple or tabernacle, of large size, made also of
silver, inside which is placed the monstrance, which is carried
in procession on Corpus Christi day. In order to distinguish
these objects one from another, the name of *viril* is given to the
object which holds the consecrated host ; it is generally made of
rock crystal, with a gold stem and mount ornamented with precious
stones. The small tabernacles are generally objects of the greatest
importance both from their artistic and intrinsic value. The description of one of them will be sufficient to give an idea of their
construction.

Although a fine custodia existed formerly at Toledo, which we
know weighed 164 pounds, Cardinal Ximenez de Cisneros wished
a finer one to be made, and caused the plan to be furnished by
competition. Diego Copin, Juan de Borgoña, and Enrique de
Arphe presented designs ; the one by Enrique de Arphe was
selected. Arphe began his work in 1517, and continued exclusively employed in this, and without the help of other master
silversmiths, until April, 1524, when he gave up the monstrance to
the authorities of the cathedral. The silversmith, Lainez, finished
in 1523 the gold and jewelled cross which is on the top. It
represents a Gothic hexagonal temple, 8 feet high, of three orders,
with all the variety and number of necessary architectural details

such as pilasters, arches, columns, pyramids, canopies, crest-work, &c., to the closing of the vaulted roof; the whole is *percé à jour*, and so delicate that it looks like lace. From the roof hang bells and incense-holders of filigree work; in the key-stone are studded precious gems. Carvings in relief, representing passages of the life of Our Saviour, appear on the base of the six pedestals; they are admirably carved. In the centre of the second order is a figure representing the Resurrection of Our Lord. On the pilasters and brackets which appear in the temple there are more than 260 statues of different sizes, all of which are executed with the same skill. This monstrance was mounted on iron wires; and Archbishop Fonseca, wishing that the whole of it should be made of silver, gave orders that Arphe himself should alter it, which he did in 1525, when the total weight was found to be 388 pounds. The *viril* was then placed inside it, this was made of the first gold brought from America. It is completely covered with precious stones, and was bought by Cisneros from Queen Isabel (the Catholic); it weighs 29 pounds of gold. The tabernacle was ordered to be gilt in 1595 by Archbishop Quiroga; this was done by the Masters Diego de Valdivieso and Francisco Merino. This splendid work of art remains in this state, and may be seen at the cathedral of Toledo; it was most fortunately saved from the rapacity of the French, by being sent to Cadiz during the war. In 1513 the monstrance at the cathedral of Cordova was also made by Arphe, it is similar in style and importance to that of Toledo. Before this, he had also finished the splendid one formerly at Leon, which was destroyed by the French, as was likewise a similar smaller one, also by Arphe, formerly at the Monastery of St. Benito, at Sahagun.

The custodia made by Juan de Arphe in 1587, a Leonese artist, and grandson of Enrique, for the cathedral of Seville, competes with that of Toledo. It is formed in the same manner as a temple, but in the Graeco-Roman style, covered with an immense number of statuettes, some of which are upwards of a foot high, and reliefs of all kinds, and delicate ornamentation, worked with the utmost skill. The chapter of the cathedral commissioned the theologian, Francisco Pacheco, to direct the subjects which were to be represented, and when it was finished Arphe published a full description of the monstrance, which he does not hesitate to call " the largest and finest work in silver known of its kind." This opinion is hardly an exaggerated one if we look at this splendid work of art. Its plan is circular, and measures 3½ yards high, and weighs 1082 pounds of silver. For details consult Cean Bermudez' " Diccionario," Descripcion de la Catedral de Sevilla, Museo Español de Antiguedades, vol. viii., p. 1.

Besides these two celebrated silversmiths there was another of the same family, the son of Enrique, and father of Juan, Antonio Arphe, an artist also of great merit, who made in 1554 the custodia which still exists at the cathedral of Santiago.

Cean Bermudez says in his " Diccionario," " that in the same manner as the city of Leon gave Spain three illustrious silversmiths, Cuenca gave them other three in the Becerrils," these were Alonso and Francisco Becerril brothers, and Christoval, the son of Francisco. They all worked at the famous and splendid custodia of Cuenca, and between them they produced a most important series of works from 1528 to 1584.

It is extremely difficult to give in so small a space the description of the works and names of the numerous artists on silver and gold work, who worked in Spain during the 16th century. At the present time, notwithstanding the innumerable objects lost, a long list would remain of the specimens which have reached us, and their different forms and applications, still visible in the churches of Toledo, Seville, Zaragoza, Palencia, Santiago, and others of the Spanish peninsula. Some idea may be gathered of the importance this art attained in Spain by looking through the following list of artists who worked in silver and gold, upwards of 450 of whom I have added to the 95 given by Cean in his dictionary. It must

be borne in mind that the objects on a large scale which reproduce an architectural model, adopt three styles during the century,
all three of them admirable as regards beauty of form. The
first is Gothic, a reminiscence of the former time, improved by
the change which had already taken place, in drawing and
modelling. The second style is known by the name of *plateresque*,
when applied to architecture, and consists in copying the general
structure of buildings in the classical style, and applying the orders
and pointed arch, while keeping to the profusion of decoration
of the earlier period, and modifying the general plan with the
object of introducing the greatest quantity of ornamentation.
The third style is the Greco-Roman ; it is more sober in decoration,
and has a greater tendency to keep to the imitation of the classical
school.

Besides the objects described, which may be considered as
original works and the most important examples of Spanish
silversmiths' work, I must mention those which came from South
America, chiefly from Mexico, which possess a certain aspect ;
they consist of carved and *repoussé* work ornamented with flora of
the country adapted in an oriental style ; others consist of filigree
work, double-headed crowned eagles are frequently met with in
the same style as those made at Cordova and Salamanca.

There are interesting specimens at the Kensington Museum
which give an excellent idea of Spanish silversmiths' work.
Besides those already described attention must be drawn to

No. 305–66. A silver-gilt cross ornamented with foliage,
statuettes of saints and the Evangelists with their emblems,
Marked $^{NOE}_{M.}$ About 1560. Height 3 feet 2 inches.

No. 302–66. Silver-gilt chalice, ornamented with foliated scroll
work and half figures beaten and chiselled. Marked Estorga.
About 1540.

No. 132–73. A silver-gilt chalice, the bowl inscribed outside
" + Sangvis mevs vere est potvs ; " the stem is of baluster form,
in several tiers, ornamented with brackets and large chatons set

with crystal, and a band of cherubim. The foot is chased with masques, festoons, harpies, and birds, and surrounded by eight semicircular projections, on which are an armorial shield and a

SPANISH CHALICE. SOUTH KENSINGTON MUSEUM.

cross set with emeralds and lapis lazuli. Engraved at bottom "S. I. de Salinas." [See woodcut.] With it is a paten dated 1549.

No. 481-75. Chalice, silver-gilt; the bowl chased in relief with the instruments of the Passion; on the knop are ten applied figures of Apostles on ground of translucent blue enamel; the foot, which has eight semicircular projections, is *repoussé* with representations of the Evangelists, cherub and other heads, the Crucifixion, and a shield with the initials L. B. P. around a crown of thorns enclosing a heart. 17th century. [See woodcut, p. 31.]

No. 314-64. Silver-gilt pax of architectural design; in the centre is a group in full relief of the Virgin giving the chasuble to St. Ildefonso. About 1540-50. [See woodcut, p. 33.]

No. 1129-64. Incense holder, boat-shaped, of rock crystal mounted in silver-gilt. Around the rim is a band of guilloche pattern, set with amethysts and garnets; on the lids a band inscribed "Oratio mea dirigatur sicut incensum." About 1540-50.

No. 93-65. Silver triptych with suspending chain, the

SPANISH CHALICE. SOUTH KENSINGTON MUSEUM.

interior painted in oils, the exterior engraved in arabesque. About 1550.

We find that Spanish jewels were as magnificent in the 16th century as were the large architectural objects for ecclesiastical use. One of the most important in richness and artistic merit was the splendid crown belonging to the Virgen del Sagrario at Toledo, which it is deeply to be regretted disappeared in 1868. This crown was made in 1556 by the silversmith Hernando de Carrion ; it then consisted of a gold circle with chiselled and enamelled ornamentation, set with pearls, emeralds and rubies. In 1574 Cardinal Loaisa wished to enrich it, and ordered a silver worker called Alejo de Montoya to add to it an upper part, formed as an imperial crown, which Montoya agreed to do by a special agreement. This addition was formed of small figures of angels of enamelled gold, in pairs supporting the side bands, which met in the upper part forming a group of allegorical figures, upon which was placed a spherical emerald, without a flaw, 1½ inches in diameter, which served as a base to the cross. The bands were studded with precious stones and ornamented inside with sub-jects of the life of the Blessed Virgin in enamel. The height of this crown was 10½ inches by 8½ wide. Montoya took 12 years to do this work—he finished it in 1586. The fine bracelets belonging to this crown, which have also disappeared, were made at the same time by Julián Hernando.

The jewels worn by the Spanish kings and grandees were equally magnificent. In the description of the gems which Prince Don Carlos, the son of Philip II., left to be distributed at his death, are included a sword the hilt of which was of solid gold enamelled in different colours : this Don Carlos bequeathed to the Grand Master of the Order of St. John ;—a halberd composed of 27 pieces of enamelled gold in high relief; and a sword with gold mount enamelled in colours with masks, medals and festoons in the Roman style, made by Rodrigo Reynalti. Consult " Coleccion de Documentos Ineditos para la Historia de España," vol. 27, Madrid, 1855. I owe to the courtesy of Count Valencia de Don Juan, the following description of arms made by *Toto platero de*

SPANISH PAX. SOUTH KENSINGTON MUSEUM.

su Alteza in 1554. [Archives of Simancas legajo, No. 37.] These arms belonged to Prince Don Carlos.

D

A gold sword, the cross of which is ornamented with masks of white, grey, and black enamel.

A gold dagger, and sword-belt belonging to the same sword, ornamented in a similar manner.

Also a gold sword, belt and dagger ornamented with figures of children in solid gold and enamel.

Although the greater part of these silversmiths were Spaniards, the Milanese artist, Jacome de Trezzo was very celebrated during the reign of Philip II. He made several jewels of great importance for the king and royal family. The splendid tabernacle which was taken by the French in 1810 from the Escorial was one of his finest works; they carried off at the same time the superb shrines, the gifts of kings and princes, and everything they could lay their hands on of gold and silver, loading ten campaign carts. Consult, "Historia del Escorial," by Quevedo. Madrid, 1849, p. 220.

At the South Kensington Museum are several objects of this kind, which will give an excellent idea of Spanish jewel work.

No. 334-70. A gold enamelled pendant, in form of a chained dog, supported on a scroll from which small pearls depend, and suspended by two chains of alternate enamelled and plain links, united to a fastening crowned by a bird.

No. 335-70. Enamelled gold pendant in form of a pelican and her young, enriched with a carbuncle and pearls, and suspended by pearl links.

No. 336-70. Enamelled gold pendant in form of a dog enriched with jewels.

No. 337-70. Enamelled gold pendant, in form of a parrot, set with hyacinth, suspended by chains.

No. 340-70. Enamelled gold pendant representing the Virgin of the Immaculate Conception.

Nos. 341 and 342-70. Pendants representing the Virgen del Pilar Saragossa, attended by saints. [See woodcut opposite.]

Spanish jewel work does not decrease during the 17th century, the number of artists who worked was very great, and the quantity of objects of all kinds which were made by them to enrich the shrines of churches, and the houses of grandees, was remark-

SPANISH JEWEL, 17TH CENTURY.   SOUTH KENSINGTON MUSEUM.

able, although their artistic merit was far inferior to the work of the 16th century.   The general decay of art, which produces in Europe the *barroco* style, appears in Spain more exaggerated and to a greater extent than elsewhere.   The objects made during this period reproduce until the beginning of the 18th century the lines and extravagant ornamentation which we meet with in architecture, the handiwork however continued to be excellent, and no expense was spared to give an aspect of richness to the objects made.

D 2

The large quantity of objects of all kinds made of silver, and the quantity also used in wearing apparel, gave rise to constant prohibitions restricting its use from the reign of Ferdinand and Isabel, and even to a far greater extent at the beginning of the 16th century. In a Decree, issued at Madrid in 1594, "it is

SILVER DISH.　SPANISH, 17TH CENTURY.　SOUTH KENSINGTON MUSEUM.

forbidden to make or sell cabinets, escritoires, caskets, brasiers, *chapines* (clogs), tables, commodes decorated with silver, either beat in *repoussé*, stamped, carved or plain, and whoever makes, sells, or buys them, is to lose them." Notwithstanding this and other restrictions which appeared in the 17th century, this abuse can hardly have been checked, judging by the number of these objects which have reached us, not counting those preserved in the shrines of Spanish churches and cathedrals.

The luxury which was apparent in this century of great decay for Spain will be found in the numerous descriptions which exist of different feasts and ceremonies.

A good idea may be nad of this style of silversmiths' work from the silver dishes in the South Kensington Museum. An engraving of one of these appears on the preceding page.

BREAST ORNAMENT SET WITH EMERALDS. SPANISH, LATE 17TH CENTURY. SOUTH KENSINGTON MUSEUM.

During the 17th century, jewellery underwent a complete transformation—the proceedings and *renaissance* forms of the Italian school were abandoned, with all their richness of sculptures, enamels, and variety of stones. Instead of this, jewels were formed of emeralds, diamonds or rubies in gold setting, *percés à jour*, producing an excellent effect. The exceptions to this rule are the objects in which enamelled work still predominates, a reminiscence of the former century. Among the finest and best examples may be mentioned the gold crown of the Virgen de los Desamparados of Toledo, made in Mexico in the

17th century. It is formed like a basket of flowers, of delicate tracery, and richly studded with fine emeralds. Several most interesting specimens exist at Kensington of Spanish jewellery of this kind, bought at the sale which took place in 1870 of the jewels belonging to the Virgen del Pilar at Zaragoza.

No. 325–70 is a breast ornament of gold scroll open work, with enamelled flowers, set with emeralds. [See woodcut on p. 37.]

No. 320–70, a gold breast ornament with five bosses and seven pendants, set with rose diamonds.

No. 406–73. Breast ornament, gold open strap work and floral filigree, the lower part an oval pendant, set with table diamonds. [See woodcut on p. 39.]

The following fine Spanish jewels of the 17th century in the Kensington Museum are also worthy of attention :

No. 330–64. A pectoral cross, with medallions containing relics.

No. 298–66. Gold filigree cross, within which is an ivory crucifix.

No. 344–70. Enamelled gold pectoral cross set with amethysts.

No. 417, 417A.–69. A pair of earrings of gold open work, branches set with white crystals.

No. 323, 323A.–70. Silver open work earrings set with rose diamonds.

No. 330 to 330C.–70. Four miniature ewers of silver filigree open work, the bodies of Chinese enamelled copper.

No. 1224–71. Silver frame *repoussé*, with the Holy Dove, and a bleeding heart encircled with thorns.

Models of the baroque or, as it is called in Spain, *Churriguesque* styles continued to be copied during the beginning of the 18th century, in the same manner as in the 17th century. At this time, as in the rest of Europe, a reaction begins in every branch of art, due in Spain to the influence of French and Italian artists who accompanied the family of Bourbon. The Academy of Fine Arts of St. Fernando was founded by a king of that House towards the middle of the century, the teaching was reduced to copying Greco-Roman models, such as they were understood at that time.

The great centres which in the 16th century had produced such splendid works of art had almost completely ceased. No great

BREAST ORNAMENT SET WITH DIAMONDS. SPANISH, LATE 17TH CENTURY.
SOUTH KENSINGTON MUSEUM.

silversmiths remained at Valladolid, Leon, Toledo, or Seville. The only localities which have preserved even to the present day the traditional forms of these ornaments are Salamanca, Cordova,

Astorga, and Santiago.   Madrid absorbed from the middle of
the 17th century the whole of this industry.   In Larruga's
" Memorias," Vol. IV., will be found every detail given on this
subject.   Several important establishments for the object of making
silver work on a large scale were founded at Madrid, the most
important being that of Tomas de Buenafuente, which passed
after to Francisco Novi.   Two Frenchmen called Isaac and
Miguel Naudin established a manufactory in 1772.   In each
the greater part of the work was machine made.   Others were
founded to cut and polish precious stones, and mount paste
stones.   This was done with great skill by Antonio Martinez in
1778, in a building fitted up for the purpose, which still exists
opposite the Botanical Garden of Madrid.   Martinez was pensioned by Charles III. in Paris and London to study the improvements in this industry.   The principal object of the manufactory was to teach the technical proceedings required in order
to extend this industry in the country, and supply a school in
which machinery, models, drawings, &c., were to be met with.
Pupils of both sexes were admitted ; machinery was made in the
workshops, and Martinez undertook to teach the manufacture of
gold, doublé, or steel trinkets, with or without enamel or stones.
Sword-hilts, buckles, snuff-boxes, needle-cases, handles for sticks,
brooches, necklaces, orders, and other different objects, were
made either of open work or enamelled gold.

Inkstands, dishes, dinner services, chocolate stands, cruets, knives
and forks, were made of silver in different styles, generally imitating the English manner.   [Consult Larruga, " Memorias Politicas y
Economicas."   Madrid, 1789.   Vol. IV., p. 116.]

The results obtained by the manufactory of Martinez were
most satisfactory; a large number of apprentices were taught
there ; but their work was completely French in character; the
manner and style of the Spanish school of silversmiths was completely forgotten.

As I have already mentioned, the traditional forms were

preserved in some localities which require to be mentioned here
in order to finish this account of this industry in Spain. An
interesting and varied collection of modern Spanish peasant jewellery exists at the South Kensington Museum. Strange to say,
although this collection was formed a very few years ago, in 1870,
it would be very difficult now to make another; for owing to
the means of communication having been of late years so much
improved in Spain, the peasantry are leaving off their national
costumes, and substituting in every detail modern fashions.
Among this peasant jewellery the silver gilt necklace and
reliquaries of Astorga, No. 1114-73, deserve special attention.
These necklaces were worn round the neck and part of the body.
The neck ornaments of gold and seed pearls made at Salamanca,
those of silver gilt of Santiago; the filigree work of Cordova
in the Moorish style, and the long earrings of Cataluña with
precious stones, are interesting reminiscences of older times.

LIST OF SPANISH GOLDSMITHS AND SILVERSMITHS.

10TH CENTURY.

Years in which they worked.		Residence.
961.	Hudzen ben Bozla, a Moor. He made a silver casket which exists still at Gerona Cathedral	Gerona.

13TH CENTURY.

1279.	Maestre Jorge	Toledo.
1283.	Modova, Pablo de	Burgos.
	Niculas (Don)	
1262.	Perez, Juan	Burgos.

14TH CENTURY.

1357.	Andreu, Raimundo de	Gerona.
1358.	Barners, Pedro	Gerona.
1325.	Bartolomé, Maestro	Gerona.
	Bernec, Pere, V. Barners	
1382 to 1393.	Capellades, Pedro	Tortosa.

Years in which they worked.		Residence.
1378.	Fernai, Rodrigo	Oviedo
1334.	Frau, Ramon	Palma de Mallorca.
1367.	Martinez, Sancho	Sevilla.
1382 to 1393.	Paris, Pedro de	Tortosa.
1373.	Perpiña, Juan	Valencia.
1370.	Ponce, Bartolomé	Palma de Mallorca.

15TH CENTURY.

1417.	Abello, Joan	Daroca.
1495.	Alcaçar, Juan de	Toledo.
1477.	Almerique	Barcelona.
1494.	Berenguer, Juan	Valencia.
1499.	Castellano	Toledo.
1454.	Castelnou, Juan de	Valencia.
1460.	Castelnou, Jayme de, son of Juan . .	Valencia.
1470.	Cetina, Mestre	Valencia.
1458 to 1463.	Diez, Pedro el Cabalan . . .	Toledo.
1494.	Diaz, Thomas	Toledo.
1417.	Diaz, or Diez Caro, Ferrando . . .	Daroca.
1418 to 1426.	Garcia de Valladolid, Alfonso . .	Toledo.
1438.	Garcia, Alonso	Burgos.
1442.	Garcia de Pielagos, Juan	Burgos.
1477.	Gomez, Garcia	Valencia.
1424 to 1459.	Gonzalez de Madrid, Juan	Toledo.
1477.	Hance	
	Lorenzo, Don	
1425.	Medina, Juan de	Toledo.
1499.	Medina, Pedro de	Toledo.
1470.	Nadal Yvo, Maestre	Valencia.
1493.	Narbona, Diego	Toledo.
1495.	Nuñez, Alonso	Toledo.
1485.	Oviedo, Fernando de	Burgos.
1487.	Pizarro	Guadalupe.
1457.	Rodriguez de Villareal, Alonso . .	Toledo.
1459.	Rodriguez de Villareal, Anton . .	Toledo.
1483.	Rodriguez, Gonzalo	Toledo.
1496.	Rodriguez, Geronimo	Sevilla.

Years in which they worked.		Residence.
1459.	Rodriguez de Villareal, Lope	Toledo.
1417 to 1423.	Roiz, Pero	Darroca.
1489 to 1491.	Ruby, Maestre	Toledo.
1416.	Ruiz de Astudillo, Alfonso	Burgos.
1431.	Ruiz de Medina	Toledo.
1426.	Ruiz, Juan	Toledo.
1498.	Ruiz, Juan	Toledo.
1404.	Sanchez, Martinez	Sevilla.
1424.	Sanchez, Anton	Toledo.
1417.	Sancho, Manuel Hernando	Burgos.
1487.	Segovia, Fr. Juan de	Guadalupe.
1418.	Valles, Juan	Toledo.
1484 to 1488.	Vigil, Pedro de	Valladolid.
	Yvo V. Nadal Yvo	

16TH CENTURY.

1586.	Abedo de Villandrando, Diego . . .	Madrid.
1531.	Aguirre, Pedro de	Toledo.
1515.	Aleman, Mateo	Sevilla.
	Aleman, Nicolas	Sevilla.
1596.	Alfaro, Francisco . . .	Sevilla.
1539.	Alonso, Juan	Toledo.
1552.	Alvarez, Baltasar	Palencia.
1568.	Alvarez, Francisco	Madrid.
1531.	Alvarez, Juan	Granada.
1560.	Alvarez, Juan	Madrid.
1538.	Alvear, Juan de	Burgos.
	Alvear, Nicolas de	Burgos.
1520 to 1521.	Andino, Cristoval de . . .	Burgos.
	Angel, Pedro	Toledo.
1565.	Anrique, Joan	Toledo.
1570.	Avila, Alonso de	Toledo.
1567.	Avila Cimbron, Diego de . . .	Toledo.
1544.	Arfe, Antonio de	Leon.
1595.	Arfe y Villafañe, Juan de . . .	Sevilla.
1506 to 1525.	Arphe, Enrique de	Leon.
1531.	Baeza, Francisco de	Granada.
	Baeza, Juan	Granada.

Years in which they worked.		Residence.
1580.	Ballesteros, Fernando de	Sevilla.
1560.	Baptista, Juan	Toledo.
1584 to 1601.	Baroxa, Gregorio de . . .	Toledo.
1534.	Becerril, Alonso	Cuenca.
. 1575.	Becerril, Cristoval	Cuenca.
1552.	Becerril, Francisco	Cuenca.
1590.	Belta, Hanz	Madrid.
	Belthae, V.—see Hanz Belthae .	
1582.	Benavente, Juan de	Palencia.
1546.	Benavente, Pedro de	Toledo.
1556.	Borgoñes, Juan	Toledo.
1538.	Buentalante, Alonso de . . .	Granada.
1586.	Camps, Bernat	Barcelona.
1547 to 1561.	Carrion, Hernando . . .	Toledo.
1556.	Carrion, Fernando	Toledo.
1586.	Castro, Juan de	Madrid.
1531.	Castro, Luis de	Granada.
1505.	Cetina, Bernardo Juan . . .	Valencia.
1546.	Comes, Gabriel	Barcelona.
1553.	Conill, Antonio . .	Barcelona.
1531.	Cordova, Anton de	Granada.
	Cordova, Juan de . . .	Granada.
1514.	Cota, Martin	Toledo.
1567.	Davila Cimbron, Diego . .	Toledo.
1558.	Davila, Diego	Toledo.
1593.	Diaz, Francisco . .	Toledo.
1526.	Diaz, Hernando	Toledo.
1586.	Dominguez, Juan	Madrid.
1513.	Donanti, Juan	Sevilla.
1564 to 1598.	Dueñas, Alonso de . . .	Salamanca.
1531.	Dueñas, Juan de	Granada.
1537.	Escripian, Luis	Toledo.
1531.	Fernandez, Diego	Granada.
1554.	Fernandez, Manuel	Sevilla.
1567 to 1593.	Fernandez, Marcos	Toledo.
	Fernandez del Moral . . .	Madrid.
1531.	Flores, Diego	Granada.
1572.	Font, Joan	Barcelona.
1555.	Francés, Juan	Toledo.

Years in which they worked.		Residence.
1561 to 1590.	Gallego, Miguel	Toledo.
1531.	Garcia, Thome	Granada.
1561.	Gallo, Gaspar	Toledo.
1555.	Goden, Juan	Toledo.
1509.	Gomez, Heros de	Valencia.
1573.	Gomez, Baltasar	
1574.	Gonzalez, Pedro	Uveda.
1513.	Gueran, Ferrer	Barcelona.
1531.	Hermosilla, Bartolomé de	Granada.
1567.	Hernandez, Gonzalo	Toledo.
1531.	Hernandez, Luis	Granada.
1567.	Hernandez, Marcos	Toledo.
1524 to 1544.	Hernandez, Pedro . . .	Toledo.
1531.	Herrera, Gonzalo de	Granada.
1524.	Herreros y Manzanas . . .	Toledo.
1585 to 1587.	Hanz, Belthae	Madrid.
1582 to 1599.	Honrado, Julian	Toledo.
1531.	Jaen, Fernando de	Granada.
1562 to 1573.	Lainez, Juan Bautista	Madrid.
1524.	Laynez, Rodrigo . . .	Toledo.
1559.	Leon, Leoni . .	Madrid.
1597.	Leoni, Miguel .	Madrid.
1531.	Lopez, Francisco	Granada.
1548 to 1570.	Lopez, Juan . .	Toledo.
1530.	Lopez de Leon, Juan	Toledo.
1508.	Madrid, Pedro de	Toledo.
1531.	Mar, Alonso de la	Granada.
1588 to 1614.	Marques, Lorenzo	Toledo.
1522.	Marquez, Cristoval . .	Toledo.
1531.	Martinez, Pero	Granada.
1544 to 1547.	Martinez, Francisco . . .	Toledo.
1553.	Mas, Miguel	Barcelona.
1534.	Masanell, Joan	Barcelona.
1517.	Mayquez, Diego	Toledo.
1500 to 1515.	Medina, Pedro de	Toledo.

Years in which they worked.		Residence.
1538.	Mendoza, Alonso de	Granada.
	Mendoza, Blas de	Granada.
	Mendoza, Diego de	Burgos.
1564 to 1601.	Merino, Francisco	Toledo.
1579 to 1586.	Montoya, Alejo de	Toledo.
1598.	Morales, Luis	Madrid.
1592.	Morales, Tomas	Toledo.
1515 to 1517.	Moran	Toledo.
1556.	Moran, Pedro Fernandez de . . .	Burgos.
1561.	Morel, Thomas du (an Englishman) . . .	Toledo.
1574 to 1590.	Montoya, Alexo . . .	Toledo.
1573.	Muñoz, Alonso	Toledo.
1598.	Muñoz, Antonio	Madrid.
1573.	Niebre, Matias de, a native of Burgundy, living at	Toledo.
1512.	Nuñez, Alonso	Toledo.
1531.	Nuñez, Francisco	Granada.
1532 to 1560.	Oña, Antonio de	Burgos.
1531.	Oñate, Juan de	Granada.
1537 to 1546.	Ordoñez, Andres	Toledo.
1507 to 1510.	Ordoñez, Pedro	Toledo.
1537 to 1528.	Orna, Juan de	Burgos.
1581.	Ortiz, Pedro	Madrid.
1529 to 1546.	Oviedo, Diego de	Toledo.
1586.	Pan, Juan	Barcelona.
1594.	Pardo, Martin	Escorial.
1534.	Parra, Juan de la . . .	Toledo.
1577.	Pastrana, Luis de . . .	Madrid.
1595.	Pedraza, Diego de . . .	Estremadura
1593.	Pedraza, Esteban . .	
1559.	Perez, Francisco	Barcelona.
1598.	Perez, Pedro	Madrid.
1535.	Pierres, a Frenchman, residing at . . .	Toledo.
1587.	Poch, Pero Juan	Barcelona.
1568.	Poggini, Juan Pablo . . .	Madrid.
1532.	Pons, Pere . . .	Barcelona.

Years in which they worked.		Residence.
1574.	Portigniani, Juan Bautista	Toledo.
1541 to 1554.	Ramirez, Pedro	Toledo.
1590.	Reynalte, Francisco de	Madrid.
	Reynalte, Juan de	Madrid.
	Reynalte, Pedro de	Madrid.
1590.	Reynalte, Rodrigo de	Madrid.
1531.	Rivera, Diego Lopez de	Granada.
1590.	Rodriguez Bermudez, Gonzalo	Madrid and Toledo.
1557 to 1586.	Rodriguez de Babia, Juan	Toledo.
1596.	Rodriguez del Castillo, Melchor	Segovia.
1551.	Rodriguez, Duarte	Toledo.
1568.	Rodriguez Machado, Juan	Toledo.
1567.	Ros, Felipe	Barcelona.
1537.	Rozas, Gregorio de	Burgos.
1538.	Rozas, Jeronimo de	Burgos.
1584 to 1590.	Ruiz, Diego	Toledo.
1531.	Ruiz, Jeronimo	Granada.
1524.	Ruiz, Julian, lapidary	Toledo.
1590.	Ruiz, Juan	Toledo.
	Ruiz, Juan, el Vandolino	Sevilla, Jaen, and Cordova.
1545.	Sabat, Benedicti	Barcelona.
1566.	Salamanca, Antonio de	Madrid.
1590.	Sanchez, Andres	Toledo.
1522.	San Roman, Pedro de	Toledo.
1531.	Sevilla, Hernando de	Granada.
1524.	Sigüenza, Pedro de	Sevilla.
1595.	Tamarit, Andreu	Barcelona.
1590.	Tello de Moreta	Toledo.
1554.	Toto.	Madrid.
	Trezzo, Jacome de, an Italian, who worked at	Madrid.
1589.	Trezzo, a nephew of Jacome	Madrid.
1590.	Urbano, Juan	Cordova.
1580.	Usatigni, Juan Alonso	Madrid.
1537.	Valdes, Antonio de	Barcelona.
1589.	Valdes, Lucas	Cordova.
1564 to 1598.	Valdivieso, Diego de	Toledo.
1593.	Valdivieso, Lucas de	Burgos.
1575.	Valla, Narcisco	Barcelona.

Years in which they worked.		Residence
1548.	Valladolid, Juan de	Toledo.
1566.	Valle, Antonio del	Madrid.
1524.	Valles, Hernando de	Toledo.
1512.	Vargas, Gutierre de	Toledo.
1563.	Vazquez, Baptista	Toledo.
1512 to 1543.	Vazquez, Diego	Toledo.
1558.	Velasco	Toledo.
1580.	Velez	Toledo.
1569.	Vergara, Nicolas de	Toledo.
1546.	Vicente, Mateo, lapidary	Toledo.
1561.	Vida, Francisco	Barcelona.
1534.	Villagran, Juan de	Toledo.
1590.	Villanueva, Juan Domingo de . . .	Toledo.
1552.	Villaseca, Alexo	Toledo.
1538.	Vitoria, Francisco de	Granada.
1538.	Vitoria, Juan de	Granada.
1528.	Vozmediano, Diego de . .	Sevilla.
1536.	Vozmediano, Juan de	Sevilla.
1561.	Ximenez, Juan . . .	Barcelona.
1537.	Ximenis, Rafael	Barcelona.
1599.	Zepes, Bartolomé de	Toledo.

17TH CENTURY.

1618 to 1627.	Adeba, Jusepe	Madrid.
1677.	Alcario, Francisco de . . .	Sevilla.
1664.	Aleman, Juan	Toledo.
1623.	Alonso, Jeronimo	Madrid.
1676 to 1714.	Alonso de Prado, Pedro . . .	Burgos.
1622.	Alvarado, Ambrosio de . .	Madrid.
1635.	Alvarez Brizuela, Blas	Madrid.
	Alvarez, Blas	Madrid.
1636.	Alvarez de Peralta, Pedro .	Madrid.
	Alvear, Andres	Burgos.
1640.	Alvear, Juan de	Burgos.
1617.	Alvear, Juan de	Madrid.
1691.	Arandas, Gaspar	Tarragona.
	Arfe, Joseph, a grandson of Juan de Arfe . .	Sevilla.
1613.	Avalos, Diego de	Madrid.
1604.	Avendaño de Tudela, Luis . . .	Madrid.
1677.	Avila, Agustin de	Sevilla.

Years in which they worked.		Residence.
1620.	Barinci, Juan Bautista	Escorial.
1624.	Baraona, Antonio	Madrid.
1638.	Barona, Pedro	Barcelona.
	Bellicis, V. Bardi	
1650.	Bardi, Bellicis	Barcelona.
1604.	Belta, Pedro	Madrid.
1602.	Benavente, Pedro	Toledo.
1645.	Belorado, Antonio de	Burgos.
1630.	Bonino, Pedro	Madrid.
1616.	Bracho, Alexandro	Toledo.
1628.	Brizuela, Gaspar Miguel de . . .	Madrid.
1622.	Calvo, Juan	Madrid.
1626.	Camanyes or Comanes, Aloy	Tortosa
1650.	Campo, Juan del	Burgos.
1646.	Campo, Juan de	Madrid.
1643 to 1664.	Carcaba, Felipa, the wife of Andres Salinas, worked at	Toledo.
1621.	Carranza Alvear, Juan de	Madrid.
1622.	Carranza, Martin de	Madrid.
1615.	Castro, Juan	Madrid.
1651 to 1670.	Ciga, Miguel de	Burgos.
1646.	Comañes, Aloy	Tortosa.
1668.	Concepcion, Friar Juan de la . . .	Escorial.
	Cruz, Friar Eugenio de la	Escorial.
1620.	Cuello, Amaro	Madrid.
1661.	Dandez, Agustin	Barcelona.
1623.	Delgado Maldonado, Miguel . . .	Madrid.
1660.	Diaz, Juan	Segovia.
1619.	Dominguez, Luis	Madrid.
1613.	Duarte, Cristoval de	Madrid.
1671.	Duran, Juan	Toledo.
1613 to 1624.	Duran, Jusepe	Madrid.
1664.	Ebrart, Pedro	Toledo.
1660.	Elizes, Alonso de . . .	Toledo.
1642.	Espinosa, Juan de	Madrid.
1640.	Espluga, Tomas	Barcelona.
	Estrada, Manuel de . . .	Sevilla.
1624.	Estrada, Sebastian	Madrid.
1655 to 1678.	Faneli, Virgilio	Toledo.
1630.	Franconio, Juan Bautista	Sevilla.

E

Years in which they worked.		Residence.
1657.	Fernandez, Andres	Burgos.
1679 to 1694.	Fernandez, Gamonal Joseph	Toledo.
1631.	Fernandez de Angulo, Miguel	Madrid.
1612.	Fernandez de Castro, Juan	Madrid.
1618.	Fernandez, Martin	Madrid.
1627.	Fernandez de Tapia, Andres	Madrid.
	Fernandez de Tapia, Juan	Madrid.
1667 to 1670.	Fortuna, Juan de	Toledo.
1629.	Gallo, Alonso	Madrid.
1615.	Gamonar, Mathieu de	Madrid.
1600 to 1635.	Garcia, Alonso	Toledo.
1622.	Garcia, Diego	Madrid.
1618.	Garcia, Francisco	Madrid.
1613.	Garcia, Martin	Madrid.
1600.	Garrido, Gaspar	Madrid.
1620.	Generino, Francisco	Escorial.
1610.	Gomez, Antonio	Madrid.
	Gomez, Diego	Madrid.
1626.	Gomez, Juan	Madrid.
1610.	Gomez, Marcelo	Madrid.
1615.	Gonzales, Gonzalo	Madrid.
1613.	Gonzales, Enrique	Madrid.
1634.	Gonzales, Francisco	Madrid.
1630 to 1640.	Gonzales, Pascual	Madrid.
1654.	Gonzales, Rafael	Segovia.
1607.	Guardia, Melchor, a native of Milan	Barcelona.
1679.	Güergo, Domingo de	Burgos.
1639.	Guigelmo, Eugenio	Madrid.
1627 to 1634.	Guigelmo, Juan	Madrid.
1618.	Heredia, Juan de	Madrid.
	Heredia, Sebastian	Madrid.
1631.	Hurtado, Luis	Madrid.
1694 to 1698.	Jaranta, Juan de	Toledo.
1650.	Landeras, Jeronimo de	Burgos.
1611.	Leal, Sebastian	Madrid.
1606.	Leoni, Pompeyo	Madrid.
1620.	Lopez, Domingo	Madrid.
1639.	Lopez, Francisco	Madrid.

Years in which
they worked.   Residence.

1611.	Lopez de Alvarado, Antonio	Madrid.
1676.	Lopez Barona, Andres	Burgos.
1617.	Lorenzo, Juan	Valladolid.
1638 to 1646.	Maestre, Luis	Toledo.
1611.	Marisanz, Pedro	Madrid.
1653.	Martinez, Juan	Burgos.
1673.	Mata, Francisco de	Burgos.
1677.	Mata, Pedro de	Burgos.
1686.	Mayares, Miguel	Madrid.
1614 to 1625.	Maymó, Bernardo	Tarragona.
1639.	Medina, Juan Bautista de	Madrid.
1628.	Medina Requexo, Bautista de	Madrid.
1641.	Mendez, Duarte	Madrid.
1614.	Mexia, Juan	Madrid.
1604.	Mimbreño, Alonso Roman	Madrid.
1641.	Miñano, Juan de	Madrid.
1626.	Miranda, Alonso de	Madrid.
1611.	Moles, Juan	Madrid.
1639.	Montero, Francisco	Madrid.
1630.	Morales, Francisco	Madrid.
	Morales, Manuel de	Madrid.
1695.	Muñoz, Juan	Madrid.
1661.	Nadal, Andres	Barcelona.
1620.	Nadal, Martin	Madrid.
1621 to 1629.	Navarrete Escarraman, Bartolomé de . .	Madrid.
1613 to 1623.	Navarro, Cristoval	Toledo.
1624 to 1628.	Navarro, Manuel	Madrid.
1626.	Nuñez, Antonio	Madrid.
1630.	Oliva, Gregorio de	Madrid.
1650 to 1675.	Ortiz de la Revilla, Juan . . .	Madrid.
1615.	Oviedo, Martin de	Madrid.
1619.	Oviedo, Pedro de	Madrid.
1611.	Paiba, Vicente de	Madrid.
1665.	Palomo, Diego	Toledo.
1640.	Pallares, Juan de	Madrid.
1628.	Pancorvo, Cristoval de	Madrid.
1624.	Paradiñas, Andres de	Madrid.
1659.	Pedraza, Bernardo de	Toledo.

Years in which they worked.		Residence.
1632.	Perez, Alonso	Madrid.
1652 to 1658.	Perez, Antonio	Toledo.
1680.	Perez de Montalto, Antonio	Toledo.
1685 to 1688.	Perez de Montalto, Miguel	Toledo.
1630.	Puig, Luis	Valencia.
1627.	Quero, Juan de	Madrid.
1632.	Quixano, Marcos	Madrid.
1617.	Ramirez, Agustin	Madrid.
1627.	Ramos, Juan	Madrid.
1628.	Reynalte, Juan	Madrid.
1660.	Riba, Manuel de	Toledo.
1624.	Ribera, Martin de	Madrid.
1617.	Rios, Esteban de	Madrid.
1626 to 1646.	Roda, Agustin	Tortosa.
1626.	Rodriguez, Bartolomé	Madrid.
1631.	Rodriguez, Eugenio	Toledo.
1645.	Rodriguez, Gabriel	Madrid.
1618.	Rodriguez, Diego	Madrid.
1613.	Rodriguez, Jeronimo	Madrid.
1617.	Rodriguez, Juan	Madrid.
	Rodriguez Bermudez, Gonzalo	Madrid.
1623.	Romano Valmaseda, Juan	Madrid.
1607 to 1625.	Ros, Pedro	Barcelona.
1617.	Rosales, Francisco de	Madrid.
1611.	Ruiz, Eugenio	Madrid.
	Ruiz, Juan Bautista	Madrid.
	Ruiz de Valdevieso	Burgos.
1675.	Ruiz de Velasco, Juan	Burgos.
1684.	Salazar, Francisco	Burgos.
1604 to 1635.	Salinas, Andres de	Toledo and Madrid.
1639 to 1670.	Salinas, Francisco de	Toledo.
1639 to 1680.	Salinas, Vicente de	Toledo.
1616.	Sanchez, Francisco	Toledo.
1659 to 1661.	Sanchez Ormachea, Pedro	Toledo.
1614.	San Martin, Juan de	Toledo.
1610 to 1617.	Santillana, Antonio de	Madrid.

Years in which they worked.		Residence.
1642.	Santo Domingo, Hipolito	Madrid.
1653.	San Vicente, Jacinto de	Burgos.
1640.	Sarabia, Cristoval de	Sevilla.
1668.	Segura, Juan de	Sevilla.
1632.	Serrano, Francisco	Madrid.
1640.	Soler, Baltasar	Madrid.
1629.	Soria, Francisco	Madrid.
1608.	Soria, Jeronimo de	Madrid.
1617.	Soria, Lucas de	Madrid.
1620.	Spagna, Juliano	Madrid.
1694.	Scase, Gaspar	Sevilla.
1662.	Suer, or Sueur, Esteban, a Frenchman who worked at	Toledo.
1671.	Tellez, Juan	Toledo.
	Tebres, Antonio	Toledo.
1677.	Tello, Mateo, a German, worked at	Sevilla.
1617.	Tofino, Alonso	Madrid.
1618 to 1623.	Valera, Domingo de	Madrid.
1619.	Valedomar, Angel de	Madrid.
1626.	Valle, Juan del	Madrid.
	Valmaseda, V. Juan Romano	
1624.	Vega, Juan de	Madrid
1672.	Velasco Ganado, Pedro	Toledo.
1625.	Velasquez, Juan	Madrid.
1627.	Villalta, Antonio	Madrid.
1600 to 1626.	Villamayor, Baltasar	Toledo.
1638.	Villarago, J.	Barcelona.
1622.	Villarroel, Andres de	Madrid.
1614.	Villegas, Martin de	Toledo.
1645.	Vivanco, Simon	Madrid.
1615.	Xabier, Antonio	Madrid.
1610.	Zabalza, Diego de	Madrid.
1615 to 1633.	Zaldivia, Lucas de	Burgos.
	Zoga, Miguel de	

18TH CENTURY.

1746.	Aguilar, Geronimo	Cordova.
1794.	Alamo, Bernardo de	Toledo.
1703.	Aragon, Diego de	Segovia.
1716.	Aranda, Alberto	Madrid.

Years in which they worked.		Residence.
1746.	Aviles, Manuel de	Cordova.
End of 18th cent.	Balmet, Bartolomé	Madrid.
1740.	Ballestero, Manuel	Cordova.
1730 to 1752.	Bargas, Manuel de	Toledo.
1702.	Bargas, Mateo de	Toledo.
1739.	Bargas y Machuca, Manuel de	Toledo.
1789 to 1797.	Bargas Machuca, Manuel Timoteo . . .	Madrid.
1753.	Bautista, Vicente	Toledo.
18th cent.	Benitez, Pedro	Salamanca.
End of 18th cent.	Buenafuente, Tomas	Madrid.
1746.	Bustamante, Franco	Cordova.
1734.	Bustos, Floro de	Sevilla.
1784.	Calzado, Jose, enameller	Malaga.
1746.	Camacho, Lorenzo.	Cordova.
1746.	Camacho, Rafael	Cordova.
1713.	Campo, Matias del . .	Soria.
1734.	Castillo, Matias del . . .	Aranda del Duero.
1746.	Castro, Damian de .	Cordova.
1748.	Castro, Diego	Toledo.
18th cent.	Chevalier, Luis Claudio, a Frenchman, residing at .	Madrid.
1728.	Colomes, Pedro, worked at the mounts of silver knives made at	Alcora.
End of 18th cent.	Conde, Domingo	Madrid.
1754.	Cros, Josef	Valencia.
	Cuerda, Feliz de la	Toledo.
1738 to 1745.	Cuerda, Jose de la	Toledo.
1722 to 1748.	Dominguez, Juan Antonio	Toledo.
1776.	Elosua, Antonio	Burgos.
1776.	Elosua, Manuel de	Burgos.
1790.	Fernandez, Pablo	Burgos.
18th cent.	Fernandez Clemente, Melchor . . .	Salamanca
1741.	Fernandez de la Fuente, Antonio . . .	Toledo.
1778.	Ferroni, Juan	Madrid.
1701.	Figueroa, Juan	Salamanca.
1688.	Fornaguera, Buenaventura. . .	Barcelona.
1790.	Gallardo, Vicente	Sevilla.

Years in which they worked.		Residence.
1710.	Gamonal y Guzman, Juan	Toledo.
1746.	Garcia, Jose	Cordova.
1760 to 1766.	Garcia Reyna, Manuel	Toledo.
1753.	Garcia Crespo, Manuel	Salamanca.
1772.	Gaudin, Isaac, a Frenchman, residing at . . .	Madrid.
	Gaudin, Miguel, a Frenchman, residing at . .	Madrid.
1714.	Gomez, Pedro	Alcala de Henares.
1746.	Hidalgo, Gabriel	Cordova.
1700 to 1717.	Jaranta, Juan de	Toledo.
1743.	Jaranta y Zapata, Juan de	Toledo.
1717 to 1732.	Jaranta, Lorenzo	Toledo.
1746.	Jurado, Jose	Cordova.
1746.	Lara, Diego de	Cordova.
1790.	Lecaroz, Antonio	Sevilla.
1745.	Lopez, Bernardino	Toledo.
1784.	Lopez, Manuel	Burgos.
1746.	Luna, Andres de	Cordova.
	Luque, Juan de	Cordova.
1700.	Llanos, Manuel de	Burgos.
1746.	Madueño, Francisco . . .	Cordova.
1790.	Mairod y Vassner, José	Sevilla.
1734.	Manrique, Franco Esteban . .	Aranda de Duero.
1784.	Marti, Jose	Barcelona.
1778.	Martinez, Antonio	Martinez.
1754.	Martinez, Estanislao	Valencia.
End of 18th cent.	Martinez, Gregorio .	Madrid.
1703.	Martinez del Valle, Jose . .	Segovia.
1693.	Matons, Juan	Tarragona.
End of 18th cent.	Mendeluce, Fermin . . .	Navarra.
End of 18th cent.	Molinez, Francisco . .	Zaragoza.
1722.	Monteman y Cusens, Lorenzo .	Salamanca.
1746.	Moreno, Manuel . . .	Cordova.
1725.	Muñoz de Amador, Bernardo . .	Madrid.
1746.	Muñoz, Francisco . . .	Cordova.
	Navas, Fernando de . .	Cordova.
1784.	Nieva, Antonio de	Malaga.

Years in which they worked.		Residence.
1770 to 1776.	Niño, Jose	Toledo.
1767 to 1777.	Niño, Jose Bernardo	Toledo.
End of 18th cent.	Nivel, Juan	Madrid.
End of 18th cent.	Novi, Francisco	Madrid.
1786.	Olivares, Fermin	Madrid.
1746.	Palomino, Jose . . .	Sevilla.
1784.	Pechenet, Juan	Madrid.
1734.	Perez de Oviedo, Francisco .	Granada.
1746.	Pineda, Manuel	Cordova.
	Quintero, José .	Huelva.
1760 to 1777.	Reyna, Manuel	Toledo.
1743.	Reyno, Tomas	Toledo.
End of 18th cent.	Roche, Nicholas	Madrid.
1715 to 1757.	Rodriguez de Castro, Juan . . .	Burgos.
1784.	Rovira, José . .	Barcelona.
1746.	Roxelio, Francisco .	Cordova.
1791.	Ruiz, Donata . . .	Burgos.
1746.	Ruiz, Juan . .	Cordova.
	Ruiz, Miguel . . .	Cordova.
1777.	Ruiz, Pedro . . .	Burgos.
1746.	Sanchez, Francisco	Cordova.
1731.	Sanchez Renentes, Tomas	Sevilla.
1767 to 1777.	Sanchez Niño, Jose	Toledo.
1731.	Sanz, Pedro	Sevilla.
18th cent.	Sanz de Velasco, Toribio . .	Salamanca.
1700.	Simancas, Francisco de	Burgos.
1716.	Supuesta, Juan	Madrid.
1731.	Tamaral, Ignacio	Sevilla.
1746.	Torralvo, Sebastian	Cordova.
1755.	Torrijos, Lucas de	Burgos.
1771.	Urqueza, Domingo	Madrid.
	Valadrez Romero, Luis	Sevilla.
1746.	Vargas, Jose de	Cordova.
	Vega, Pedro de la	Cordova.
1754.	Vicente, Bautista	Valencia.
1728.	Vicente, Luis	Valencia.

Years in which they worked.		Residence.
1734.	Villa, Andres de	Sevilla.
1713 to 1715.	Zurreño, Antonio	Madrid.
1799 to 1800.	Ximenez, Manuel	Toledo.

I owe to the courtesy of Baron Ch. Davillier the names of the following artists, which appear in his "Histoire des Principaux Orfèvres Espagnols," Paris, 1879.

Perez de las Cellas, Antonio, a native of Saragossa; he worked at Rome in	1456
Ruiz, Alonso; he worked at Toledo in	1431
Ferrandez, Garci; he worked at Toledo in	1431
Pielagos, Juan Garcia, Burgos	1442
Fernai, Rodrigo, a Frenchman, who worked at Oviedo in . .	1368
Bells, Antonio, Barcelona	1458
Closes, Francisco, Barcelona	1464
Rodriguez de Villareal, Lope, Toledo	1466
Sano, Salvador, Barcelona	1475
Zobarola, Francisco, Banet	1480
Jujuce, a Valencian Jew, Pamplona	1356
Freset, Perrin, Rodez, Conrat de, } Frenchmen working at Olite, Navarre, in . .	1444
Bonte, Daniel de, a German, working at Olite, in Navarre . about	1400
Valdubia, Maestro Ferrando, Rome	1525
Fuente, Gonsalvo de, Rome	1539
Alfonso, Rome	1546

IRON WORK.

NUMEROUS iron mines have existed in Spain, especially in the Cantabrian provinces, and have been worked from very early times. They are mentioned by Pliny, lib. 34, cap. xii., and have given rise to the development of excellent metal works in the Spanish Peninsula: although in many localities this tradition has been continued until our days, the Basque Provinces have in all times excelled in this artistic industry.

The want of durability and the little care taken of objects of iron-work, owing to the insignificant value of the material employed, prevent us from being able to mention any important examples of a very early date. After drawing attention to some interesting specimens which have reached us from the Spanish-Arabs, we must begin the history of iron-work in Spain in the second half of the 15th century; it continues to progress in the 16th, and produced undoubtedly at that period works which were unrivalled in Europe. The *rejas* or chancel screens enclosing chapels in the cathedrals of Toledo, Seville, Granada, Salamanca, and other churches in Spain, of which it is much to be deplored no drawings or photographs exist, deserve the especial attention of those who follow this industry in the present day, owing to the beauty of their forms, and the inexhaustible variety of models which they present to the manufacturer.

Besides specimens of Iron-work connected with arms which will be described in a separate article, the most interesting examples of Moorish manufacture which have reached us are keys of most delicate tracery; their perfect state of preservation shows that they have only been used as symbols of cities or fortresses, which on given occasions were offered to kings or great people. Even in the present day the ceremony is still kept up of offering a key to the foreign princes who stay at the royal palace of Madrid, and in a similar manner as far back as the Middle Ages, keys have been presented to Spanish sovereigns on their visiting such towns as Toledo or Seville, and a ceremonial is gone through of swearing to uphold their privileges, a reminiscence probably of what occurred when these towns were conquered from the Moors.

One of these keys at Valencia, belonging to Count de Trigona, measures 9½ inches long, and was originally gilt; its handle or bow is closed, and covered with delicate work in relief. The wards are ornamented in the same manner with a combination of several words written in Cufic letters of difficult interpretation. Round the handle we can read most distinctly in Arabic the name of the artist: "It was made by Ahmed Ahsan."

This key appears to be of the 13th to 14th century. Two similar ones existed in the town hall of Valencia of a most monumental character; they were considered of great antiquity, but it has been ascertained that they were made in 1632, by the locksmith Juan Marti.

In the shrine of the Cathedral of Seville there are two interesting keys (*see* woodcut); one of them is of iron, the other of silver, of a similar style. For further details see "Museo Español de Antiguedades," vol. ii., p. 1. The first, which is represented to the right, is of genuine Moorish workmanship; the wards are covered with letters in Cufic characters, which several oriental scholars have tried to interpret, without coming to a satisfactory conclusion, probably owing to the confused, or double meaning of the letters. It is supposed with good foundation that this was the identical key which was given to King St. Ferdinand, the conqueror of Seville, in 1248, the day he took possession of the city. The silver key, to the left of the plate, has traces of gold and niello work, representing in the upper part, ships, castles and lions. Round the handle runs an inscription in Hebrew—" The King of Kings will open; the King of the whole Earth will enter." In the wards appear in delicate open work carving the following words in Spanish, "God will open; the king will enter. Dios abrirá; rey entrará." It may be affirmed to have been made in the 14th century, and in that case, symbolizes some event of the life of King Pedro the Cruel, a great protector of the Jewish race. Five Moorish keys of a similar kind, but inferior merit, may be seen in the local Museum of Segovia, and the Archæological Museum of Madrid.

The objects of iron-work made by the Christian artists of this period in Spain must have been good, for although no specimens exist, we have at any rate historical information which confirms this. In the Consistorial Ordinances of Barcelona, Capmany, "Memoirs," vol. i., we find that ironsmiths formed an extensive guild in the 13th century; in 1257 four of its members formed

MOORISH KEYS IN THE
CATHEDRAL OF SEVILLE.

part of the chief municipal council; this guild increased in importance in the following centuries. The Ordinances of Seville of the 15th century, which were reformed in 1502, and those of

Toledo, also re-enforced in 1582, give an idea of what was done by workers in bronze, the methods of workmanship and other details of interest. The Ordinances of Seville mention *rejas* made in Biscay, and give a good idea of the styles adopted by the iron-masters there. The Ordinances of Granada repeat almost exactly the former prescriptions.

The Cathedrals and large churches in Spain lent themselves in an admirable manner to the construction of objects of all kinds in iron work, especially the railings enclosing the side chapels, or sepulchres, and the double screens required for the *Capilla Mayor* and *Coro*, owing to the ancient Spanish custom of constructing the choir in the centre of the principal nave of the cathedral. Hence we meet with names of the iron-masters, *rejeros*, mentioned in early documents as attached to the different cathedrals in the same manner as painters and architects. We find Bartolomé Morey working at Palma de Mallorca in 1389 to 1397. He was succeeded by his son Juan, from 1401 to 1407. See Piferrer, "Recuerdos y Bellezas de España." Maestro Basil worked at Burgos, and Maestro Pablo at Toledo and its dioceses towards the end of the same century. Maestro Juan Francés worked at Toledo in 1482. By this same artist is the beautiful *reja* of the Capilla Mayor of the *Colegiata* of Alcala de Henares; it is signed, " Maestre Juan Francés, maestro mayor de las obras de fierro en España." From this time the names of iron-masters are well known and numerous; we may safely affirm that those who lived in the 16th century have left us the most important works.

One of the finest specimens of this artistic industry is the splendid *reja* which divides the nave at the royal chapel of Granada. Its immense size has enabled the artist to carry out a splendid ornamentation in the " plateresque style," combined with reliefs on a large scale of figures of apostles and saints, terminated at the upper part with a wide band of ornamentation of leaves and flowers, crowned with a Rood, with the Virgin and St. John on

either side. The splendid balustrades and supports are forged
with the hammer; the figures and circular piers are formed of
large plates, *repoussé* and carved in the most admirable manner,
and give a good idea of the difficulties of this work, which the
artists of this time had overcome, long before the various
technical facilities of the present day existed. The ornamentation
of this *reja* was originally gilt, and the figures are painted in oils.
It was made about the year 1520 to 1530; in the lock, formed
as a Gothic pinnacle, is a small inscription, "Maestro Bartolome
me fec." This same artist worked at Jaen and Seville. Cean
Bermudez calls him "sculptor and iron-master."

Two most important specimens of iron-work exist also at the
cathedral of Toledo, enclosing the *Capilla Mayor* and *Coro.*
The *reja* of the Capilla Mayor is 42 feet wide by 19 inches high;
it rests on a pediment of marble ornamented with masks and
bronze work, upon which rises the *reja*, which is divided hori-
zontally by means of a frieze of ornamentation, and this again
vertically in five compartments. In each vertical division there
is a pilaster of four sides formed of *repoussé* plates, carved with a
fine ornamentation in the renaissance style, this is again terminated with life-size figures in high relief of bronze. The second
compartment rises upon the band which divides it in an horizontal sense; it follows the same decoration in its pilasters, and
is terminated by a series of coats of arms, torches, angels, and a
variety of foliage which finishes the upper part. Upon the centre,
hanging from a thick chain supported from the roof, is suspended
a life-size Rood, of admirable effect, which completes the decoration. In several spots there are labels with mottos in Latin; in
one of them appears the following inscription, and the date of
1548 when this splendid work was finished: "Anno MDXLVIII.
Paul III. P. M. Carol. V. Imper. Rege. Joannes Martinez Siliceus.
Archipiscopus. Tolet. Hispaniae. Primat." The railings of this
reja are silvered, and the reliefs and salient points gilt. The
artist who made it was Francisco Villalpando, a native of Valla-

dolid ; this model was chosen among those of several artists, who presented their plans in competition before the ecclesiastical authorities; it is calculated that ten years elapsed before it was finally finished in 1548. Villalpando was greatly distinguished likewise as a sculptor and architect. In 1563 a book was printed after his death of a translation he made of the work on architecture by Sebastian Serlio. Other remarkable bronze works of art, which will be described further on, were also by him.

The *reja* of the coro, which is placed opposite that of the Capilla Mayor, is almost exactly similar in size. It is less rich in ornamentation, but so pure and sober in its general lines, and its ornamentation is so perfect, that it is perhaps superior to the other. This *reja* consists of a single architectonical body, divided in six vertical compartments, covered with bas reliefs of such delicate work that they appear rather to be by the hand of a silversmith than by an iron-master. An innumerable number of figures are combined with the ornamentation in the base, terminations of the columns and coronation; in the same manner it is full of banderoles with Latin mottos, and gilt and silvered; it was finished in 1548, as we see by the inscription. This *reja* was made by Domingo de Cespedes, a native of Toledo, with the help of his son-in-law, Fernando Bravo; the design was also chosen by competition, and it was finished in seven years. Both these admirable models of iron-work belong to the best productions of the renaissance school, and contain models which might be adapted with great advantage to ironwork of every description in the present day.

It would be an interminable task to describe the multitude of railings similar in richness and good taste to these which happily survive in Spanish cathedrals and churches. It is sufficient to call attention to the following. The *reja* of the Capilla del Condestable in the cathedral of Burgos, by Christoval de Andino in 1523, has been considered one of the finest specimens of its kind, owing to the perfection with which every detail is carried

out.   A contemporary writer in describing it says : " Good workmen, and those who wish that their work may have authority
an l be blameless, must endeavour to be guided by ancient
models, as your fellow-citizen, Cristoval de Andino ; his works
are thereby more elegant and excellent than any others which
I have seen up to the present time ; if not, judge of his work
by looking at the *reja* which he is making for your lord the
Condestable, which is undoubtedly superior to all those which
have hitherto been made in Spain." Sagredo—" Medidas del
Romano," quoted by Cean Bermudez.   In the centre of the
upper part, towards the middle, appears the inscription : " Ab.
Andino, A.D. MDXXIII."   The *reja* of the *coro* of the cathedral of Seville, made by the iron-master, Sancho Muñoz in
1519, a native of Cuenca, is also very remarkable ; besides the
finer ornamentation which covers it, it has figures of kings and
prophets representing the genealogy of Our Lord.   The *reja*
belonging to the *capilla mayor* of the same cathedral was the
work of Friar Francisco de Salamanca, 1518–1533 ; it is covered
with an open-work ornamentation, figures of angels and bas-reliefs,
and is terminated in the upper part with a representation of the
Entombment of Our Lord.   The large *reia* of the cathedral
of Cuenca, made by Arenas in 1517, those at Palencia, by
Andino, 1520, and Rodriguez, 1555 ; the one at the church of
Sn. Juan de la Penitencia, Toledo ; the beautiful railing at the
chapel of Palenzuela, in the cathedral of Salamanca, 1524, and a
number of objects of smaller size, such as iron pulpits in the
cathedrals of Barcelona, and in some chapels at Burgos, Avila,
Palencia, and Toledo, several of which are anterior to the 16th
century, are all worthy of the student's especial notice.   Among
these objects of smaller dimensions special reference must be
made to the fine and picturesque *reja* surrounding the sepulchre
of Archbishop Diego de Anaya, in the chapel of Sn. Bartolomé,
in the cloister of the cathedral of Salamanca.   The beauty of
its details and the open-worked inscription which surrounds it,

place it at once among the finest specimens of ironwork of the 15th century. The two window *rejas* at the house called "de las Conchas" in the same town—an admirable specimen of Burgundian architecture, although restored—may be quoted as excellent models of ironwork applied to civil buildings.

Iron pulpits have been made in Spain with great success. Two interesting examples of the end of the 15th century still exist at the cathedral of Avila. They are hexagonal in shape, and supported by lions' claws; they were originally gilt. One of these pulpits is ornamented in the Flamboyant style, the other in good Renaissance; consult Sir Digby Wyatt's "Architect's Note Book in Spain." Friar Francisco de Salamanca made two interesting iron pulpits for the cathedral of Seville; they are covered with bas-reliefs representing the Evangelists and subjects taken from the Acts of the Apostles and the Apocalypse. The pulpit at the parish church of Sⁿ· Gil de Burgos must also be mentioned. Mr. Street, notwithstanding his want of sympathy with every object not strictly of the Middle Ages, says: "It is of very late date, end of the 15th century, but I think it quite worthy of illustration. The support is of iron, resting on stone, and the staircase modern. The framework at the angles, top and bottom, is of wood, upon which the ironwork is laid. The traceries are cut out of two plates of iron, laid one over the other, and the ironwork is in part gilded, but I do not think that this is original. The canopy is of the same age and character, and the whole effect is very rich at the same time that it is very novel. I saw other pulpits, but none so old as this."

Among the applications of iron to decorations of civil architecture must be specially mentioned the nails and knockers on the doors of houses, which are so characteristic of Toledo and other old Spanish towns. This style was imitated from the Moors. Some doors still exist at the Alhambra, Granada, covered with enormous heads of nails of a half-spherical form with embossed pattern. These same nails are constantly to be found on old

Spanish houses, to which are added in the angles pieces of iron of a most artistic order.   A large number of these nails from Toledo, are in the Kensington Museum.   Examples of two are given.

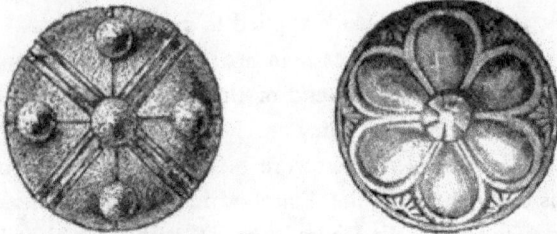

SPANISH NAIL HEADS.   SOUTH KENSINGTON MUSEUM.

After the 16th century this industry loses its artistic interest and importance.   Ironwork becomes simply practical and useful, and ceases to reproduce the grand carved and chiselled works of former times.   The artistic objects are reduced to specimens on a small scale : door-locks, of which an excellent example exists at the church of Calatravas, Madrid ; a weighing machine, made by the locksmith Salinas for the Mint in the 17th century, which was exhibited at the Special Loan Collection of Scientific Apparatus at Kensington in 1876, the fine ornamentation of the clock of the cathedral of Seville, made in the last century by Friar Josef Cordero, and the very remarkable iron locks made by Millan at the beginning of the present century, for the rooms at the palace of the Escurial, called " Piezas de Maderas finas."   The art of inlaying iron with gold and silver, constitutes in Spain a special industry ; the principal artists who carry it out at the present time with great skill are Messrs. Zuluaga at Madrid, and Alvarez at Toledo.   The splendid sepulchre of General Prim at the church of Atocha, Madrid, made entirely of damasquiné iron-work, is worthy of the greatest commendation ; the fine vases and shields of *repoussé* ironwork inlaid with gold, made by Alvarez of Toledo, are artistic and excellent revivals of the Milanese work of the 16th century.

IRON MASTERS.

Year in which they worked.	Name.	Locality of their Residence.
1520.	Avila, Fr. Juan de	Guadalupe.
1527.	Andino, Pedro	Seville.
1540.	Andino, Christoval	Toledo.
1557.	Arenas, Hernando	Cuenca.
1523.	Bartolmé, El Maestro	{ Jaen and Seville.
1555.	Barco, Alonso	Palencia.
1559.	Brabo, Hernando	Toledo.
1579.	Cela, Juan Tomas	Zaragoza.
1541.	Cespédes, Domingo de	Burgos.
1561.	Corral, Ruy Diaz del	Toledo.
1604.	Celma, Juan Bantista	{ Aragon y Galicia.
1692.	Conde, Sebastian	Seville.
1797.	Cordero, Fr. Josef	Seville.
1537.	Delgado, Juan	Seville.
1540.	Domingo, Maestro	Toledo.
1518.	Elias, Joan de	Palencia.
1519.	Esteban, Maestro	Seville.
1494.	Frances, Juan	Toledo.
1555.	Herreros, Llorente	Palencia.
1522.	Idrobo, Diego	Seville.
1524.	Juan, Fray	Seville.
1518.	Lopez, Juan do Urisarri	Palencia.
1531.	Lemosin	Cuenca.
1518.	Muñoz, Sancho	Cuenca.
1389.	Morey, Bartolomo	{ Palma de Mallorea.
1555.	Moreno, Benegno	Palencia.
1565.	Pedro, Maestre	Palencia.
1533.	Palencia, Antonis de	Seville.
1607.	Peñafiel, Luis de	Toledo
1510.	Prieto, Fernando	Seville.
1512.	Prelojero, Juan	Palencia.
1555.	Rodriguez, Gaspar	Palencia.
1607.	Rodriguez, Bartolomé	Toledo.
1607.	Silva, Francisco de	Toledo.
1533.	Salamanca, Francisco de	Seville.
1518.	Urisarri, Lopez	Palencia.
1561.	Villalpando	Toledo.
1518.	Yepes, Juan de	Seville.

BRONZES.

Objects of bronze of native origin are less frequently met with in Spain than those of silver and iron. Many foreign artists worked at this industry, the history of which only begins in the 16th century. The specimens of bronze work made by the Moors will be described in their proper place. It is true that examples of bronze made by the Iberians and Romans are frequently met with in excavations; they consist chiefly of hatchets and other arms, bracelets, fibulas, etc., but they are similar in every respect to objects of the same kind found in other European countries. During the Middle Ages, objects of enamelled gilt bronze were used on a very large scale in churches; specimens of a very high order may be seen in Spain, such as the splendid altar at San Miguel de Excelsis in Navarre; that at Santo Domingo de Silos, and the statuette of the Virgin de la Vega at San Esteban, Salamanca. These objects were, however, probably made at Limoges, or in some other locality out of Spain. We hardly can trace any bronze of this period but cathedral bells. One was made at Puig-Valencia as early as A.D. 622, melted in 1550, the only trace of the early work being the inscription and date, which are given by contemporary authors.

Another bell, about half a foot high, of A.D. 875, exists at the Local Museum of Cordova, with the inscription: "*Offert hoc munus Samson abbatis in domum Sancti Sebastiani martyris Christi, Era* DCCCCXIII." We find the name of "*Joannes Calcena me fecit Anno Domini* 1306," on a bell at the cathedral of Valencia, and on one of Lerida was to be read : " *Fecit factum per magistrum Joannem Adam Anno Dei* 1418 *in mense Aprili ;* " the author appears to have been, by reference to the documents of the church, " *de burgo Sanctæ Mariæ Turlensis diocesis regni Franciæ,*" for details see Villanueva, vol. ii., p. 147—152, xvi. 88.

Before entering into the renaissance period, I must mention some remarkable specimens which have reached us, the work of the Spanish Arabs. Probably the most ancient and interesting is a sculpture representing a stag, now at the Provincial Museum of Cordova, which evidently belonged to a fountain. It was found in the ruins of the palace of Medina Az Zahra, the construction of which corresponds to the time of Abd er Rahman III., (961); it is undoubtedly work of this period, and probably belonged to this palace, so celebrated by Oriental writers. The fragments of a bronze fountain and several lamps, at the Museum of Granada, are of a later date ; they were found in the excavations of the early city of Illiberis, which was abandoned in the 11th century, when its inhabitants chose the present site of Granada. The fragments, which are supposed to have belonged originally to a fountain, consist of a small temple 22 inches high, of an hexagonal base, with twelve small columns supporting bands of open work, frescoes, cupola, and turrets: in the angles are birds. There are six lamps, all of which are mutilated and incomplete ; their form and object is indicated by the remains of chains which suspended them. Some of them are half melted, giving testimony to the conflagration which the mosque suffered in the time of the Arabs. Other bronze fragments have been found in the same locality. All these objects are artistic in their general lines, but the workmanship is indifferent, and the ornamentation heavy and coarse.

A bronze lion and a mortar, found some years since in the province of Palencia, are more artistic in form and general details. The mortar was found near Monzon, and the lion not far from it. Remains still exist of a castle, which was founded by the Arabs, in the locality, and which at the beginning of the 11th century was in the hands of the Christians; it is highly probable that these objects belonged to its Moorish inhabitants. If we take into account how frequently we find Oriental remains in this locality, both these objects may be safely classified as belonging to the 10th century, although there are details in their ornamentation which appear rather to be of a later period. The lion is 12½ inches high by 14½ inches long; an aperture in the lower part which communicates with the mouth of the animal, appears to suggest that it belonged to a fountain, the water of which issued, or not, owing to the movement of the tail, which rotates and acts as a key. The shape of this lion recalls those at the Alhambra; its forms are stiff and angular, in the conventional Oriental manner of reproducing animated beings. The surface is covered with ornamentation, the mane is arranged in mannered and symmetrical curls, like those so common in Assyrian sculptures. On the back and two sides is the following inscription in Cufic characters :

بركة كاملة نعمة شاملة

" Perfect blessing. Complete happiness."

This object is similar in detail and the inscription to a bronze griffin at the cemetery of Pisa ; it belonged to the collection of the painter Fortuny, and at the sale in 1875 it was bought by Mr. E. Piot.

The mortar is circular in form, and is surrounded by twelve prismatic sections. Two lions' heads serve to support the hanging rings or handles. The whole of the outside is most delicately carved with arabesques, among which are to be met frequently figures of birds and quadrupeds. See " El arte en Esp.," vol. iii., Madrid, 1864. The following inscription in elegant Cufic characters runs round the upper part: it is repeated twice. " Complete blessing, and ever-increasing happiness and prosperity of every kind, and an elevated and happy social position for its owner." From the richness of the ornamentation of this object, it is probable that it was used to pound aromatic drugs.

A bronze lamp of a similar ornamentation was found some years ago at Cordova—it is not unlike in form and shape Roman lamps of the same kind made of earthenware. It is engraved all over, and the subject of a dog pursuing a hare appears often repeated. None of these objects of bronze work are however equal in importance to a lamp made during the reign of Mohammed III. of Granada, now at the Archæological Museum, Madrid [See Plate.] It is composed in its base of a body destined to hold the light, upon which is supported a large four-sided piece in the form of a pyramid, which is completed with an octagonal body which surmounts it. Four graduated balls suspend it. The height of this lamp is 2½ yards, and taking into account its general structure, it appears as if the chains or intermediate pieces are wanting, which probably existed on the inverted bell of the base. The manufacture and elegance of decoration of this object is of a very high order, and may be compared with bronze work of Damascus. The greater part of the pieces are covered with pierced open work, and the motto of the Kings of Granada, "There is no conqueror but God." In the lower part of the large pyramid, truncated in four sides, is a long inscription in Arabian characters, stating the lamp to have been made by order of Mohammed III. year of the Hegira, 705 (A.D. 1305).

The remaining objects of bronze work of Spanish-Moorish production are less important. They are interesting notwithstanding. The spherical perfume-burners which were used to roll on the pavement are highly artistic and might be adopted in the present day. One or two bronze buckets of a well exist at the Madrid Archæological Museum, with some small objects of little importance found at Cordova. This artistic industry has continued until the present day in Spain in the form of

MOORISH LAMP. ARCHÆOLOGICAL MUSEUM, MADRID.

objects of domestic use, such as brasiers, mortars and lamps, several of which preserve their ancient traditional form.

In metal work as in architecture, a large number of instances exist in Spain in which the Christian and Moorish styles are blended—as an example of this style may be mentioned the fine bronze gates of the cathedral of Toledo. These doors, which are 18 ft. high by 12 ft. wide, are covered on both sides with bronze plates; the outer side is decorated with a geometrical Moorish design and small Arabic inscriptions, alternating with castles and a number of Arabic mottoes. In one of the side bands and in the lower part may be read in Spanish the following inscription:

" Estas puertas fueron acabadas en el mes de Marzo era de mil c ccc. setanta e cinco años."

"These doors were finished in the month of March, in the era of 1375 years " (A.D. 1337).

The fine doors of the cathedral of Cordova, del Perdon, are similar in style. They are made of wood and covered with bronze plating, and Gothic and Arabic inscriptions,—the word " Deus," and

الملك كله الله

"The empire belongs to God, all is His." Round these doors, alternating with the arms of Castille and Leon, is the following inscription. " Dia dos del mes de Marzo de la era del Cesar de 1415 años, (A.D. 1377.) Reinante el muy alto et poderoso D. Enrique, rey de Castilla." These doors were restored in 1539.

The Puerta del Perdon of the cathedral of Seville is similar in style, and a good example of moresque bronze work.

Returning to the bronze work of the Christian artists of the renaissance period, the general rule which may be established with reference to statues is that they have been made by foreign artists. This is the case with the splendid groups of figures at the high altar and presbytery of the Escorial by Pompeyo Leoni, the equestrian statue of Philip IV. by Pedro Tacca, and others of a similar kind. One of the very few exceptions to this rule occurs in Bartolomé Morel, a Spaniard, the author of the statue called the "Giralda" on the tower of the cathedral of Seville, the desk of the choir, and *Tenebrarium* at the same church. These objects were all by him, and are among the finest specimens of bronze work in Spain. The *Tenebrarium* is described by Cean Bermudez in his "Descripcion artistica de la catedral de Sevilla," p. 129, in the following manner: "This object is better executed and more graceful in design than any of its kind in Spain. It consists of a triangular candelabrum, which is used during matins in the three last days of Holy Week with fifteen tapers, which are extinguished on reading each psalm.

"It was designed and executed by Bartolomé Morel in 1562. Juan Giralte, a native of the Low Countries, and Juan Bita Vazquez helped him to make the statues which are at the head of this candelabrum, and Pedro Delgado, a sculptor of great renown, worked at the foot.

"It is 8 yards and a half high, and the triangular upper part is 3 yards wide: it is surmounted by fifteen statues which represent Our Saviour, the Apostles and two other disciples or evangelists. In the vacant space of the triangle there is a circle ornamented with foliage, in the centre of which is a figure in high relief of the Blessed Virgin, underneath is a medallion bust of a king. This centre is of bronzed wood, and is supported by four small bronze columns, below which are four caryatides, resting on a nobly designed border ornamented with lions and other animals in the renaissance style." See woodcut on next page.

Villalpando distinguished himself at the cathedral of Toledo in the same way as Morel at Seville. The splendid *reja* at the Capilla Mayor with the fine gilt bronze pulpits, the bas-reliefs of the doors of Lions, 1564, the font, and railing surrounding the altar of the Virgin in the coro were all made by him. The pulpits, made as it is asserted out of the bronze sepulchre of Dn. Alvaro de Luna are octagonal, six of their sides are admirably decorated

THE TENEBRARIUM IN THE CATHEDRAL OF SEVILLE.

with bas-reliefs of exquisite work divided by pilasters and terminated by a finely designed frieze. The door of Lions is covered in a similar manner with bronze plates ornamented in the finest renaissance style; the knockers are models in their way. In the opposite door del Reloj, these reliefs have been copied in 1713 by the silversmiths Zurreño y Dominguez.

Notwithstanding the great merit of these works, the stands for the choir books are even finer and more exquisite in detail. They are made of gilt bronze and represent subjects from the life of St. Ildefonso, the Prophet David and the Apocalypse. They were modelled and designed by Juan Navarro in 1562, and carved by Nicolas de Vergara and his son some years afterwards.

Two artists, natives of Aragon, were very famous during the same century for their bronze work. One of these, Celma, made the pulpits of the cathedral of Santiago, which are finely ornamented with busts between the columns, and bas-reliefs representing subjects of the lives of the saints, and a fine design of leaves and flowers. In one of the inscriptions may be read: "*Joannes Baptista Celma, Aragonentis patria pingendi artifex salutis anno 1563. Compostellæ faciebat.*" The other artist was Cela, the author of the fine reja del coro of the church of the Pilar at Saragossa, dated 1574–79.

Two gilt metal Monstrances of Spanish work of the 16th century are in the South Kensington Museum. No. 4310, 57, represents an architectural shrine, decorated with strap and cartouche-work, columns, and arcades in the renaissance style; it is dated 1537. See woodcut on next page. The other, No. 190, 66, has an ornamented stem, with knob, on which stands a triangular shrine with kneeling angels; above is a smaller shrine surmounted by a crucifix.

Objects of bronze work of the 17th century which are not by Fanelli, Tacca, or other foreigners, are less numerous; most of them show signs of the decline of art at this period. The chiselled and openworked altar frontal, at the burial-place of the

SPANISH MONSTRANCE, DATED 1537. SOUTH KENSINGTON MUSEUM.

kings of Spain at the Escorial, is a very fine work of its kind.
The shrine of the Sagrario de la Santa Forma, also at the

Escorial, is an excellent piece of workmanship—both these objects were made by lay brothers of the convent. Friar Eugenio de la Cruz and Friar Juan de la Concepcion, silversmiths, worked during the reign of Philip IV. at chiselling these and other objects of bronze.

The exaggerations and bad taste, which were so common in every branch of artistic industry, were as prominent in bronzes—the bas-reliefs of this metal which ornament the back of the high altar of the cathedral of Toledo, at the "Transparente," are generally mentioned as models of bad taste. They are by Narciso Thomé; the architecture, painting, statues and carvings in marble, jasper and bronze are by the same person, as appears in the inscription which he placed there at its termination in 1734.

On the accession of King Charles III. from Naples in 1759, these defects were corrected, in part owing to the classical influence which became so general in Europe, and continued to the early part of the present century. The silver manufactory of Martinez founded in Madrid under his auspices, has already been mentioned in treating of silver work. Objects of bronze of all kinds were made there in this classic style, and at the porcelain manufactory of Buen Retiro, where splendid tables were made of pietre dure, mounted in bronze. The most important objects there produced may be seen at the chapel of the royal palace of Madrid, and the palaces of Aranjuez and the Escurial.

ARMS.

THOSE who have a taste for the study of prehistorical monuments in Spain, will find a very extensive collection of arms and other utensils of this period at the Muséo Arqueologico, Madrid, which have been found in different localities of the country. They chiefly consist of hatchets, knives, and lance and arrow points made of flint, and are similar in form to those which have been discovered in the north and centre of Europe. There are therefore, constant analogies between the implements used by the primitive Iberians, and those of other European races of the prehistoric period.

The arms and weapons of the following age, known as the age of bronze, are less common in Spain, although a few specimens exist in the Muséo of Madrid, and the "Academia de la Historia." They chiefly consist of swords, daggers, and lance and arrow points. The hilts are formed of the same material as the blade in some instances, in others they consist of a blade fitting into a wooden or ivory handle. The blades are cut on both sides; they are straight, and finished off in a point; in the centre runs a thick rim made for the purpose of strengthening the blade, and that it should not bend. One of these specimens measures 30 inches long. The daggers are about one-third smaller, with the same rim in the centre; the bronze hilt is nailed to the blade, and the lance and arrow points are of the same kind. These weapons are similar in style to the numerous examples found in other countries, especially England. The hatchets are also the same, their manner of being fixed on to their handles and their size and weight being identical with the English ones. One of the few specimens which varies from this general rule, is a dagger, with a cylindrical horn-like hilt, belonging to Sᵗ. Villaamil : it was found at Galicia with other interesting arms. (Consult Muséo Español de Antiguedades, iv. 63.)

The probable antiquity of these weapons always remains a matter of doubt; this is especially the case with stone implements. When on their discovery the geological structure of the soil has been studied, some evidence exists on which to ground an opinion; but this is very seldom the case in Spain, and Messrs. Prado, Villanova, Botella, and MacPherson, are among the few and most trustworthy geologists who have investigated this subject. With reference to bronze implements, Spanish authors have a tendency to attribute them to prehistoric times. I see no reason to justify this opinion, and it appears to me that when this subject has been studied in a more satisfactory manner, it will appear that these arms were used during the Roman domination at the same time as the iron ones.

In reaching the Iron period, already within historical times, we find that the Spanish people, when once under the Roman rule, used the well known arms and utensils which will be found reproduced in all elementary books on archæology. In this, as in every other sphere, the Romans imposed their civilization on the races they conquered. Some important exceptions, however, exist to this general rule. The Spanish swords must have been excellent in quality, since the Romans adopted them after the Carthaginian war : they were however, never able to imitate the manner in which they were tempered. Suidas says : *Romani patriis gladiis depositis Hannibalico bello Hispaniensium assumpserunt . . . . sed ferri boni atem et fabrica solertiam imitari non potuerunt.* The locality where the best swords were made in Spain was Bilbilis (Calatayud, province of Aragon), the birthplace of the poet Martial, who, when praising the waters of the river

Jalon and the excellence of its quality for tempering metals, says, *Salone qui ferrum gelat.* These swords were wide, and cut on both edges ; their points were sharp, and all of them had in the centre signs of a central groove running down its length. Several specimens may be seen at the Museo Arqueologico, Madrid, which are 15 or 19 inches long. The Spaniards used also swords of another form, which were known by the name of *falcata,* from falx, sickle ; the blade was curved, and it has been supposed to be the genuine Spanish model. The blade was widened in proportion from the hilt to the point, which was very sharp : it cut like a sickle in the interior curve, and only a small part was sharpened in the opposite side. The best specimen, which exists in the Madrid Museum, is 22½ inches long. The weapons made at Toledo must have been very famous during the Roman period : Gracio Falisco, a poet of the time of Julius Cæsar, says, in mentioning them : *Ima toletano præcingant ilia cultro ;* the sword manufactory there attained afterwards great importance.

I must end by mentioning the *funda,* or slings, and leaden plummets (*glandes*), which were thrown so dexterously by the slingers of the Balearic Islands. The slingers of this province are mentioned with great praise by ancient authors. (V. Smith, Dictionary of Greek and Roman Antiquities. *Funda.*)

During the Visigothic domination, some modifications must have been introduced in the form and number of the arms used, probably owing to the tradition of the Gothic race, and the Byzantine or Oriental influences, which they accept in every sphere ; but the names and explanation of these weapons, given by San Isidoro in his " Etimologies," lib. xviii., indicate that the Roman system was adopted as a general rule. The chief modification which may be established for the Visigoths, and the greater part of the European races, is that from their time the breast-plates and metallic pieces, which served as a protection for the legs and arms, fell into disuse, and were substituted by coats of mail or chain armour. This is deduced from San Isidoro's not describing

G

these metallic plates; although he gives numerous details on
different sorts of coats of mail, including those made of coarse
stuffs woven in Silisia.   At this time, the use of planks or boards
to protect the body was abandoned, and did not prove acceptable
until the end of the 13th century, when they again became very
generally adopted in Spain.

During the 13th and 14th centuries, the Spanish Christians
continued to use the same weapons as in other European states.
The history of Spanish arms, in like manner with its artistic
history and civilization, is similar to that of other nations; it frequently occurs that objects of this kind are classified with those
of other countries, the only exceptions to this general rule being
those which result from the Moorish conquest and influence.

The Arabs, after they took possession of Spain at the beginning
of the 8th century, imported, with their arts and industries, special
arms and weapons, the greater part of which were copied from
Persian models ; their swords, helmets, and shields deserve special
attention ; in other weapons the difference is not so great ; and,
indeed, in the two first it is chiefly confined to their decoration.

None of the arms made by the Moors have been so justly
celebrated, or so delicately worked as their swords.   An Arabic
author, El Camus, says the Arabs had as many as 1000 names to
designate swords.   In the first years of the Hegira, their historians
praise the swords made at Yemen, and in India ; later on, those
of Syria ; Damascus was, however, the great centre where arms of
all kinds were made.   Several interesting Arabic manuscripts are
known on this subject, such as the *Treatise on steel blades* in the
library of Gotha, that on *Different kinds of arms, with the properties
of lances, swords, and horses*, in the Library of Leyden, and
numerous articles by Oriental scholars, which have appeared in
the "Journal Asiatique," and other reviews.   The manufacture
in Syria decayed in the 15th century ; other centres gained in
importance, specially those in Egypt, Morocco, and Spain, which
had rivalled the East in this industry during the Middle Ages.

The Arabs introduced their forms and manner of decorating arms when they invaded the Peninsula; it is, however, highly probable that the traditions still existed at Bilbilis and Toledo of the manner of tempering steel. It is known that Abd-er Rahman II. (A.D. 822–852) reformed the manufacture of arms at Toledo, and that in A.D. 965, Al Hakem II. sent a rich present of specimens made in the locality to Don Sancho, King of Leon. Notwithstanding the high reputation of the industries of Cordova, the great centre and court of the Spanish Arabs during the earlier period of their domination, "it never became famous for its working steel," as Fernandez Gonzalez tells us in his study on Spanish-moresque swords, from which much of this information has been derived. (V. Mus. Esp. de Antiguedades, v. i. and v.). Almeria, Murcia, Seville, and Granada were greatly distinguished in this manufacture during the domination of the Arabs in Spain.

We know that Almeria, during the 12th and 13th centuries, " was also famous for the fabrication of all sorts of vases and utensils of iron, copper, or glass." (Mohamadan Dynasties in Spain, by Al-Makkari, vol. i. p. 51.) Abou Said, in writing in the 13th century of Murcia, says, " Objects are made there of latteen and ron, consisting of knives and scissors, with an ornamentation in gold. Other similar utensils, proper for the outfit of a bride, or a soldier, in such large quantities, that the mere thought of it confuses the imagination."

The same author, when speaking of the swords of Seville, says, " The steel which is made at Seville is most excellent ; it would take too much time to enumerate the delicate objects of every kind which are made in this town." These industries must have continued in the hands of the Moors after the town was conquered by Spaniards in the 13th century. In the following century we find in the will of King D⁰. Pedro, " I also endow my son with my Castilian sword, which I had made here in Seville, ornamented with stones and gold."

No specimens of Hispaño-moresque swords exist previous to the 15th century. We possess some highly interesting examples of this period, all, or the most part, of which were made at Granada, the last centre of civilization of the Spanish Arabs. The most important are the sword, dagger, and double-handed sword and knife, which, with the authentic costume, belonging to Boabdil, the last king of Granada, are now in the possession of the Marquis of Villaseca, at Madrid. These objects were gained by an ancestor of the marquis, who took Boabdil prisoner in 1482 at the battle of Lucena. In compliance with the chivalrous practice of the time, the arms of the conquered king went to the conqueror, and have been kept as heirlooms since that time.

The sword of Villaseca is 39 inches long, this includes 12 inches of the hilt. (See woodcut.) "The steel blade," says S'. Fernandez, in his article, vol. v. p. 395, "is of a later date, and appears to have been added to the sword after the older one had disappeared. It is a Toledo blade, marked with the letter S, similar to the one used by Alonso Sahagun the elder, and with a hollow line in the centre."

I am of opinion, however, that it may be the original blade, for the other sword, which still exists at Granada, of the same kind, has likewise a blade marked T, Toledo. This coincidence appears to suggest that those made there were preferred, and in both instances they exactly fit the sheath, which is the original one.

The hilt of this fine sword is formed of solid gold, enamelled in blue, white, and red. This decoration runs along the pommel and cross bars. The axle is made of ivory carved with the utmost skill. Two octagons are on each side, with the following inscription in semi-Cufic letters:

$$\text{و بالغ في}$$

(may you) "obtain your object." On the other side:

$$\text{بقاء}$$

"in saving his life."

SWORD OF BOABDIL. VILLASECA COLLECTION, MADRID.

Four shields surround in the upper part this axle, which contains the following inscription in rather illegible characters :

بسم الله القدرة لله ولا الله الا هو العبطه لله الواحد

"In the name of God, power belongs to him, there is no other divinity but he, happiness proceeds from God alone."

In the lower part in similar shields we read :

الآبة هى لله لانه اول مرة لا يعلمون بالله الجاهلون ونذرهم فى طغيانهم

"Miracles belong to God, for certainly the ignorant do not know God at first, for it is their habit to err."

On the pommel is the following inscription :

قل الله واحد هو لم يلد ولم يوبد

Say, He alone is God, Eternal God, who neither created, nor was engendered."

Under the pommel, on green enamel, appear the following letters :

قل هو

الله

احد الله

الصمد لم . . . .

Say, " The only God, Eternal, not . . '

On the other side :

يلد

فلم يو . . .

لد فلم يا

كن له كفوا احد

" was neither created, nor engendered, and has no equal."

On a band which appears under the axle, on enamel, are the following letters:

الله

هو

الرحمان

الرحيم

" God is clement and merciful," and on the other side :

الله

هو خير

احفظ

" God is gifted with the best memory."

The learned archæologist and orientalist, Dⁿ Pascual de Gayangos, is of opinion that this sword was worn hanging round the neck, between the shoulder blades. A small bag, *tahali*, probably hung also from the leather girdle, which still exists in the collection of Villaseca.

The *montante*, or double-handed sword, has an iron cylindrical hilt inlaid with ivory. On it appears the motto of the kings of Granada :

ولا غلب الا الله

" God alone is the conqueror."

The blade, part of which is wanting, is marked with the crescent.

The dagger is superior in artistic merit. The hilt is made of iron, ornamented with ivory delicately engraved in arabesques. The blade is damascened in gold, with inscriptions on one side, repeating :

السلامة العز الفايم السعد الدايم

" Health, permanent glory, and lasting happiness [belong to God "].

On the opposite side :

ـﺮﻓ ﻒﻌﻓ

" It was made by Reduan."

The scabbard of this dagger is most beautiful, its chapes are made of silver enamelled in green, and the remainder is of crimson velvet embroidered in gold, from which hangs a fine tassel of silk and gold thread. A small eating knife is fitted into this same scabbard, which possesses no artistic interest.

The woodcut on the next page will give a good idea of the blade of a Moorish dagger of the 15th century.

A sword of a similar kind to the one already described may be seen at Granada at the *Administrador's* of the Generalife. It belongs to the marquis of Campotejar, a descendant of Sidi Jahia, a Moorish prince who was converted to Christianity. The marquis of Vega de Armijo has an interesting sword of the same kind, and two others exist at the Museo de Artilleria, Madrid, which belonged to Aliatar; Boabdil's sword is at the Royal Armoury. The Hispano Arab sword, which for centuries had been in a saint's hand at the church of San Marcelo, Leon, is now at the Museo Arqueologico, Madrid.

The Spanish Moors used helmets similar in form to those of the Christians, though their manner of decoration was different; after the importations made by the Crusaders, the similarity must every day have been greater. The *almofar*, which appears by its name to have been originally oriental, and which is constantly named in Spanish documents from the poem of the Cid, was a protection for the head, of a similar form to those used in France and other countries, consisting of a hood made of chain armour, covering the head and leaving the face free ; upon it was placed the hood or helmet. Some helmets exist at the Royal Armoury of Madrid of Spanish Moorish origin ; among them are two very remarkable ones, which have been attributed to Boabdil, the last king of Granada. (Nos. 2345, 2356, of the Catalogue.) They are decorated with gold filigree, niellos, and geometrical ornamentation in the best oriental style, most admirably worked, and different in this respect to the helmets used in this time. Another interesting helmet, which belonged to this ill-fated monarch, exists in the province of Almeria.

The *adargas*, or shields, are more varied: they were frequently adopted by the Christians. They were generally round, with a salient point in the centre, *ombilicus*, or a sort of iron grating made for the purpose of entangling the adversary's sword. These shields were of wood or thick cowhide, *vacaries*, and were decorated outside in a variety of ways, sometimes with pierced iron plates or bands of leather, forming arabesques; and at other times with an ornamentation of iron, and leather embroidered with gold and silver, with rich hanging tassels and pendants. Shields of a prolonged form were also very constantly used, terminating in a semicircle in the upper part, and in the lower by a sharp point or a semicircle at the top and bottom, as may be seen in the paintings of the Sala de la Justicia at the Alhambra. A good collection of round shields may be seen at the Armoury at Madrid: they are not earlier in date than the 15th century, the most interesting among them are Nos. 233, 253, 389, 595, and 607 of the Catalogue. Some of them are exquisite in work and detail. These shields, although belonging to the

MOORISH DAGGER,
15TH CENTURY.

latest period of the middle ages, were used before this time,
for they appear on the ivory casket existing at the cathedral of
Pamplona, [V. Ivories, p. 130], dated A.D. 1005, and in miniatures
of Spanish MSS. of that date. One of the best examples, which
may be mentioned to confirm these indications, will be found in
a MS. at the British Museum (Add. ii., 695), which was painted
during a period of twenty years in the monastery of Silos, near
Burgos, and finished and completed A.D. 1109. Mr. Shaw, in
his " Dresses and Decorations," vol. v., reproduces some of these
figures, and says : " The figures which form our plate represent
Spanish warriors of the later part of the 11th century, and are
interesting on account of their remarkable resemblance to the
Anglo-Norman soldiers on the celebrated Bayeux tapestry. This
resemblance is observable in the style of the drawing, as well as
in the costumes. It is highly probable that the military habits of
this period were borrowed from the Saracens. This supposition
is strengthened by the fact that Arabic inscriptions in Cufic letters
are found among the ornaments of the several robes still preserved which belonged to German and Frankish barons of the
10th and 11th centuries. One peculiarity of our Spanish warriors
is the round shield with the elegant ornaments on the disc."

These may be considered the chief varieties of Spanish arms
in the Middle Ages. In other instances the French and Italian
forms are adopted. The manufacture of arms was not reduced
then as at a later date to the monopoly of the Government or to
determined localities. Besides the arms made at Toledo, those
of Seville, Granada, Valencia, Zaragoza, Barcelona, the Basque
provinces, and Cuellar, were very famous. Readers of Shake-
speare will remember Falstaff's *bilbo*, a rapier made at Bilbao in the
Basque provinces. The principal merit of these arms consisted
in the manner in which the artist tempered his metal. It was
generally done at night in order to distinguish in the darkness
the exact colour of the heated steel in dipping it into the water.
The swords known by the name of *perrillo* were highly esteemed

in Spain during the 15th and 16th centuries ; they were marked
with a figure resembling a dog.   Cervantes mentions and praises
these blades in his "Rinconete y Cortadillo " and "Don Quixote."
They were made by a Moor of Granada, who it is stated had
been swordsman of King Boabdil, and became a Christian under
the name of Julian del Rey.   His godfather was King Ferdinand,
and besides working at Granada he did so at Zaragoza and
Toledo.   When an artist of merit excelled in a given locality, it
absorbed all the fame of this industry.   During the Renaissance
larger centres of this industry were established in large towns, and
the fame of the objects they produced was concentrated there.
Toledo absorbed the importance in the industry of sword making.

We find that the Municipal Ordinances of the Middle Ages
give very little information by which we can judge of the merits
of the objects produced.   A Guild of Armourers existed at Barcelona as early as 1257, and of Sword makers from the 14th century ;
but the information given concerning this subject is very slight. ·
We find more details in the Ordinances of Toledo, Seville, and
Granada, whence we learn that manufactories of arms existed in
these towns.

The sword manufactory of Toledo acquires its greatest importance during the Renaissance period until the end of the 17th
century, when it terminated.   It was re-established again in 1760
under the patronage of the Government, and continues to work in
the present day.   Don Francisco de Santiago Palomares wrote, in
1772, an "Account of the Sword Manufactory of Toledo," the
manuscript of which exists at the Academia de la Historia (E. 41).
The most interesting part of this study consists in the details
given upon the manner of tempering the blades.   The names he
has collected of the most remarkable artists, are taken from the
original dies of their marks which existed at the Archives of the
Ayuntamiento at Toledo.   These marks have been published in
the "Catalogo de la Armeria," Madrid, 1849, from which I copy
them.   It must be borne in mind that Palomares, after quoting

the text by the Poet Gracio Falisco, which I have given at the beginning, does not establish any definite fact which enables us to study the historical progress of this manufactory during the Middle Ages. The author says, p. 111: "At the beginning of this industry there was no centralization or monopoly in this manufactory, some armourers formed a guild, placing each artist in his proper place. The kings of Castille granted them privileges of different kinds."

Bowles says, in his "Introduction to the Natural and Geographical History of Spain," that the steel used at the manufactory of Toledo was taken from an iron mine existing at a league from Mondragon, the only one then known in Spain.

The celebrity of Toledo blades has excited the curiosity of many who wished to ascertain the cause of their great excellence and renown. Some supposed the sword manufacturers of Toledo possessed a secret for tempering their arms: it was not so, however; their only secret being the waters of the Tagus and the fine white sand on its banks. This sand was used for cooling the steel: when the steel was red-hot, and began to give forth sparks, it was uncovered a little and sprinkled with sand, and sent on to the forgers. As soon as the blade was ready it was tempered in the following manner: a line of fire was made and the blade placed in it in such a manner that only four-fifths of its length should touch the fire. As soon as the blade was red-hot it was dropped perpendicularly into a bucket of Tagus water; when cold, if it was found to be bent, a small portion of sand was poured on the yoke, the blade was placed upon it, and beaten until properly straightened. After this the fifth part of the blade was fired, and when red-hot was seized with tongs and rubbed with suet, which soon began to melt; after this the blade was sent to the grinding-stones, and finished by being polished by wooden wheels with emery powder.

Charles the Third, a year after he became King of Spain, re-established officially the manufactory of arms of Toledo. He placed it in a building near the Miradero Alto, and the works began in 1761. The king soon found the building too small for the purpose, and ordered his architect, Sabatini to build the present one, outside the town near the river Tagus, which was finished in 1783, and from this time has been under the superintendence of the Royal Artillery. Not a single sword maker existed in 1760 of any note who was competent to be placed at the head of the works, and it was found necessary to bring a proper person from Valencia.

Palomares, who was present, says: "As soon as the building was ready and disposed for working, Luis Calisto, a famous sword maker, began to work. Calisto was a native of Valencia, and more than 70 years of age when he was appointed. Other artists were chosen at the same time by the Director. In the short space of time in which that chief master armourer lived, he made most excellent weapons; he was most skilful, and was probably imitated by his successor."

Names of the Sword Makers of Toledo.

The numbers given correspond to the plates of their marks, given in "Catalogo de la Real Armeria."

1. Alonso de Sahagun, el *viejo*, 1570.
2. Alonso de Sahagun, el *mozo*.
3. Alonso Perez.
4. Alonso de los Rios ; he also worked at Cordova.
5. Alonso de Cava.
6. Andres Martinez.
7. Andres Herraez ; he also worked at Cuenca.
8. Andres Munesten ; worked at Calatayud.
9. Andres Garcia.
10. Antonio de Baena.
11. Antonio Gutierrez.
12. Antonio Gutierrez, a son of the former.
13. Antonio Ruiz, 1520 ; he used the initial letter of his name.
14. Adrian de Zafra ; worked at Sn. Clemente.
15. Bartolomé de Nieva.

16. Casaldo y Campañeros ; worked at Cuellar and Badajoz.
17. Domingo de Orozco.
18. Domingo Maestre, el *viejo*.
19. Domingo Maestre, el *mozo*.
20. Domingo Rodriguez.
21. Domingo Sanchez ; called el Tigerero.
22. Domingo de Aguirre.
23. Domingo de Lama.
24. Domingo Corrientes ; worked also at Madrid.
25. Fabrian de Zafra ; hijo de Adrian.
26. Francisco Ruiz, el *viejo*, 1617.
27. Francisco Ruiz, el *mozo*.
28. Francisco Gomez.
29. Francisco de Zamora ; worked also at Seville.
30. Francisco de Alcozer ; worked at Madrid.
31. Francisco Lurdi.
32. Francisco Cordiu.
33. Francisco Perez.
34. Giraldo Reliz.
35. Gonzalo Simon, 1617.
36. Gabriel Martinez.
37. Gil de Almau.
38. Hortuño de Aguirre, 1604.
39. Juan Martin.
40. Juan de Leizalde ; worked at Seville.
41. Juan Martinez, el *viejo*.
42. Juan Martinez, el *mozo*, 1617.
43. Juan de Almau, 1550.
44. Juan de Toro.
45. Juan Ruiz.
46. Juan Martinez de Garata.
47. Juan Martinez Menchaca ; he lived at the beginning of the 16th century, and worked at Lisbon, Seville, and Madrid.
48. Juan Ros.
49. Juan Moreno.
50. Juan de Saludo.
51. Juan de Meladoria.
52. Juan de Vargas.
53. Juan de la Horta, 1545.
54. Juanes de Toledo.
55. Juanes de Algruniva.
56. Juanes de Muleto.
57. Juanes, el *viejo*.
58. Juanes de Uriza.

59. Julian del Rey, the Moor; he worked for Boabdil, King of Granada, 15th century.
60. Julian Garcia; worked also at Cuenca.
61. Julian de Zamora.
62. José Gomez.
63. Jusepe de la Hera, el *viejo*.
64. Jusepe de la Hera, el *mozo*.
65. Jusepe de la Hera, el *nieto*.
66. Jusepe de la Hera, el *visnieto*.
67. Jusepe del Haza.
68. Ignacio Fernandez, el *viejo*.
69. Ignacio Fernandez, el *mozo*.
70. Luis de Nieves.
71. Luis de Ayala.
72. Luis de Belmonte.
73. Luis de Sahagun.
74. Luis de Sahagun.
75. Luis de Nieva; worked at Calatayud.
76. Lupus Aguado, 1567.
77. Miguel Cantero, 1564.
78. Miguel Sanchez.
79. Melchor Suarez; worked at Lisbon.
80. Nicolas Hortuño de Aguirre, 1637.
81. Pedro de Toro.
82. Pedro de Arechiga.
83. Pedro Lopez; worked at Orgaz.
84. Pedro de Lerzama; worked at Seville.
85. Pedro de Lazaretea; worked at Bilbao.
86. Pedro de Orozco.
87. Pedro de Belmonte.
88. Roque Hernandez.
    Sarabal; used no mark.
89. Sebastian Hernandez, el *viejo*, 1637.
90. Sebastian Hernandez, el *mozo*; he worked also at Seville.
91. Silvestre Nieto.
92. Silvestre Nieto.
93. Tomas de Ayala, 1625.
94. Zamorano, el Toledano.

Nos. 95, 96, 97, 98, and 99, are the marks of sword makers whose names are unknown.

Miguel y Manuel Fernandez; worked at Toledo in 1786.
Pedro de Barreta; at Bilbao at the end of the 16th century.

The following names may be added to this list—

Luis Calisto, 1760; and the four following artists are mentioned by Palomares as working at Toledo.
Juan de Valladolid.
Sebastian Herbás, 1617.
Manuel Ruiz, 1700.
Ignacio Fernandez, 1708.
Juan Orenga, 15th century; worked at Tortosa, and mentioned in the "Corvacho" of the Arcipreste de Talavera, fol. xi.
Martin Garro, v. p. 120, "Almanaque de la Industria."
Alonso Gutierrez, master of sword making at Madrid in 1625.

This artist, and the eleven following, are mentioned in original documents at the Academia de San Fernando.

Francisco de Borja, sword maker and gilder; Madrid, 1634.
Gaspar Martin, sword maker; working at Madrid in 1637.
Juan Mazon de Santorcas, sword maker and gilder; Madrid, 1636.
Juan de Medina; Madrid, 1620.
Lorenzo de los Rios; Madrid, 1585.
Miguel de Berrio; Madrid, 1575.
Pedro Casado, sword maker; Madrid, 1636.
Francisco de Elias, an apprentice of Pedro Casadós.
Francisco de Salinas; Madrid, 1636.
Acheza —— ; Toledo.
Camilo, 1500.

Two fine rapiers are in the Kensington Museum, Nos. 626, '68, and 2214, '55, which belong to the 16th and 17th centuries, and give a good idea of this industry of Toledo. Woodcuts of these appear on the opposite page. One of the blades is marked with the name of Francisco Ruiz. A large and most important collection of rapiers, swords, and other arms exists at the Royal Armoury of Madrid.

The breastplates are unusually fine, but the finest among them are by Milanese artists. A good example, which has been considered Spanish, was formerly in the Bernal Collection (see woodcut on p. 98); it gives an excellent idea of the artistic importance attained by this industry.

The saddles used in Spain were similar to those of other

European countries, for we find the same names adapted to the Spanish language. In the poem of the Cid, 13th century, and

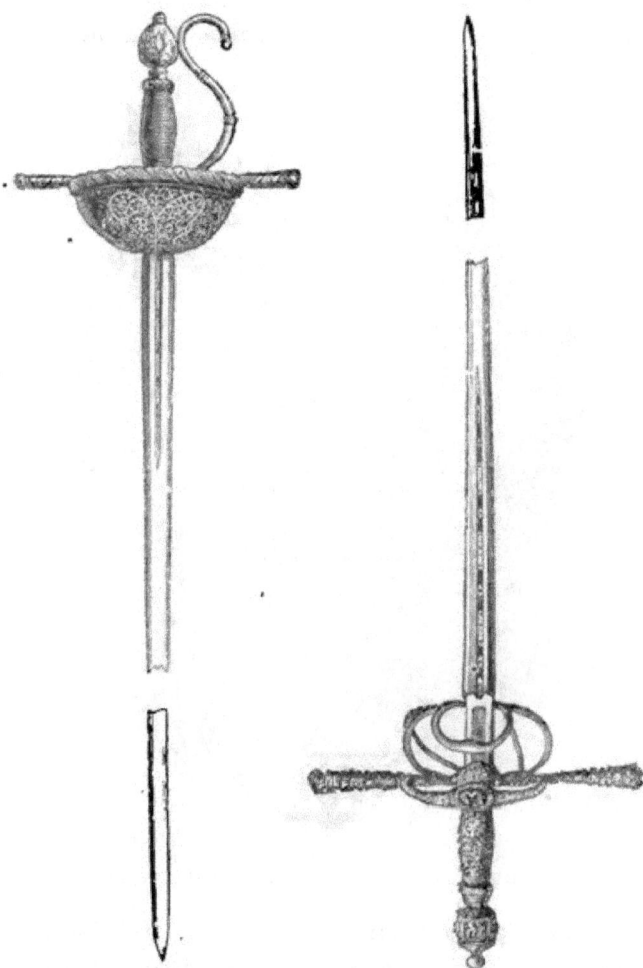

SPANISH RAPIERS. SOUTH KENSINGTON MUSEUM.

other works of the Middle Ages, *gallega* and *barda* saddles are mentioned which were peculiar to Spain. The *gallega* saddles were called so from being made in Gallicia; the *barda* proceeded from the Moors. We find no details which explain their exact structure.

A very remarkable collection of saddles of every description may be studied at the fine collection of armour at Madrid ; among

BREASTPLATE, FORMERLY IN THE BERNAL COLLECTION.

them are two of special interest—No. 2311 of " Catalogue of Armoury "—traditionally supposed to have belonged to the Cid, and No. 1310, which was used by King James the Conqueror in the 13th century. The Cid's saddle (see woodcut) is intended for a war-horse ; its bows are covered with black metal plating, orna- mented with a design of leaves and pilgrims' shells, partially gilt,

and the word " Fides," considered to be the Cid's devise. Much
has been written on the origin and authenticity of this saddle.
Cervantes alludes to it in the 49th Chapter of "Don Quixote,"
Part I. For further details see " Catalogue of the Armeria."

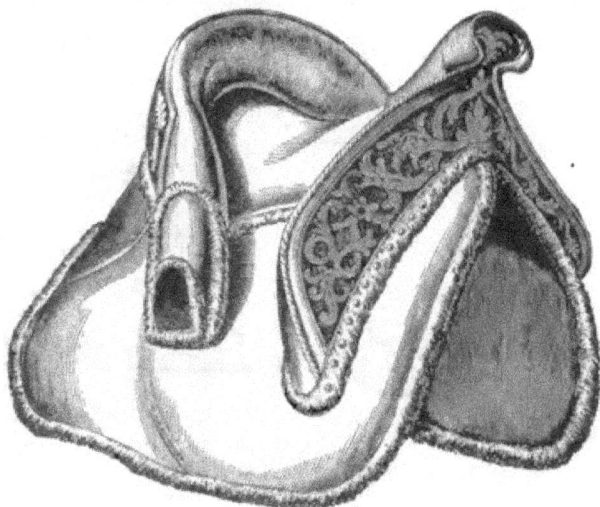

SADDLE OF THE CID. ARMOURY, MADRID.

The greatest novelty which was introduced during the Renaissance period was the use of fire-arms. The only names of ancient
artists that I have met with, who had any connection with the
manufactory of large pieces of artillery were Pedro Burgues, an
iron master of Barcelona, who lived in 1393 ; Rodrigo de Almanza,
and Pedro Colomer, who made fire-arms at Barcelona in 1413 ;
and the Moor, Alfarax Darhin, an iron master of Tarazona ; V.
Fernandez Duro. [Museo Español, vol. v. p. 18.]

Portable fire-arms were introduced into Spain towards the
middle of the 15th century. Count Clonard, in treating this subject
in the " Memorias de la Academia de la Historia," ix. p. 214,
says:—" Alfonso de Palencia tells us the *espingarda*, or large hand
musket (see woodcut), and *arbatana* culverin, were used in the

insurrection at Toledo in July, 1467. He assures us they had been very recently invented and named. They had been mentioned as early as 1449. In the siege of Toledo, Don Alvaro de Luna could not be kept back from the dangerous position in which he had placed himself, notwithstanding the shower of

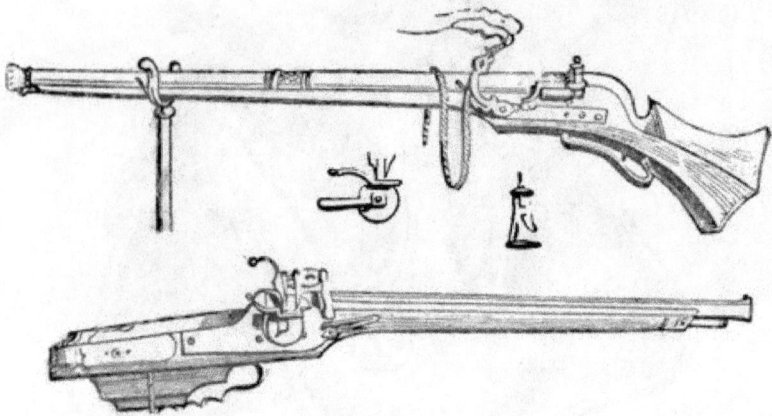

SPANISH MUSKETS.

stones, rockets, arrows, and shots of *espingardas* which were thrown into the town."

At the same time as these portable fire-arms were used in Spain, the ancient *bal'estas*, crossbows, so generally used in the Middle Ages, were very popular. Several artists became very famous in their manufacture. Alonso Martinez de Espinar enters into many details of this implement in his rare volume on the "Arte de Ballesteria y Monteria," Madrid, 1644, 4to, from which I copy the following passage, p. 11:—"The crossbow is more secure and less dangerous than the arquebuse; for it has never been known that a man's life has been lost by breaking the string or cord, two things which are dangerous, but not to a considerable extent. The crossbow has many advantages over the arquebuse: it kills, but does not frighten game; this cannot be done with the arquebuse, for the sound it makes alarms and frightens the game, and is heard everywhere. Once set, its shot is secure ; which is not the case with the arquebuse, which often misses fire.

"This weapon has been used in Spain from very early times, and has been made by the best masters ; the most famous among them were— '

> Azcoitia el Viejo.
> Pedro de la Fuente.
> Christoval de Azcoitia.
> Juan Hernandez.
> Juan Perez de Villadiego.
> Juan Azcoitia.
> Vzedo.
> Hortega.

"The only famous maker of crossbows of the present time is Juan de Lastra."

Espinar does not mention the name of Miguel, a crossbow maker of Zaragoza, or another celebrated maker who lived at Barbastro. The ambassador Salinas alludes to them both in an hitherto unedited letter written to King Ferdinand of Hungary, the brother of the Emperor Charles V. He says :—"Before I was able to find a lodging in this town of Monzon (Aragon), which was about five or six days, I went to Balbastro, Barbastro, and there occupied myself in making a pair of crossbows for your Majesty. I believe they are so made that they will satisfy the desires which were required ; they were made in my presence and according to my wishes, and as your Majesty is annoyed when they do not go off as you wish, I determined to make them in the following manner : One of them weighs l. ounces, which is considered here a very great weight. I, knowing your Majesty's wishes, had another made of lvi. ounces, that is to say $3\frac{1}{2}$ lbs. of Castille, carved and worked in such a manner that the cords should not break ; and that it be pleasant to shoot, I can affirm your Majesty that the maker is the best which exists in Spain, and yet he has never made so fine a crossbow as this one which is now sent to your Majesty ; and if not to your liking, I do not expect you ever will be pleased with one. I have sent them to Victoria in order that the screws may be made to fit the cords, and have ordered them to be made without delay; and as soon as they are ready they are to be sent to Bilbao to be forwarded to Flanders to the Queen, to whom your Majesty must write, in order that whatever you may wish may be done with them. When we leave here, it is said, we are to go to Zaragoza, where your Majesty will stay ten or twelve days. I will order two crossbows from *Maestro Michel,* who competes with the maker at Barbastro. I will do the same with these as the others. I entreat your Majesty should provide that the best of the two should not be lost. I am thoroughly satisfied with it, and am sure it will please your Majesty. From Monzon, 27th day of August, MDXXXIII." (Copy of a letter by Martin de Salinas to Ferdinand, King of Bohemia and Hungary, MS. fol. Acad. of History, c. 71).

Martinez de Espinar gives in his " Arte de Ballesteria," p. 41, the names of the best Spanish arquebuse or musket makers, and says : " The first cannon brought to Spain came from Germany ; the artist who made them used the following marks :—

" Two heads.

" A vase.

" A vase and pine.

" A pair of tongs.

" Flames.

" A knife.

" An excellent artificer worked formerly in Italy called Lazari Cominaz, but many bad cannons have been attributed to him.

" The best Spanish masters were—

" Maestre Simon, él viejo.

" Maestre Pedro, his brother, who made at Madrid excellent cannon and locks.

" They came over with the Emperor Charles V., and worked also for the Kings Philip II. and III., and marked the pieces they made with three sickles.

"Maestre Simon had four sons; all of them followed his profession. Felipe and Simon Marcuarte have worked for Philip III. and IV. Simon Marcuarte is still alive. They mark with a sickle in a shield, and make also excellent hunting-knives, archers' knives, halberds, and other things. Pedro, their brother, is also an excellent artificer.

"Juan Salado worked in several localities, and died at Salamanca. He was an excellent arquebuse maker. His mark was the letter of his name and a horse.

"Sanchez de Mirveña, his son-in-law, followed him. He marked with a lion and his initials.

"Gaspar Fernandez was brought by King Ferdinand from Salamanca, and the arms he makes are the best in Spain.

"Pedro Muñoz worked at Seville. He was surnamed El Toledano, and marked with all the letters of his name.

"Juan de Metola did the same.

"Leguizamo worked at Seville. He marked with his name and two stags.

"Francisco Hernandez used his full name.

"Andres Herraez was a native of Cuenca. He made every sort of arm, and marked with an eagle and his initials.

"Maestre Cristoval de Ricla marked with an X.

"Pedro Palacios with P P."

A fine musket exists by Palacios at the Royal Armoury of Madrid —No. 427. By Cristoval de Ricla there is a cannon of worked iron, No. 2319, mounted on its gun-carriage, with the following inscription, "Hizome en Ricla Cristoval Frisleva año, 1565." A fine gun, also at the Armeria, is by the same artist.

Juan de Espinar does not mention the following artists, who lived at his time at Madrid. I find their names given in original documents in the Library of the Academia de San Fernando.

Bartolomé de Orgaz 1643
Juan de la Cruz 1629
Juan de Mazo 1613

Juan de Pozo 1625
Juan de Zuazo, armourer of his Majesty 1645
Lucas de Ros, armourer of his Majesty 1623-1628
Matias Suezo, was arquebusier of the guards of Seville in . . . 1625
Rafael Villato in 1625
Pero Matia appears in documents of the archives of Simancas as musket-maker living at the Alhambra at the end of the 16th century.

By extracting the information on this subject which is given in the introduction to the Catalogue of the Armoury, we find this list can be brought down to our time :—

Gaspar Hernandez had two excellent pupils.
Domingo Garcia and Juan Belen, who marked with a lion with a lifted paw. He was appointed gunsmith to King Charles II. in 1699.
Alonso Martinez was an excellent artist ; he marked his work with the letters of his name.
Luis Santos, 1739.
Nicolas Bis.
Matias Baeza, gunsmith of King Philip V., 1739.
Alonso Martinez, 1732.
Diego Esquivel.
Juan Fernandez, appointed in 1726.
Diego Ventura, appointed gunsmith to Charles III., 1760.
Luis Santos.
Matias Baeza, 1740.
Francisco Bis.
Ignacio Barcina.
Sebastian Santos, 1752.
Gabriel de Algora, appointed gunsmith to Ferdinand VI., 1746.
Juan Fernandez.
Manuel Sutil, an excellent artist.
José Cano, 1740.
Joaquin Celaya, 1749.
José Lopez.
Diego Ventura.
Benito San Martin.
Juan Santos.
Francisco Lopez, a great artist, gunsmith of King Charles III., in 1761.
José Cano.
Diego Alvarez, 1775.
Joaquin Celaya.
Salvador Cenarro, 1762.

Antonio Gomez, 1762.
Pedro Ramirez.
Agustin Bustindui.
Sebastian Santos.
Pedro Fernandez.
Gabriel de Algora.
Agustin Ortiz, 1761.
Miguel Cegarra, 1768.
Francisco Lopez.
Francisco Garcia, 1788.
Isidoro Soler, 1792.
Francisco Targarona, 1792.
Gregorio Lopez, 1792.
Agustin Ortiz.
Pedro Fernandez.
Carlos Rodriguez.
Antonio Navarro.
Diego Alvarez.
Valentin Lopez.
Juan de Soto.
Carlos Montargis, 1783
Manuel Cantero, 1792.
Hilario Mateo.
Antonio Gomez.
Juan Lopez.
Ramon Martinez.
Basilio Escalante.
Manuel Soler.
Melchor Alvarez, **the** first gunsmith who **forged spiral cannon** in Spain,
    and made double-barrelled guns.
Gregorio **Lopez.**
Aquilino **Aparicio.**
Ramon Zuloaga.
Eusebio Zuloaga.

*** The marks used by these artists are given in plate 9 of " Catalogo de la
Armeria de Madrid," 1849.

Daggers, knives, scissors, and other small arms made in Spain,
have been famous from early times. A good example of a dagger
is No. 2238, 55 at the Kensington Museum. A great number of
towns have been distinguished for this industry, such as Albacete,
Murcia, Alcazar de San Juan, and Guadix, where even in the

present day much cutlery is produced. The cutlery made in Spain
preserves the traditional Moorish forms. Al Makkari says, in
speaking of these objects, in his "Moham. Dyn. in Spain," vol. i.,
p. 93 :—"Murcia was likewise famous for the manufacture of
coats of mail, breast-plates, and steel armour inlaid with gold ;
all kinds of instruments of brass and iron, such as knives, scissors,
and other trinkets, and especially weapons and other warlike instruments, wrought in such perfection as to dazzle with their
brightness the eyes of the beholder." The translator adds, p. 393 :
"Several towns in the province are renowned for this industry.
At Albacete there are several manufactures of well-tempered
scissors, daggers, and knives, which, from the shape of their
blades, betray their Moorish origin. Since the expulsion of the
Moriscos, the Spaniards have kept up this manufacture, and
daggers and knives of the end of the last century are often met
with bearing Arabic inscriptions and verses from the Koran. I
have seen one which on one side has the following inscription, ' I
shall certainly kill thy enemies with the help of God,' and on the
reverse, 'Fabrica de Navajas de Antonio Gonzalez, Albacete,
1705.'"

Sr. Rico y Sinovas has published an interesting article on iron-
work in the "Almanaque de el Museo de la Industria," 1872.
He gives the names of the following artists who were famous in
this industry.

Aguas, Juan ; he worked at Guadix in 1735.
Albacete, signed Cel, 18th century.
Ambrosio, worked at Mora in the 18th century.
Arbell, Ramon, worked at Olot, Cataluña, in the 17th century.
Beson, Manuel, worked at Madrid.
Castellanos, el *viejo*, worked at Albacete in 1766.
Castellanos, el *mozo*, worked at Albacete in the 18th century.
Castello, Gregorio, 16th century.
Cerda, Miguel de la, worked at Madrid and Segovia in 1590.
Diaz, Pedro, worked at Albacete in the early half of the 18th century
Escobar, Cristoval, 16th century.
Escobar, Juan, 17th century.

Fernandez Manso de Payba, Jose, master cutler of the 18th century.
Garcia de la Torre, Teodoro, 18th century.
Garijo, master cutler of Albacete ; he worked in 1771.
Gomez, Mateo, worked at Albacete in 1659.
Grande, Juan, 1643.
Gutierrez, worked at Chinchilla, 1701.
Herrezuelo, el *viejo*, worked at Baeza in 1643.
Herrezuelo, el *mozo*, worked at Baeza in 1643.
Horbeira, Angel, worked at Madrid in the second half of the 17th century.
Lallave, Juan, locksmith of Madrid in 1820.
Leon, worked at Albacete early in the 18th century.
Llorens, Pablo, worked at Olot in 1699.
Moro, worked at Madrid late in the last century.
Ramirez, Juan, worked at Mexico in 1590.
Romero, worked at Albacete in 1769.
Rosel, worked at Mora.
San José, worked at Jaen in 1673.
Selva, Juan, worked at Cartagena in 1780.
Segura, worked at Mora towards the end of the last century.
Sierra, Juan, worked at Albacete in 1771.
Sosa, Madrid, 17th century.
Torres, Albacete, 17th century.
Vicen Perez, worked at Albacete in 1674.
Vilarosa, Antonio, worked in the 17th century.
Vicen Perez, Julian, worked at Albacete in 1710.
Zervantes, Francisco, Toledo, 17th century.

The following artists' names may be added ; they consist of master cutlers of Madrid, and are to be found in a bundle of original documents at the Academy of San Fernando.

Alcocer, Francisco, 1635.
Baltanos, Lucas de, 1611.
Castillo, Rafael del, 1625.
Cuenca, Francisco de, 1613.
Fuente, Pedro de la, worked at Mora and Madrid in 1628.
Garcia, Bartolomé, 1642.
Gonzalez, Marcos, 1624, 1625.
Heras, Antonio de las, 1611.
Luzon, Andres de, 1611.
Martin, Alonso, 1643.
Martinez de Machuca, Pedro, 1611.
Morel, Alonso, 1643.

Rodriguez de Quiñones, Pedro, 1611.
Torres, Antonio de, 1622.
Valsarias, Lucas de, 1611.

The following names of artists are given in Calomarde's
" Historia Politica de Aragon."

Ferrara, Andres, Zaragoza, 16th century.
Picado, Jeronimo, Calatayud, 1722.
Nieva, Luis, Calatayud, 17th century.
Munester, Andres, Calatayud, 18th century.

FURNITURE.

It is difficult to give an account of the furniture used in Spain from the earliest times, owing to the absence of specimens belonging to the Roman or Visigothic period. We are safe, however, in affirming that, during the domination of the Romans, the same models were used in Spain as in Rome itself, the similarity between objects of other kinds which exists, and the continual habit of the Romans of imposing their culture on the countries which they conquered, is sufficient to justify this idea. During the first period of the Christian era until about the 11th century, other objects which have reached us as gold and silversmiths' work, seem to prove that all industrial art work, including furniture must have been Classic, Byzantine, or Oriental in form, according to the period in which these styles predominated. The Roman or Classical style must have lasted for a considerable time, if we judge by the texts given by San Isidoro, in his " Etymologies," lib. xx., cap. xi. and xii. San Isidoro lived in the 7th century of our era. We find he mentions the words, *de lectis et sellis, de vehiculis*, which refer to furniture of the Roman period; but we do not meet with any distinctive terms which can be applied to the time in which he lived, on the contrary he comments on phrases and alludes to the forms of objects in the same manner as Rufus, Varrus, and other classical writers.

At the invasion of the Arabs in the beginning of the 8th century the Byzantine element increased in its application to furniture. During the reign of the caliphs, contemporary authors tell us that luxury of decoration of every kind was carried to a great extent. The description of the pulpit or *minbar* of the mosque of Cordova will give an idea of its richness. Al Makkari, in his "History of Mohammedan Dynasties in Spain," says, "the length of the Mihrab was 8 cubits; its breadth, 7 cubits; the height of its dome, 13 cubits. There stood on one side a pulpit, constructed by Alhahem, equalled by none other in the world for workmanship and materials. It was made of ivory and exquisite woods, such as ebony, sandal, Indian plantain, citron wood, aloe, and so forth, at the expense of 3,575 dinars : the steps by which it was ascended were nine in number. Another writer says it was formed of 36,000 pieces of wood fastened together by gold and silver nails, occasionally encrusted with precious stones, and its construction lasted for seven years; eight artists being daily employed on it," vol. i. p. 222.

Edrisi, who lived at Cordova at the beginning of the 12th century, describes this pulpit in the same manner. It was to be seen in the cathedral of Cordova as late as the 16th century, when it was destroyed, and its materials employed in the construction of an altar. An Arab *minbar* is in the South Kensington Museum, which came from Cairo, and although belonging to the last centuries of the Middle Ages, it will give an idea of this structure and its elaborate workmanship.

The oldest specimen of furniture which exists in Spain, belonging to Christian art, is the shrine of San Millan de la Cogulla, in the province of La Rioja, described in *Ivories*, p. 134. This casket or shrine was made by the orders of King Sancho el Mayor, in 1033, in order to preserve the relics of San Millan. It is of wood, covered with 22 compartments of highly interesting ivory plaques, representing episodes from the life of the Saint. The names of the artists, *Apparitio* and *Rodolpho*, appear on it. In 1808 the French stripped the shrine of its gold and silver ornaments, but, most fortunately, left the casket and its ivory carvings behind.

Another interesting object, which is useful for illustrating furniture in Spain in the 12th century, is the Bishop's throne in the cathedral of Gerona. It is of white marble of one piece, covered with a simple ornamentation in excellent taste, in a similar style, and for the same purpose, as the throne of San Clemente in Rome. It is raised at the back of the altar, and is ascended by thirteen steps. The Bishop sits on this throne after the first purification, and continues there until the Offertory, when he descends and finishes the mass at the altar ; owing to the existence of this chair, one of the most ancient rites of Catholicism has been preserved at Gerona.

Mention must also be made of the shrine in which the remains of Queen Urraca are kept in the cathedral of Palencia, and the Cofre del Cid in the cathedral of Burgos, although they are more interesting for their antiquity than their artistic merit.

During the 13th century furniture in Spain must have been similar to that used in other countries, it was influenced by French and Italian forms ; from which, as was the case in architecture, these models were constantly copied. Some idea of this is given in the triptych known by the name of the Tablas Alfonsinas, which is fully described in Gold and Silver Work. (See woodcut on p. 17.)

The principal novelty which we find in Spain in this industry consists in the combination of the Christian and Moorish styles applied to furniture. A very remarkable specimen exists at the Academia de la Historia, consisting of a reliquary, triptych or armoire of very large dimensions, formerly in the church of the Monasterio of Piedra in Aragon. It is 13 feet wide and 8 feet high. When the two doors are closed six compartments appear on each, surrounded by a border headed by a wide cornice. This cornice is divided in sixteen spaces formed by arches adorned with stalactite ornamentation in the Moorish style ; inside each span is painted the figure of a saint. In the twelve compartments which form the doors there are subjects from the life of

Our Lord, beginning with the Annunciation, and ending with the Descent from the Cross painted in excellent taste. The border which surrounds these doors is formed of a beautiful geometrical ornamentation, in the purest Oriental style; in the upper and lower part appears the following inscription in Gothic characters, which gives us the date in which this object was made.

Tabernaculum hoc vocabitur aula Dei quia vere Dominis est in loco isto. Fuit autem constructum ad honorem et reverentiam sacratissimi corporis Domini nostri Ihu Xpi et pasionis ejusdem nec non ad honorem = et reverentiam sanctissime genitricis ejusdem et totius celestis curie et sanctorum . . . at fuit . . . depictum anno MCCCXC. anima ordinatoris requiescat . . . sinu salvatoris. Amen.

When this triptych is opened several compartments appear, formed by cusped Gothic arches, placed within others; in the form of a mitre divided by pinnacles. The ornamentation which fills the vacant space between the arches, and the seven banderoles in the lower part are in pure Gothic style, without a reminiscence of Moorish art. In the central banderole appears the name of *Dopnus Martinus Poncii Abbas*, the abbot of the monastery where this reliquary was made, and the person by whom the expense was probably borne. The inside of the doors is divided into two horizontal zones, which include half the total size. The upper zone is covered with geometrical tracery, similar to the outer borders. The lower one is divided into four compartments for each leaf of the door, eight within two, which are formed by cusped Gothic arches; within these spaces are painted standing figures of angels holding musical instruments in their hands and nimbi round their heads. The details and forms of the instruments and delicate ornamentation of the costumes and carpets, constitute one of the most beautiful details of this triptych. These details and several of the architectural lines of the Gothic part of this ornamentation denote an Italian influence, probably Sicilian. for this province belonged then to the crown of Aragon.

This triptych is richly gilt, and painted inside and out, and is one of the finest and most remarkable specimens of the kind which exist in any country. A plate may be seen in " Mus. Esp. de Antiguedades," vol. vi., p. 307.

A very interesting specimen of this combination of styles is a recess or cupboard of the 14th century, which is at the Kensington Museum, No. 1764, 71, [see woodcut.] It is 5 feet 4 inches high, by 8 feet wide ; and is composed of an outer arch, with the tympani ornamented with fine arabesques in relief, made of stucco, —representing vine tendrils, leaves, and flowers, similar to those which appear in the Cosa de Mesa and other Moorish houses at Toledo. The arch is surrounded by two Latin inscriptions in Gothic characters, of which only the following words are legible + Autem transies per medium ilorum . . . . mente +. The first of these is from St. Luke, iv., v. 30, a passage often quoted by alchemists.

This arch serves as a portal to the cupboard, which is about a foot deep, and is divided into two compartments with two rows of shelves. Each of these is supported by a series of Moorish arches, the tympani of which are ornamented with tracery, or an ornamentation of leaves in a geometrical and Oriental manner. On the rim of the upper part is repeated the following inscription in African characters :

اليمن و الاقبال

" Felicity and Fortune."

On the lower shelf are the following words in Spanish in Gothic characters : + Dios : te : salve : estrella : de : la : mannana : medicina : de : los : peccadores : reina + " Hail ! morning star ; medicine of sinners ; queen."

This " Alhacena," or cupboard, existed formerly in the court of an old house at Toledo, known by the name of "Casa de la Parra," and is constantly called " Botica de los Templarios," the Templars' dispensary, probably because the Templars occupied the parish of

1

"BOTICA DE LOS TEMPLARIOS." FROM TOLEDO. SOUTH KENSINGTON MUSEUM.

St. Michael, in which the house stands, and because the word "medicine" is mentioned in the inscription.

In order to increase the list of these objects, which are unfortunately so rare, it is necessary to mention the organ case, decorated with fine Moorish tracery, in the chapel founded by Diego de Anaya, Archbishop of Seville in 1374, .in the cloister of the cathedral of Salamanca.

Another specimen of furniture of interest of the 14th century is the shrine or casket containing the remains of San Isidoro, existing in the parish church of San Andres at Madrid. This casket is 7 feet 5 inches long; the cover is formed of two plain surfaces, forming a roof, which leaves a triangular pediment at each end. The shrine is made of wood, covered outside with a coat of painting in distemper, and is decorated with a series of painted compartments simulating pointed tricuspid arches let into others which are mitre-shaped; in the interior spaces are painted a series of representations of the life of ·the saint. This object is extremely interesting: it is evidently of Spanish ·workmanship, although it has great resemblance with the Italian *cassoni* of the same period. See vol. iv. "Mus. Esp." p. 593, and "Monumentos Arquitectonicos"—livraison 67.

. The most important period of artistic furniture in Spain must be looked for in the 15th and 16th centuries: we find in this time works decorated with sculptured figures and most delicate and exquisite ornamentation. Nothing gives a better idea of this than the choir seats of Spanish cathedrals. The cathedrals in Spain are different to those of France and the north of Europe owing to the circumstance that the choir, or *coro*, is placed in the middle of the central nave, in the traditional form of the primitive basilicas, such as San Clemente at Rome, with the difference however, that towards the last centuries of the Middle Ages the *pluteus* or walls that surround it, which are elevated about one yard from the floor, were turned into an enclosure or wall four or five yards in height. A space is therefore set apart in the middle of the church, which, although spoiling the general effect of the nave, becomes, as is the case in most Spanish cathedrals, a museum of artistic objects of all kinds. The side facing the presbytery or high altar is enclosed by a *reja*. [See Iron and Bronze work.] In the three remaining sides stalls are placed against the wall, forming two rows, one near the floor, and the other raised about a yard from the lower ones. The general system adopted is a row of stalls separated from each other by the arms; the backs of the lower ones serving as stands for the books which are used by those who sit in the upper range. The subsellæ are prolonged and form canopies, pinnacles, crest-work, and other varied ornamentation resting on columns. They are usually made of walnut wood, and there is not a single vacant space which is left uncovered with figures or ornamentation in relief: the effect produced by the whole is admirable. The number of seats varies according to the size of the choir, or importance of the church.

It is probable that the earliest wood carvers who worked in Spain came from Flanders or Holland, if we judge by the decided Germanic character of the figures and ornamentation, and frequent mention made of foreign masters ; but this industry very soon took root in Spain, and Spanish artists soon equalled or excelled their masters. The most important choir stalls carved in the Gothic style in Spain belong only to the last years of the 15th and beginning of the 16th century ; those in the Renaissance style come immediately afterwards, and include the whole 16th century.

One of the finest is that of Leon, it is in the purest German-Gothic style, and may be considered as a masterpiece in its way : the large figures are as delicately carved as the small ones. The representations of the " Last Judgment " and " Tree of Jesse " are as beautiful as can be imagined. The choir at Zamora is also in the German style ; the large figures which ornament it are splendid in effect. These stalls are fully described in "The Ecclesiologist," in the following manner : " The stalls, though not remarkably early, are very fine. The bishops, as usual, at the centre of the west nave; then three dignitaries on each side; then at each extremity of the west end a door into the nave; then on the north and south sides respectively twenty stalls with subsellæ, which also are returned. All the panelling is very fine: but that at the back of the subsellæ I will give at full, because the types of, and legends concerning Our Lord are so remarkably well chosen, that they may be useful as giving ideas to our own church builders, and might be introduced with great advantage in stained glass." "Ecclesiologist," vol. xiv., p. 363.

The stalls at the cathedral and church of Sto. Tomas of Avila, and cathedral of Burgos are also very fine. · The *coro* at Barcelona is extremely picturesque; at the backs of the stalls are placed the coats of arms of the knights of the Golden Fleece, in a similar manner to those of St. George's Chapel at Windsor; among these we find the arms of Henry the VIIIth. In 1519 the Emperor Charles V. held at Barcelona a chapter of this Order, the only one which has ever been held in Spain.

It would take too much space to enumerate the choir seats in Spain worthy of notice; those at Toledo rank as the most important, as including the last period of the Gothic and best Renaissance styles. This *coro* contains 45 stalls in the lower, and 71 in the upper part. Mr. Street fully describes the lower part in his "Gothic Architecture in Spain," p. 252, and says: "The lower range of stalls, fifty in number, are the work of Maestro Rodrigo, circa A.D. 1495; and the upper range were executed, half by Berruguete and half by Felipe de Borgoña, A.D. 1543. The old stall ends are picturesque in outline, very large, and covered with tracery, panels and carvings with monkeys and other animals sitting on them. The upper range of stalls is raised by four steps, so that between the elbows of the lower stalls and the desk above them, are spaces filled in with a magnificent series of bas reliefs, illustrating the various incidents of the conquest of Granada. They were executed whilst the subjects depicted were fresh in the minds of the people, and are full of picturesque vigour and character. The names of the fortresses are inscribed on the walls ; in some we have the siege, in others the surrender of the keys; in others the Catholic monarchs, accompanied by Cardinal Ximenes riding in triumph through the gates." The upper stalls, although considered by Mr. Street "heavy dull Paganism," are among the most important artistic works existing in Spain. Their sculptures and ornamentation reproduce the Renaissance Italian style in its finest period. Columns of red jasper are combined with the walnut-wood carvings, and the termination of the upper part which rests on the wall is of white marble carved by the same artists.

Choir stalls, sharing the fate of other architectural works, followed the general path of decay after the 16th century. Those stalls at the cathedral of Malaga, which were carved in the 17th century by José Michael, Pedro de Mena, and Luis Ortiz, are worthy of mention: the figures in high relief at the back are very fine. This falling off of artistic feeling is particularly observable at the cathedral of Cordova; the stalls there, which were carved by Pedro Duque Cornejo in the 18th century, are admirable in richness of ornamentation, but the whole decoration is in the worst possible taste. The fine lecterns which are placed in the centres of the choirs are often good examples of carving. An admirable model of this style exists at the cathedral of Zamora.

In treating of furniture of other kinds, the silver chair or throne of Dⁿ Martin de Aragon must figure in the first instance. It is described in "Gold and Silver Work," p. 19. In these and other objects which are not Oriental in style, constant reminiscences are observable of the similarity of ideas and forms with Italian or French objects. The large chests or *cassoni* of different sizes which are constantly met with in museums, or in private collections, are similar to objects of the same kind which abound in Italy. Some are covered with fine Gothic or Renaissance carvings in the same taste as the choir stalls, and are ornamented also with good iron-work. Some of them were made in the province of Cataluña of inlaid ivory, imitating in a coarse manner Florentine and Milanese work. These objects were of the end of the 15th and beginning of the 16th century. An excellent example exists at the cathedral of Toledo, near the Puerta de los Leones, consisting of an iron coffer covered with carved and repoussé work.

A fine cupboard of walnut wood may be seen at the same cathedral which is unrivalled for its beauty. It is composed of an architectural order with six pilasters, forming five vacant spaces completely covered with medallions, groups of children, flowers, and a multitude of subjects of ornamentation in reliefs, terminating with a frieze crowned with candelabra and salient points. This piece of furniture was made in 1549–1551, by the sculptor, Pedro Pardo, for holding vestments of the clergy. In 1780 a reproduction was made by Gregorio López Durango : the original and the copy face each other in the room which is passed on entering the Sala Capitular. As Spanish carved wood work of the beginning of the 16th century may be mentioned the specimens at the Kensington Museum, Nos. 245 and 246–64, of two panels with armorial shields.

During the 16th, but more especially the 17th, century it became very fashionable in Europe to use secretaires or cabinets to a great extent, which, if we calculate by those that still are found in private houses in Spain, have never been so numerous in any other country. A great variety of every description may be seen at the South Kensington Museum. In looking through old inventories at Madrid, the number of these escritoires which decorated the rooms of the Palace is almost incredible. Many of them came from Italy, Flanders, or Germany. In a memorial drawn up by Pedro Gutierrez and presented to the King, begging for protection for this industry, he says : "The cabinets and escritoires, *contadores y bufetes*, which were worth 500, 600, and 700

reales when brought from Germany, are now made in Spain for
250 and 300 reales each." (Acad. de la Hist., N. 6, vol. iv.
371.) The quantity and importance of those brought from Germany is to be inferred from an edict promulgated by Philip III.,
in Valladolid in 1603, in which "cabinets of every kind coming
from Nuremberg are not allowed to enter the country," ib. 518.

These cabinets were made in a great variety of ways. Some
were, as we have seen, copied in Spain from foreign models, but
the greater number constituted a characteristic industry of the
Peninsula. Some were covered with wood carvings in a similar
style to the large armoires in the Sala Capitular at Toledo.
Others were known by the name of *Vargueños*, because the great
centre of their manufacture is supposed to have existed at the
village of Vargas in the province of Toledo. These cabinets are
effective ; their geometrical ornamentation is a reminiscence of
the Oriental style, and the iron work outside is very striking. A
good specimen may be seen at the Kensington Museum, No. 1073,
'71; a woodcut of the upper portion is given on the next page.

We also meet with cabinets and armoires with glass doors
covered with tortoise-shell and gilt bronze. A splendid series
of inlaid work of tortoise-shell, ebony, mother-of-pearl and
ivory is preserved at the Sacristy of the Cartuja at Granada,
made by a friar of the same convent, Manuel Vazquez, at the
beginning of the last century. Cabinets of ebony, inlaid and
covered with repoussé silver work, must have been very generally
made in Spain ; silver was used to so great an extent after the
conquest of America, that a law was issued in 1574 prohibiting
with the utmost rigour the making and selling of this kind of
merchandise, in order not to increase the scarcity of silver. " No
cabinets, desks, coffers, braziers, etc., shall be manufactured of
silver."

Cabinets of inlaid ivory or different coloured woods which were
originally imported from Italy and Germany were constantly reproduced in Spain, as will appear by the following dialogue :—

" How much has your worship paid for this cabinet? It is worth more than 40 ducats. What wood is it made of? The red one is made of mahogany from the Habana, and the black one is made of ebony, and the white one of ivory. You will find the workmanship excellent. Here you will find a finer cabinet.

VARGUEÑO CABINET. SPANISH. 16TH CENTURY. SOUTH KENSINGTON
MUSEUM.

Where was it made? It was brought with these chairs from Salamanca." (" Dialogos Familiares," by J. de Luna, Paris, 1669, p. 111.) Among cabinets inlaid with bone or ivory there is a peculiar style in which furniture brought from the Portuguese possessions in the East was imitated in a rough way. Some also have reached us in which the drawers are covered with embroidery in silks of different colours, exquisitely worked. In the 17th century furniture of different kinds was covered with embroidered silks. At the Kensington Museum there is an interesting coffer, which came from the Convent of Loeches, and was originally the gift of Count Duke de Olivares, Philip the IVth's minister.

The cabinets decorated with *pietre duri*, which are frequently
met with in Spain were of foreign make.   Madame d'Aunoy, in
describing the house of a grandee of Spain in her "Voyage
d'Espagne," p. 56, vol. ii., Lyon, 1643, says, "et de grands cabinets
de pièces de rapport enrichis de pierreries, lesquels ne sont pas
faits en Espagne : des tables d'argent d'entre eux, et des miroirs
admirables tant pour leur grandeur que pour leurs riches bordures,
dont les moins belles sont d'argent.   Ce que j'ai trouvé de plus
beau sont des *escaparates ;* une espèce de petit cabinet fermé d'une
seule glace et rempli de tout ce qu'on se peut figurer de plus
rare."   Cabinets ornamented with paintings on glass, or copper,
or enamels came from Flanders, and some rare specimens of
damasquine work were most probably Milanese manufacture.

In Cean Bermudez "Dicc Historico de los Profesores de Bellas
Artes" appear among the sculptors' names, those of the artists
who carved the most important stalls of the cathedrals, and other
works of art of a similar kind, but the names of those who made
cabinets have never yet been published.   I have been fortunate
enough to be able to collect the following from unpublished
documents which exist at the Library of the Acad. de San
Fernando at Madrid.   They worked in the 16th and 17th
century.

Aguayo, Urban de, wood carver .	1623
Carpintero, Francisco, wood carver	1630
Garcia, Marcos, wood carver of his Majesty.	1637-42
Gomez, Juan, carver in wood .	1598
Gorostiza, Juan de, carver in wood	1627
Higares, Nicolas de, carver in wood	1625
Hispano, Francisco, carver in ivory	1618
Hoz, Martin de la, carver in wood .	1624
Lara, Benardino, de, carver in wood	1612
Lozano, Pedro	1622
Marcos, Juan, carver in wood	1636
Martinez, Andrés, carver in wood	1622
Martinez, Dionisio, carver in wood	1621-25
Martinez, Gabriel, carver in wood	1623
Murga, Tomas de, carver of his royal Highness	1614

Osoz, Martin de, wood carver 1623
Parezano, Alonso, wood carver of his Majesty 1623
Pelegrin, Joan, wood carver 1614
Peña, Jeronimo de la, wood carver 1622
Quero, Melchor de, carver in wood 1586
Radis, Francisco, master maker of cabinets in ebony and ivory . . 1617
Riofrio, Martin de, wood carver 1612
Riofrio, Tomas de, wood carver 1626
Rodriguez, Bernardo de, wood carver 1624
Rodriguez, Domingo, wood carver 1633
Roxo, Domingo, wood carver 1630
Sanchez, Matias, wood carver 1565
Santana, Juan de, wood carver 1617
Sierra, Francisco de, wood carver 1634
Spano, Jeronimo, wood carver 1617
Torres, Juan de, wood carver 1658
Velasco, Lucas de, master in painting and gilding cabinets . . . 1633
Zorrilla, Domingo 1642

Large arm-chairs of a quadrangular form, with arms, back and seat of leather or embroidered stuffs, were used to furnish rooms at the same time as these cabinets; tables, and frames inlaid with ivory, tortoise-shell, ebony, bronze and silver, were hung on the walls; side-boards, beds, and braziers were made of inlaid woods or silver. Women during the 16th and 17th centuries sat on low stools on the ground. The beds were made of rich brocades embroidered with gold, (*vide* Madame d'Aunoy), trimmed with point d'Espagne, and on the splendid carpets were placed silver braziers which burnt crushed olive stones. The walls were covered with tapestry and rich silks, and from very early times stamped, painted or gilt leather *guadameciles* were used in Spain to a very great extent. These *guadameciles* were imitated in France and other countries in the 16th and 17th centuries; a very large quantity of this stamped leather is to be met with in England. The Baron Ch. Davillier has lately published an interesting notice on this subject, from which I take the following information. ("Notes sur les cuirs de Cordoue, Guadameciles d'Espagne," Paris, 1878.)

The word guadamecil applied to this leather comes from the village of *Ghadames* in Africa, celebrated from the 12th century for this industry.   It was imported by the Moors into Spain, and Cordova became from the beginning of the Middle Ages the great centre of this production, although other towns, such as Seville, Granada, Toledo, and Barcelona, exported these leathers also. The chronicler Ambrosio de Morales, in his "Las Antiguedades de las ciudades de España," Alcala, 1575, says, p. 10, "A great commerce is produced by the exportation of skins, and many have been enriched by it, those prepared at Cordova are so excellent, that now in Spain any goat hide prepared in any locality is called Cordovan.   Guadamecis are made of leather, and are so well fashioned in Cordova that none can compete with them ; they are exported to the Indies and all Europe.   They produce much for the town, and beautify the principal streets, for the hides are hung out to dry after they are painted and gilt, and it is a fine sight to see the walls covered with such variety of colour and form."

A good collection of these guadameciles is in the South Kensington Museum. See Nos. 471 to 485, '69, and 1651 to 1654, '71.

At the end of the 17th and first half of the 18th century, the Baroque or Churrigueresque architecture had such influence over furniture, that although exaggerated examples were very common, they reached in no country to such a pitch as they did in Spain. As specimens, the enormous *retablos* over the high altars made of gilt carved wood may be mentioned, which are so frequently to be seen in Spanish churches.   The exuberance of uncouth heavy ornamentation destroys the regularity and harmony of the general effect.   Chairs and tables were made then in the same style, and the *cornucopias* or decorated mirrors which adorn Spanish churches and sacristy, belong to this period.   The name of *cornucopia* was given in allusion to the horn of abundance.

The French influence of the last century brought the same hions fasfor furniture into Spain, and we also find there the styles known as Louis XVI. and Empire. Spain follows the general rule; porcelain plaques from the manufactories of Alcora and Retiro were let into furniture, and gilt bronze mounting were very much used. The most important specimens of furniture of the early present century are the splendid rooms inlaid with metal work at the Palace, called Casa del Labrador at Aranjuez, and those known by the name of " Piezas de maderas finas," at the Palace del Escorial. The description given by J. Quevdo, in his " Historia del Real Monasterio de San Lorenzo," Madrid, 1849, gives a good idea of their importance; he says, p. 343, " This series of four small rooms were decorated at a cost of 28,000,000 of reales (£280,000). The pavement, friezes, windows, and doors, are made of the most delicate inlaid work representing landscapes, vases and festoons of flowers, which look as if they were painted with a brush. King Charles IV. helped in this work, and they were finished in 1831 under the direction of Angel Maeso. The splendid iron work was made by Ignacio Millan. It is of polished iron inlaid with gold, and most exquisite in workmanhip."

IVORIES.

No artistic industry in Spain has left behind so little historical information as ivory carving. Only a very small number of examples of this art have reached us which are of undoubted Spanish manufacture, but a group exists among them which has been but little examined or studied; it is worthy of the utmost attention, on account of its artistic character, and the inferences which may be drawn from it.

We find no allusion in the works of Pliny or St. Isidoro to the existence of the industry of ivory carving in Spain during the Roman and Visigothic dominations. An interesting example of ivory work of the Roman period, consisting of a consular diptych may be seen at the cathedral of Oviedo, which, although certainly not carved in Spain, must not be overlooked here, in order that it may be included among the number of the carvings which have reached us of this period. The two leaves of this diptych are complete, and in a perfect state of preservation: they are 16 inches long by 6 inches wide; in the centres are two medallions in relief with a bust of the consul, who is represented in the act of throwing down with his right hand the *mappa* or handkerchief, and holding in his left hand a sceptre. The right angles are ornamented with masks, the rest of the surface is plain. The two following inscriptions run along the upper part of the leaves: FL· STRATEGIVS APION. STRATEGIVS APION V. ILL: COM. DEVV. DOMM. ET· CONS· OR.

Flavius Strategius Apius. Strategius Apius, illustrious man, count of the most fervent servants, and consul in ordinary.

This consul belongs to the period of Justinian, by which emperor he was invested with this dignity in A.D. 539. We do not know how this diptych came to Spain; it is generally supposed that it belonged originally to the shrine of the cathedral of Toledo, from whence it was removed to Asturias, with other relics, to be concealed there during the invasion of the Arabs at the beginning of the 8th century. The student will find further details in " Corpus Ins." by Hübner. " Monumentos arquitectonicos." " Mus. Esp. de Antiguedades." Vol. i. p. 385.

From the invasion of the Arabs, which began early in the 8th century, and on the foundation of the empire of the Caliphs of Cordova in the year 756, an era of grandeur began for the Arabs in Spain, coinciding with their independence from the Caliphs of Damascus, which lasted for more than two centuries; during this time Cordova became the most important literary and scientific centre in Europe. The direct influence of the East and Constantinople may be traced without interruption from this time on the culture of the Spanish Arabs. At times this culture was transmitted by the objects of every kind which the Spaniards received from the East, at others by the influence exercised by the artists who established themselves on the territory of the Caliphate of Cordova. The greater part of the industrial arts, which were imported at this time, became naturalized in the country, and we find them developed in every locality of the Peninsula, and although we do not possess any positive historical information stating this fact, which distinctly bears on ivory carvings, we are safe in affirming that the industry existed among the Spanish Arabs in a very high state of perfection during the last years of the Caliphate. The description and details of the most important ivories which have reached us of this period confirms this opinion.

At the South Kensington Museum there is a cylindrical box No. 217-'65 with rounded cover. I copy Mr. Maskell's description of this object, of which a woodcut is given. (Vide " Ivories,

Ancient and Mediæval, in the South Kensington Museum,"
Lon don, 1872.)

" This beautiful box is carved throughout, except the bottom of
it, with interlacing narrow bands forming quatrefoils, in which on
the cover are four eagles.　These have spread wings and stand

IVORY BOX.　MOORISH.　IOTH CENTURY.　SOUTH KENSINGTON MUSEUM.

erect; well designed and most delicately executed.　A small knob
serves to lift the lid.

Round the side, each quatrefoil is filled with a star having a
leaf ornament.　The same decoration is repeated in the spaces
between the larger quatrefoils on the cover.

The whole is carved in pierced work, except a band which
forms the upper upright portion of the box, round the side of the
lid.　This band has an Arabic inscription :

بركة من الله لعبد الله الحكم المستنصر بالله امير المومنين

" A favour of God to the servant of God, Al Hakem al Mostanser

Billah, commander of the faithful." He was a Caliph who reigned at Cordova, A.D. 961–976."

Another very interesting oblong box is preserved in the same Museum, No. 301–'66. The cover and sides are carved with scroll foliated ornament: the hinges and clasp are of chased silver inlaid with niello. Round the sides, immediately below the lid is the following Arabic inscription in Cufic characters:

بسم الله هذا ما عمل الأنثة السيدة الله عبد الرحمن امير المومنين رحمة الله عليه
و رضوانه

"In the name of God. This (box) was ordered to be made by Seidat Allah, the wife of Abdo-r-rahman, prince of the believers. God be merciful and satisfied with him."

IVORY BOX. MOORISH. IOTH CENTURY. SOUTH KENSINGTON MUSEUM.

This inscription must allude to Abd er Rahman III. the first Caliph of Cordova who bore the title of Emir, el Mumenin. The formula "God be merciful," &c., denotes that he was dead when it was written. He died A.D. 961. (See woodcut.)

Another casket, undoubtedly the most important in size which is known of this period, proceeds from Sanguesa, in the province of Navarre, and is now preserved in the treasury of the cathedral of Pamplona.

This splendid box, hitherto undescribed, is 15 inches long, by 9¼ wide. A wooodcut is given opposite. It is completely covered with carvings in relief, within circular cusped medallions, with figures in the centres representing different subjects: men seated, hawking, or struggling with wild beasts, and numerous single figures of lions, stags, and other animals. The intermediate spaces contain an ornamentation of leaves and flowers which is accommodated to the geometrical style of Saracenic art. Round the upper part of this box appears an Arabic inscription in fine Cufic characters.

بسّم الله بركة من الله وغبطة وسرور وبلوغ امل فى صالح عمل وانفساح اجل
للحاجب سيف الدولة عبد الملك بن المنصور و فقه الله مما امر بعمله على يدى
الفتى الكبير نمير بن محمد العامرى مملوكه سنة حمس و تسعين و ثلث ماية

"In the name of God. The blessing of God, the complete felicity, the happiness, the fulfilment of the hope of good works, and the adjourning the fatal period (of death), be with the Hagib Seifo daula (sword of the State), Abdelmalek ben Almansur. This (box) was made by the orders (of the said Hagib), under the inspection or direction of his chief eunuch, Nomayr ben Mohammad Alaumeri, his slave in the year of 395, [A.D. 1005].

In the centre medallion, on the opposite side to the lock, is represented the standing figure of a man who is attacked by two lions. He holds on his arm a shield, upon which is engraved an inscription, with the following religious formula: "There is no God but God," or a similar one, for the characters are very illegible and confused. In the centre of this shield may be read عمل حير, "made by Hair," undoubtedly one of the artists who made the box. Another artist's name may be read with difficulty in a similar inscription which appears on one of the medallions on the left side: it is written on the thigh of a stag, which is attacked by a lion عمل عبيدة, "it was made by Obeidat." Three other inscriptions of a similar character appear in other

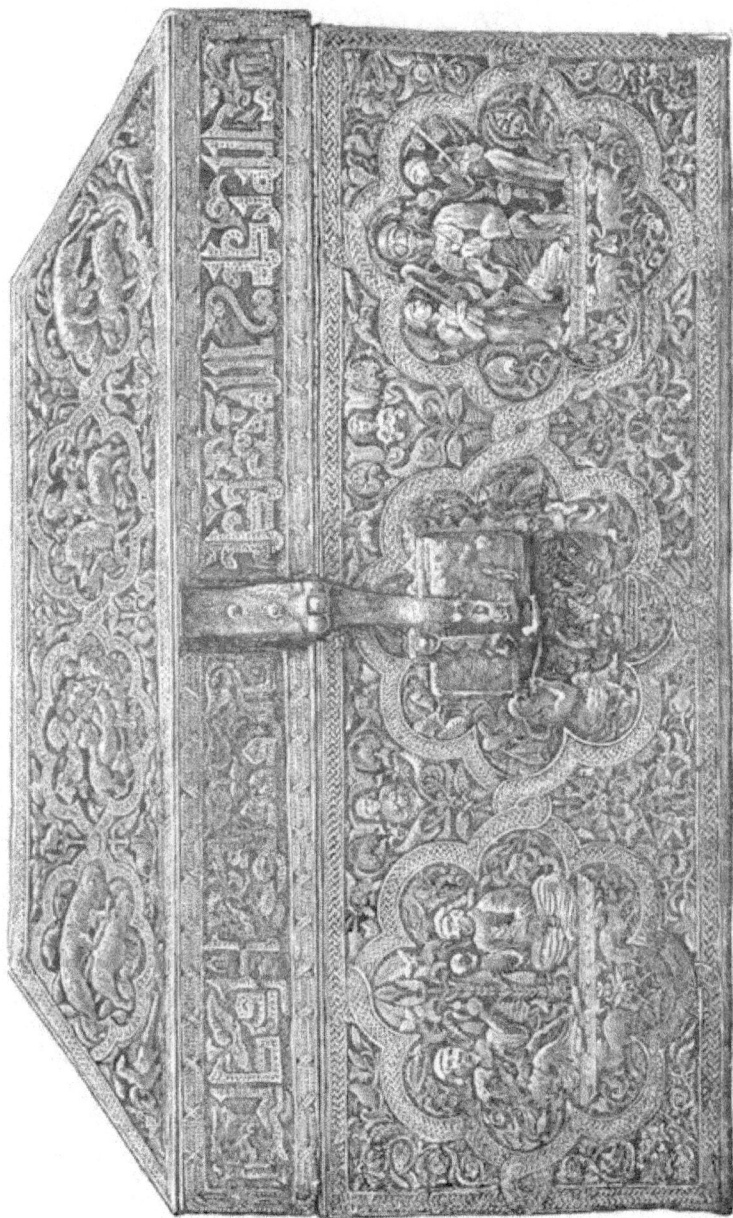

MOORISH CASKET. 11TH CENTURY. CATHEDRAL OF PAMPLONA.

parts of this box, which probably give the names of other artists, but I have been unable to decipher them.

Among other artistic objects in the shrine of the cathedral of Braga, in Portugal, there is an ivory box of the same period, and the inscription, which runs round the cover, mentions the same persons:

"There is no God but God, and Mahomad is his prophet. In the name of God, a blessing, prosperity and fortune for the Hagib Seifo, d. daula, for this work, which he ordered to be made by the hands of"—here the inscription has been broken off —"his principal eunuch." (Vide 'Artes e Letras,' No. 6, 3rd series, p. 94, Lisbon, 1874.)

Both these caskets were made for Hadjeb Abd el Melik, a minister of Hischem the second.

It is necessary to add to them an ivory diptych, preserved at the Provincial Museum of Burgos, which, as we find by the following inscription, was also made for Abder Rahman III. (A.D. 912–961).

هذا ما عمل الإمام عبد الله عبد الرحمن امير المومنين

"This was ordered to be made by the Iman servant of God Abder Rahman, prince of believers."

Two other boxes of the same artistic character, belonging to a private collection, must also be mentioned. They are both cylindrical, and are terminated by a spherical cover. They measure 7½ inches high, by 4⅜ wide, and are covered with a profuse and splendid ornamentation of figures and animals. Round the lid of of one them is a band, with the following inscription in fine Cufic character :

بركة من الله ونعمة وسرور وغبطه للمغيرة بن امير المومنين رحمه آلله مما عمل
سنة سبع وحمسين وثلث ماية

"The blessing of God and his favours, joy, and prosperity, for

Almogueira, son of the Prince of the faithful, whom may God have forgiven. It was made in the year 357 [A.D. 967]."

Almogueira was the son of the Caliph of Cordova, Abder Rahman III.

On the other may be read in similar characters—

[بسم الله الرحمن الرحيم بركة] ويمن و سعادة لرياض بن افلح صاحب الشرطة العليّ

عمل في سنّه تسع و حمسين و ثلث مايـة

("In the name of God, clement and merciful, blessing")—this part of the inscription is missing—" and prosperity and happiness for Riyadh ben Aflah, captain of the superior guard. It was made in the year 359" [A.D. 969].

The style of the objects which we have hitherto described is undoubtedly Oriental, and we must seek in Persia the origin of this industry. There is, however, every probability that these seven ivory boxes were made in Spain by Spanish Arabs, or artists who had settled there from the East. On all these carvings the names of Spanish historical persons appear, and it is hardly possible that they were ordered in remote countries, especially as some of these objects are small and comparatively unimportant. It must also be borne in mind that we find in contemporary authors many details on the luxury and magnificence of this period of the Spanish Arabs, and the great height which the arts and industries had reached at that time.

The ivory carvings which I have described present all the characteristics of the Oriental school, which was copied by European Christian sculptors during the 11th and 12th centuries. We find in Christian productions of this period, too constantly to require any further comment, the same geometrical traceries, flowers, leaves, animals, and birds. The subjects represented on monuments of Christian art have been erroneously interpreted by modern ecclesiologists who have endeavoured to demonstrate the

symbolism of these figures in a purely Christian sense with only
the unsatisfactory result of checking and leading astray art students
of the Middle Ages. It is of the utmost importance to go to the
primitive sources from which this art is derived in order to illustrate this important theory. The Oriental school of sculpture was
soon transmitted, either through the influence of the Spanish
Arabs, or by other means, to Christian artists. As an interesting
example of this may be mentioned the shrine which King Dn.
Sancho ordered to be made, A.D. 1033, in which to deposit the
bones of San Millan, still preserved in San Millan de la Cogulla,
in the province of La Rioja, Spain. This fine shrine is 4 feet
6 inches long, by 2 feet 3½ inches high. It is of wood, and
covered with gold plates and inlaid stones and crystals. Between
this metal work are placed 22 plaques of ivory carved with subjects representing passages from the life of the saint, and single
figures of the princes, monks, and benefactors who helped to
defray the expense of this work of art. Among them there are
two small figures with the names of Apparitio Scholastico,
Ramirus Rex. These have been generally supposed to be the
artists' names. A sculptor is also represented carving a shield,
and near him is one of his workmen. Underneath these figures
ran formerly an inscription, of which the first part only remains,
containing the name of the artist—"(Magis) tro et Rodolpho
filio."

Two other interesting specimens remain of Spanish Moresque
art of the 11th century. One is a casket at the South Kensington
Museum, No. 10, 66, which Mr. Maskell describes as "richly
carved in deep relief with foliage and animals in scrolls interlacing
one another, and forming larger and smaller circles. The top
and each side is a single plaque of ivory; the sloping lid at the
front and back has two panels. On the two are two animals, like
does; a large bird stands on the back of each, attacking it with
his beak. The sloping sides have, in the large circles, men on
horseback, and animals fighting. The intermediate spaces are

completely filled with foliage, and smaller beasts. Similar subjects are repeated in the circles on the panels forming the lower sides of the casket, and among them are two groups of men and women sitting ; one blowing a horn, another playing on a guitar, another holding a cup in one hand and a flower in the other." There is no inscription on this casket, but in one of the medallions on the lid there is a bust which is carried on the back of a horse, and which is probably a representation of the prince for whom the casket was made.

The other example of this period is that known as the cross of Don Fernando, at the Archæological Museum at Madrid. This cross is 20½ inches by 14. On the front is a figure in high relief of Our Lord with the inscription : IHE. NAZARENVS REX IVDEORVM. In the upper part is represented the figure of Our Lord at the moment of his Resurrection, and in the lower a symbolical figure of Adam ; both these figures are in high relief. Underneath may be read in two lines,—

FERDINANDVS REX.
SANCIA REGINA.

At the back of the cross appears in the centre the Lamb of God: in the four corners the emblems of the Evangelists. Besides these purely Christian symbols, the ground work is covered with foliage, circles interlacing each other, figures of animals of different kinds, and men struggling with wild beasts. The whole · of the ornamentation corresponds to the style of decoration of the moresque objects which I have already described. King Ferdinand I. died A.D. 1065, his wife Sancha A.D. 1071 ; and documents exist proving that in 1063 they gave this interesting work of art with other artistic objects to the Church of San Isidoro of Leon, where it remained until 1870, when it was given up by the authorities of the church to the Museum at Madrid. The following woodcut represents the back of the cross :—

BACK OF CROSS OF KING FERDINAND I. ARCHÆOLOGICAL
MUSEUM, MADRID

These different specimens represent, in my opinion, the most satisfactory view of the art industry of ivory carving during the 10th and 11th centuries. Several other examples of oriental carving in ivory still exist in Spain in the shrines of different cathedrals; others of less artistic interest may be seen at the Archæological Museum at Madrid. These caskets are for the most part not ornamented with carvings in relief, but are decorated with inscriptions painted in gold and colours. The most important are :—

A large casket at the Archæological Museum of Madrid, decorated with painting in red and green, and a fine inscription in Cufic characters.

A similar casket at the same museum, decorated with a design painted in green, red, and blue; an inscription in cufic letters runs round a band in the upper part.

عمل محمد بن السراج

"Made by Mohammad Ben Assarag."

An ivory casket at the Real Academia de la Historia at Madrid, with an ornamentation and inscription painted in the style of the former ones and the shield of arms of the Kings of Aragon. The inscription reproduces several Suras of the Koran, and the arms of the house of Aragon were probably added when the casket came into the possession of some person belonging to the family.

A casket exists at the Church of Santo Domingo de Silos (province of Burgos), which merits a special mention on account of what has remained to us of the inscription.

This casket is 13¼ inches long by 7½ inches wide and high. It is ornamented in part with foliage and flowers in the moresque style, alternating with hunting subjects, men shooting with bows and arrows, riding upon lions, fantastic animals and leopards mounted on the back of bulls. The work is inferior in art to the caskets at Pamplona and South Kensington. On a band which runs round the four sides of the lid is an inscription in Cufic characters, of which unfortunately the two longer sides have been destroyed, and have been substituted at a very early period by bands of cloisonné enamel, evidently belonging to other caskets. On the two sides an inscription remains, upon which may be read the year Hegira 417 (A.D. 1026); the name of the artist who carved it, Mohammad Ibn Zeiyan, and the two first letters of the town in which it was made (probably Cuenca)

.... لصاحبه اطال الله بقاه مما عمل بمدينة قو..... سبع عشرة واربع ماية عمل محمد ابن زيان عبده اعزه الله

". . . . . for its owner (may God lengthen his days.) It was made in the town of Cu[enca] in the year 417. (A.D. 1025.) By Mohammad — ibn Zeiyan, his servant. May God glorify him."

In the geography of Edrisi, an Oriental author who describes Spain in the beginning of the 12th century, only two names of towns are mentioned which agree with this inscription, Coria and Cuenca قورية قونكة. The first of these towns was always a less important centre than Cuenca. Edrisi praises the woollen fabrics made at Cuenca, and there is every probability that this casket was carved there, as there is also an ivory monstrance at the cathedral of Perpiñan, which has likewise an inscription in Cufic characters, stating it was made for the Hageb Ismail.

بركة من الله عمل بمدينة قونكة للحجب اسمعيل

"The blessing of God. Made at the town of Cuenca, for the Hageb Ismail."

Villanueva in his "Viage por España," Vol. 5, p. 144, mentions two large ivory caskets with Cufic inscriptions which still exist at the cathedral of Tortosa, Cataluña.

Another of a similar description is preserved in the Treasury of the cathedral of Bayeux.

This casket is, as M. André tells us in a pamphlet on "Antiquites Arabes de la Normandie," Rennes, 1869, O.^m 42 L. by O^m 28 W. and 13 H. It is decorated with bands of enamelled metal, and covered with a fine running design of peacocks and other birds. Round the lock runs the following inscription in Cufic characters :

بسم الله الرحمن الرحيم بركة من الله و نعمة شاملة

"In the name of God, clement, merciful, the blessing and His benefits complete."

These ivory caskets were made originally to hold perfumes, jewels, or precious stones. For besides the Arabic inscriptions which allude to this, we find the idea distinctly expressed in an inscription in Cufic letters on a casket which came from Cordova belonging to the Caliphate. This casket was exhibited at the Paris Exhibition in 1867 ; I do not know where it is at present.

It appears at first sight difficult to explain why the Spanish Moors decorated these objects with the representations of animated beings, against the precepts of the Koran, and the reason why these objects of undoubtedly Moorish origin have been preserved until the present day in the treasuries of Spanish cathedrals. The prohibition of the Koran to represent animated beings is, however, not so strict as is generally supposed; it is reduced to the following sentences. "O Believers ! Wine and games of chance, and statues and the divining arrows, are only an abomination of Satan's work ! Avoid them that ye may prosper." [Sura v. ver. 22.] Later commentators on the Koran have added the severest prohibitions against painters and artists who represented animated beings, but to very little effect, and we find in contemporary authors numerous details of the specimens of sculptures and paintings which were in the houses of Moorish magnates. Coins, textile fabrics, furniture, and other objects which have reached us, leave no doubt that the representations of animated beings were constantly used by the Spanish and Eastern Arabs from the first century of the Hegira.

The fact that these Moorish caskets should have been used for preserving the relics of saints in Spanish churches, is explained by the custom common in the middle ages in Spain and other countries, of offering war spoils and treasures brought from long and distant peregrinations, and even objects of natural history, to the different churches. Alligators may still be seen hanging in churches in Seville, Toledo, Valencia, etc. The Moors did the same thing : the famous warrior Almanssor, the minister of Hischem II. at the end of the 10th century, carried off the bells from the cathedral of Cordova, and had them turned into lamps and used at the mosque of Cordova. We find in ancient writers frequent mention of the custom of Spanish Christians of offering these ivory caskets to the churches, as trophies taken in their warfares with the Moors. The ecclesiastical authorities probably placed them at the time with other valuable objects in the treasuries of the churches, filling them with relics, for such is the manner in which they are found ; they have remained untouched from the earliest times and are constantly mentioned in local histories of the cathedrals. We must not suppose that the ecclesiastical authorities ignored their Mohamedan origin, for we find at every step during the middle ages the names of priests who knew and interpreted the Arabic language. The principal reason why these objects of Oriental art have been preserved, is, that the hatred of race and belief between Moors and Christians was by no means as great as has been supposed by modern authors, and certainly never went so far as to destroy objects of industrial and artistic interest. In the year A.D. 1275, certain privileges were granted to Moorish workmen who were set apart and ordered to repair the Mosque at Cordova, at that time already converted into a christian cathedral. During the 13th, 14th and 15th centuries a large number of parish churches were built in Spain in the Moorish style, either by Oriental architects, or Spaniards who had adopted their architecture, and numerous examples might be given of inscriptions and details of ornamentation which confirm most fully these theories.

Objects of ivory carvings of the middle ages, posterior to the 12th century, are frequently met with in Spain. Among the most remarkable is the Virgin de las Batallas, in the cathedral of Seville. This image belonged to St. Ferdinand, early in the 13th century, and the tradition exists that it was carried on the king's saddle in battle. The fine ivory diptychs at the Escorial and Archæological Museum at Madrid must also be mentioned, and a large number of ivory caskets, and fragments, existing in the same Museum and in different Spanish churches.

Notwithstanding, however, the numerous examples of ivory carvings which are still to be met with in Spanish churches and cathedrals, I find no information which enables us to affirm that this artistic industry existed in Spain during the 16th, 17th, and 18th centuries. We find artists mentioned who carved in wood, iron, and silver work, and numerous details of their work, but ivory carvers are never mentioned, if any existed, their number must have been comparatively small ; and I am led, therefore, to suppose that the specimens existing in Spain were imported from Italy or France, and for this reason it is necessary to end at the Renaissance the history of ivory carving in Spain.

The inlaid ivory work so constantly used in Spanish furniture of the 16th and 17th centuries, cannot be included in this notice on ivory carvers, owing to its limited character, and the use to which it was employed. One branch of sculpture must be mentioned representing sacred images, which were carved in the 16th and 17th centuries by natives of the Philippine Islands or the Portuguese Colonies. They are frequently met with in Spain, and are remarkable for their bad and careless modelling, a

mannered unartistic style, combined with the exaggerated rigidity
so common in Chinese and Indian productions.   As examples of
this style of art may be mentioned the representations of St.
Erasmus, and the Immaculate Conception (Nos. 9069, '63, 183,
'64), in the South Kensington Museum.

POTTERY AND PORCELAIN.

Roman and Visigothic.—Hispano Moresque earthenware.—Painted, glazed and lustred pottery.—Terra-cotta.—*Azulejos* (Tile decorations).—Pottery made at Talavera, Valencia, Seville, Triana, Zamora, Puente del Arzobispo.—Unglazed pottery.—Bucaros.—Alcora ware and porcelain.—Buen Retiro porcelain.

ROMAN AND VISIGOTHIC.

THE productions of Ceramic Art have constituted from the earliest times a very important industry in Spain. Fragments of vases of greyish-coloured paste, ornamented with bands or zones, are constantly found in excavations in different localities. It cannot, however, be determined whether they were importations, or imitations made in the Spanish Peninsula. The earliest mention which we find of this industry in Spain is in Pliny (Lib. xxx., cap. xii., line 19, Edition of Paris, 1526-7), who, in praising vases of pottery made in different countries, mentions those of Saguntum (Murviedro) near Valencia. An epigram by Juvenal (Sat. v. xxix.), and several by Martial (iv. 45, viii. 6, xiv. 108) on the same subject, prove that the pottery from the eastern coast of the Mediterranean was very famous at that time.

Count Lumiares, in his work on pottery of Saguntum ("Barros Saguntinos," Valencia, 1779, 8vo), mentions having examined more than 1500 specimens of pottery of different kinds, which he classifies in four groups: grey pottery, cream-coloured pottery, yellow pottery and red glazed ware, with ornamentation in relief (Samian ware); this ornamentation constitutes, in my opinion, the only distinctive feature of the pottery made at Saguntum.

L

Remains of this pottery are very frequently found in the ruins of former Roman cities; a much larger number of specimens of all kinds have appeared since Count Lumiares wrote his book, none however differ materially from the terra-cottas of the Roman period found in Italy, or in other countries. Some of the marks are identical with those given by Birch and several authors who

SAMIAN BOWL.

have written on Roman pottery; hence it would appear that this industry was imported into Spain, or the forms and marks copied there to a very large extent.

The number of inscriptions and potters' marks met with on the vases and fragments found in Spain is very great. Students who take a special interest in this subject will find full details in Dr. Emile Hübner's important work, "Inscrip. Hispaniæ Latinæ," Berlin, 1869. This writer has collected the greatest number of inscriptions. He mentions 43 which appear on bricks, 36 on vases and drinking vessels, 63 on lamps, 579 on vases of red pottery, 115 inscriptions of doubtful reading, 21 which are incomplete, and 56 written by hand. He gives us, besides, other marks without inscriptions, representing hands, horses, rabbits, butterflies, bees, flowers, etc. In an inedited history of the ancient city of Emporion (Cataluña) [MS., Acad. of Hist., Madrid], the author, Dr. Joaquin Botet y Sisó, has collected 198 potters' marks. A large number are still unpublished which have been met with on fragments of pottery found in Extremadura and

Andalucia ; we may therefore confidently assert that the number amounts to upwards of 1500.

During the Visigothic monarchy, after the downfall of the Roman empire, which lasted until the invasion of the Arabs in the 8th century, the same style of ceramic industry, copied from the Romans, continued in Spain. No special study has been made of the pottery of this epoch, but, judging by the large amount of fragments of vessels for domestic use, which are constantly found in ruins of the Visigothic period, there can be no doubt that pottery continued to be manufactured in Spain. What San Isidoro, who died in 636, says in his "Etimologies, Book xx.," confirms this opinion, and undoubtedly refers to vessels similar to those of the Roman period. (*De vasis Escariis, potoriis vinariis et aquariis, oleariis, coquinariis et luminariorum.*)

After the Roman domination and Visigothic monarchy, ceramic art in Spain may be divided into the following groups :—

1st. Objects imported by the Moors into Spain ; these consist of remains of pottery belonging to the first period of their invasion ; lustred wares, manufactured in the Peninsula, which attained great importance during the Middle Ages, and still continue to be made in the present day ; terra-cottas, and green and white glazed pottery ; and lastly tiles, *azulejos*, of bright colours in the Moorish style.

2nd. Pottery of a distinct Italian style, made principally at Talavera ; porous, unglazed, coloured pottery, *bucaros ;* white, unglazed pottery, made at Andujar and La Rambla.

3rd. Pottery and porcelain made at Alcora, and the porcelain manufactory of Buen Retiro, near Madrid.

HISPANO MORESQUE EARTHENWARE.

The Spanish Peninsula was invaded by the Arabs about the year 711 A.D., and they absorbed for several centuries the industries of the country. Ceramic Art attained great importance

L 2

in their hands during the Middle Ages and Renaissance period, for even while the pottery works established at Talavera, Seville, and other localities, manufactured pottery to a very great extent, which was chiefly imitated from Italian models, the Moorish style still continued, and has never been interrupted in the province of Valencia down to the present day.

The Arabs had as early as the beginning of the 12th century, if not even before, established the industry of metallic-lustred pottery in Spain. It remains to be seen what were the leading characteristics of the pottery of the period of the greatest importance of the Spanish Moors from the 8th to the 11th century.

Cordova, the capital of the independent Caliphs of Damascus, was the centre from which works of art of all kinds of a high order were largely exported. The ruins of the palaces at Medina Az zahra have, it is deeply to be regretted, never been excavated, and Granada is the only locality where some fragments of Moorish pottery may be studied belonging to this time.

Granada was almost unknown in the 8th century; the ancient Roman town of Illiberis, about six miles from the present site of Granada, had alone any importance : it was one of the bishoprics of Andalucia. The Arabs first settled in the remains of the Roman city : in the 10th century they removed to the spot occupied by the present town, and Illiberis was then abandoned. Roman remains are frequently found at Illiberis, as are also vestiges of the Moorish occupation, chiefly consisting of objects in bronze and fragments of pottery. These specimens are decorated with arabesques in green and black on a whitish ground. Some interesting examples may be studied at the small *Museo Provincial* at Granada, which certainly belong to the 10th or beginning of the 11th century. One of these fragments has unreadable Arabic letters ; another is decorated with a stag ; the most remarkable is a plate fourteen inches in diameter, in the centre of which is represented a falcon on a horse's back. The form and every detail of the horse, the plaited tail, ending in the form of a trident, all are identical with one on which is mounted a man holding a hawk in his hand, carved on the ivory casket described on page 133 as dated 359 of the hegira (A.D. 969), and probably of Cordovese manufacture. Both these objects possess a very decided Persian character, and undoubtedly belong to the date ascribed; for besides the circumstance of their having been found in ruins of this period, the shape of the horse is conclusive; its character changes soon after, as we find in the miniatures of the MS. of the 13th century at the Bib. Nationale de Paris, containing the "Séances de Hariri." It is almost impossible to assert whether this pottery was made in, or imported into Spain. One argument in favour of its Spanish-Moorish origin is that the glaze and paste are similar to pottery which we know was manufactured at Granada. The common earthenware proceeding from that locality is decorated in much the same manner.

Soon after the fall of the Caliphate, metallic-lustred ware was made in Spain : Edrisi, the most remarkable Arabic geographer of the Middle Ages, in describing Calatayud, says : "Here the gold-coloured pottery is made which is exported to all countries." ("Descrip. de l'Afrique et de l'Espagne," Leyde, 1866.) Edrisi was born in the year 1100. He studied at Cordova, and finished writing his book in 1154. The circumstance of this pottery being mentioned in the 12th century as excellent enough for exportation, certainly makes it appear probable that the *fabrique* already existed at an earlier date, especially when we bear in mind that Calatayud was conquered in the year 1120 by the Christians, and it is impossible to suppose that they established an Oriental industry there which was foreign to their culture, or to the contemporary Christian art. This text of Edrisi's has hitherto not been properly interpreted. In Jauber's translation (Edrisi, Paris, 1836-40), he interprets the word *guidar*, غذار, *lutum purum* of potters, as the name of a gilt textile, perhaps because in his time it was difficult to believe in the existence of metallic-lustred pottery. In the Edit. of Leyden, by Messrs. Dozy and Goeje, the sense of the word is properly given; indeed, Jauber himself translates it by *porcelain* in the chapter of this volume which refers to China.

This text of Edrisi's has never yet been quoted by writers on Ceramic Art; but once known it is impossible for a moment to state that the earliest manufacture of Moorish lustred ware was that at Malaga, an opinion which has been supported hitherto on the quotation from Ben Batutah's works, which will be given later on. I regret to have found no other allusion to the lustred ware of Aragon until the 16th century. No mention is made of it in the geographical texts published by Juynboll, Al Makkari, or other Arabic writers. From what we know of Aragon in the 16th century, it was a great centre of this industry, and its productions rivalled those of Valencia and Andalucia.

The next text which alludes to this manufacture is given by Ben Batutah, a celebrated traveller, who, after travelling for twenty years in the East, went from Tangiers to Granada, from 1349 to 1351. Passing by Malaga, he says: "At Malaga the fine golden pottery is made which is exported to the furthermost countries." ("Voy. d'Ibn Batoutah," Paris, 1853-58, vol. iv. p. 367.) This text has been constantly reproduced and commented upon, since Baron Charles Davillier first drew attention to it in his interesting little *brochure* on "Faïences Hispano-Moresques."

The next time I find lustred pottery mentioned is in the 15th century. Eximenus, in his "Regiment de la cosa publica," Valencia, 1499, in speaking of the excellent things made in the kingdom of Valencia, says: "The twenty-seventh excellent thing is that some artificial objects are made there which bring great renown to the country, for they are excellent and beautiful, and are now to be found in other localities . . . . but above all is the beauty of the gold pottery so splendidly painted at Manises, which enamours everyone so much, that the Pope, and the cardinals, and the princes of the world obtain it by special favour, and are astonished that such excellent and noble works can be made of earth."

Lustred pottery had already attained great importance in Aragon early in the 16th century. We find in a deed granted at Calatayud in 1507, that "Muhamed ben Suleyman Attaalab, an inhabitant of the suburb of the Moors at Calatayud, and an artificer of lustred golden earthenware, engaged himself with Abdallah Alfoquey of the same locality, to teach him the said industry, in the space of four years and a half, from the date of the deed." ("Estado social de los mudejares de Castilla, by Fernandez y Gonzalez," Madrid 1866, p. 437.) At Muel, a village in the province of Aragon near Zaragoza, this industry existed to a great extent in 1585. In the travels of Henrique Cock ("Relacion del viage hecho por Felipe II. en 1585," por Henrique Cock, publicado por Morel Fatio y Rodriguez Villa, Madrid, 1876,) we find the following interesting details of the manner in which this pottery was made, p. 30 :—

"Almost all the inhabitants of this village are potters, and all the earthenware sold at Zaragoza is manufactured in the following manner. First the vessels are fashioned of a certain ingredient the earth furnishes them in that locality, in the shape they may require. Once made, they bake them in an oven fitted for the purpose. They then remove them to varnish with white varnish and polish them, and afterwards make a wash of certain materials in the following manner: twenty-five pounds, *one arroba*, of lead, with which they mix three or four pounds of tin, and as many pounds of a certain sand which is to be found there. All these ingredients are mixed into a paste like ice; it is broken into small pieces and pounded like flour, and kept by them in powder. This powder is mixed with water, the dishes are passed through it, and they are rebaked in the oven, and keep their lustre. Afterwards, in order that the pottery may be gilt, they take very strong vinegar, mixed with about two reales (a small coin equivalent to 6*d.*) of silver in powder, vermilion, and red

ochre, and a little wire. When all is mixed together, they paint
with a feather on the dishes any decoration they may like, rebake
them, and then they remain gold-coloured for ever. This was
told me by the potters themselves."

But nothing can be compared in exactitude to the following
receipt of the manner of preparing this lustred ware, which I was
fortunate enough to find in a manuscript in the British Museum.
(Egerton, No. 507, MS. fol. 102).

Count Florida Blanca wishing in 1785 to establish at Madrid a
manufactory of metallic-lustred ware, had the following report on
the actual state of the industry sent to him from Manises with
full details of the manner in which it was required to be carried
out.

"After the pottery is baked, it is varnished with white and
blue, the only colours used besides the gold lustre ; the vessels
are again baked; if the objects are to be painted with gold colour,
this can only be put on the white varnish, after they have gone
twice through the oven. The vessels are then painted with the
said gold colour and are baked a third time, with only dry rose-
mary for fuel.

"The white varnish used is composed of lead and tin, which
are melted together in an oven made on purpose; after these
materials are sufficiently melted, they become like earth, and
when in this state the mixture is removed and mixed with an
equal quantity in weight of sand : fine salt is added to it, it is
boiled again, and when cold, pounded into powder. The only
sand which can be used is from a cave at Benalguacil, three
leagues from Manises. In order that the varnish should be fine,
for every *arroba*, 25 pounds of lead, 6 to 12 ounces of tin must be
added, and half a bushel of fine-powered salt : if a coarse kind is
required, it is sufficient to add a very small quantity of tin, and
three or four *cuartos* worth of salt, which in this case must be
added when the ingredient is ready for varnishing the vessel.

" Five ingredients enter into the composition of the gold colour :

copper, which is better the older it is ; silver, as old as possible ;
sulphur; red ochre, and strong vinegar, which are mixed in the
following proportions: of copper three ounces, of red ochre twelve
ounces, of silver one *peseta* (about a shilling), sulphur three
ounces, vinegar a quart; three pounds (of twelve ounces) of the
earth or scoriæ, which is left after this pottery is painted with the
gold colour, is added to the other ingredients.

"They are mixed in the following manner : a small portion of
sulphur in powder is put into a casserole with two small bits of
copper, between them a coin of one silver *peseta*; the rest of the
sulphur and copper is then added to it. When this casserole is
ready, it is placed on the fire, and is made to boil until the sulphur
is consumed, which is evident when no flame issues from it. The
preparation is then taken from the fire, and when cold is pounded
very fine ; the red ochre and scoriæ are then added to it; it is
mixed up by hand and again pounded into powder. The preparation
is placed in a basin and mixed with enough water to make a sufficient paste to stick on the sides of the basin ; the mixture is then
rubbed on the vessel with a stick ; it is therefore indispensable
that the water should be added very gradually until the mixture is
in the proper state.

"The basin ready prepared must be placed in an oven for six
hours. At Manises it is customary to do so when the vessels of
common pottery are baked ; after this the mixture is scratched off
the sides of the basin with some iron instrument; it is then
removed from there and broken up into small pieces, which are
pounded fine in a hand-mortar with the quantity of vinegar
already mentioned, and after having been well ground and
pounded together for two hours the mixture is ready for decorating. It is well to observe that the quantity of varnish and
gold-coloured mixture which is required for every object can only
be ascertained by practice."

Excellent lustred ware was made at Murcia, and in several
villages of the province of Valencia ; a good example exists of

this pottery at the museum (see woodcut); none, however, was so important as the manufactory of Manises. Diago, in his "Anales del reyno de Valencia, 1613-40," repeats the words of Eximeno:

PLATEAU, PROBABLY OF VALENCIA. SOUTH KENSINGTON MUSEUM.

"That the pottery made at Valencia is painted and gilt with so much art, that it has enamoured every one, so much so that the pope, the cardinals, and princes send for it, astonished that things of such beauty can be made of earth."

This and similar texts relating to the exportation of Spanish pottery explains the fact of these specimens being so frequently met with in Italy. Pottery of a dark copper-coloured lustre is made at the present time at Manises, and the imitations and forgeries to be met with at the dealers' shops in Madrid are made in that locality.

I have mentioned the different historical texts which allude to this industry, and the technical receipts showing the ingredients employed to give the lustre. It is now no longer possible to doubt that this pottery came originally from the East. This opinion has gained ground of late years; for among the objects discovered by Sir Henry Layard at Nineveh, and in more recent excavations in Ephesus and Asia Minor, fragments of pottery have been found with metallic lustre. This and other important examples of artistic culture undoubtedly arose in Persia. No examples which may be mentioned can give a better or more distinct idea of this than a comparison between the Persian and Hispano-Moresque wares at the South Kensington Museum. The technical proceedings and effect produced by the metallic lustre on a white ground, with touches here and there of blue, are exactly the same in both cases. The principal difference consists in a greater richness and variety of ornamentation which we find in the specimens brought from Persia, especially those covered with a turquoise blue lustre, those of a dark blue and metallic lustre, and those on which gold is applied *en froid*, of which I know no similar examples in Spain. It is possible they may have existed in the mosques, but no traces remain of mosques built by the Spanish Moors during the 13th, 14th, and 15th centuries. The mosques at Cordova and Toledo which still exist are of an earlier date. If we judge by the mosque of Amru at Cairo, and others of the same early period, tile decorations were not used in their ornamentation, and it appears probable that this industry only became important after the 10th century. The similarity of objects used in Spain and Persia is constantly observed by travellers in that country. Ruy Gonzalez de Clavijo, who was sent there as ambassador from the King of Castille from 1403 to 1406, gives a most interesting description of tile decoration, by which we find they were used in the same manner as in Spain. ("Historia del gran Tamorlan," Seville, 1582, fol.) Another Spanish traveller, Silva de Figueroa, in a MS. belonging to Don Pascual de Gayangos, in describing his embassy to Persia in 1618 mentions the manner in which these tiles were used. I do not quote from many other travellers, for their remarks are hardly so valuable as those of Spaniards, who were accustomed to see these objects in their native country.

After mentioning the historical sources from which I have traced the manufactory of Hispano-Moresque lustred ware in Spain, it is advisable to enumerate the most important examples which have reached us belonging to the 14th century, or to an earlier date.

The fine vase at the Alhambra, Granada. (See woodcut.)

A vase of the same character which exists at the Archæological Museum of Madrid.

A vase of the same kind, which belonged to the painter, Mariano Fortuny, and which was sold at the sale of his art objects in Paris, April 30th, 1875. (*Vide* "Atelier de Fortuny," Paris, 1875.)

A fragment of another vase, which belonged also to Fortuny, and was sold at the same time.

A fragment of a vase at the Museo of Granada; it is similar to the others in form and size, but without metallic lustre.

A large plaque, or *azulejo*, which belonged also to Fortuny.

The *azulejos*, or tile decorations of the house known by the name of Cuarto Real de Santo Domingo at Granada.

Several dishes and bowls at the Kensington, Madrid, and Cluny Museums, which belong to this period.

Baron Charles Davillier in his article on Hispano-Moresque lustred ware, in "Atelier de Fortuny," Paris, 1875, says that interesting specimens of this pottery exist also at the Museum of

Stockholm, and the Cathedral of Mezzara in Sicily, but that he had not had the opportunity of studying them.

All these objects have hitherto been considered to have proceeded from Malaga, writers on ceramic art derived their evidence

MOORISH VASE AT THE ALHAMBRA.

from the text already mentioned, given in Ben Batutah's travels, the only one which alluded to the existence of this industry in Spain before the 15th century; but since I have found in Edrisi's Geography a manufacture mentioned of lustred pottery which existed at Calatayud at the beginning of the 12th century, that is to say, more than *two centuries* earlier than Ben Batutah's travels, I consider it extremely difficult to classify them.

The fine vase at the Alhambra is 4 feet 5½ inches high by 8 feet 2½ inches in circumference. It is decorated in the centre with two antelopes, and a series of elegant traceries of knots, stems, and leaves which cover the body of the vase. The colours employed are brown and blue on a yellow ground, the metallic lustre is extremely pale, of a mother-of-pearl colour. The following inscriptions are repeated all over the vase in African characters:

اليمن و الاقبال

Felicity and Fortune.

عافية باقية

Permanent prosperity.

A similar vase was at the Alhambra until the beginning of the present century; it disappeared at that time, and its present whereabouts is unknown. Drawings exist of this vase which have been published in Lozano's "Ant. Arab. de España," and Murphy's Atlas of "Arabian Ant. of Spain."

The fine vase at the Museo Arq. of Madrid is similar in style. It has been reproduced in a chromo-lithograph in Mus. Esp. de Ant. VI. p. 435. Both these vases are decorated with colours which are disposed in quite a distinct manner to all the other specimens of this pottery hitherto known. The vase at Granada is ornamented in the centre with two antelopes, and from drawings which have reached us of the companion vase, we find birds are introduced in the decoration of the handles. Animals combined with ornamentation are never met with in the immense number of Moorish traceries of all kinds which may be studied at Granada. This circumstance has induced me to consider these objects to have been brought from Persia, for Ben Batutah tells us that several Persians of importance had settled at Granada;

and it is highly probable that a direct communication existed
between these two countries. It is fair, however, to mention a
detail which is against this argument. The arms of the Moorish
kings of Granada appear on the vase which has disappeared from
Granada, and although it may have been ordered from Persia, it
is also possible that it was made in the province of Andalucia.

The vase which belonged to Fortuny, and the large *azulejo*,
Nos. 42, 44 (*vide* "Atelier de Fortuny"), are very different in
style. They have no colours, and their metallic lustre is very low
in tone, a common circumstance in Hispano-Moorish pottery.
The following inscription,

عزه لمولانا السلطان ابى الحجاج

"Glory to Our Lord the Sultan Abul Hajaj," [A.D. 1333–1354]
occurs on this tile, an inscription very frequently met with also on

TILE PROBABLY FROM THE ALHAMBRA ; FORMERLY IN THE MARRYAT
COLLECTION.

the walls of the Alhambra. Abul Hajaj carried out works of restoration to a very large extent at the Palace. The two large tiles
on either side of the entrance-door of the Cuarto Real de Santo
Domingo at Granada, although not so fine as the vase and tile
which belonged to Fortuny, are similar in general character, and
it is safe therefore to consider these objects, and others of a similar
kind, to have proceeded from the manufacture of Malaga mentioned by Ben Batutah, or other pottery works of the same kind,
which probably existed at that time in the province of Granada.

Metallic-lustred dishes have at times an even surface without
ornamentation in relief, and sometimes are ornamented with ribs
and convex dots, which appear to suggest that they are meant to
imitate the structure of nails, bars, or other work common to
metal vessels, in the manner of Etruscan vases.

The finest specimens of Hispano-Moresque ware at the Kensington Museum are—

No. 8968-'63. A vase which belonged to the Soulages Collection. Mr. Fortnum, in his " Majolica, Hispano-Moresco, Persian,
Damascus and Rhodian Wares, at the Kensington Museum,"
London, 1873, describes this vase as spherical on a trumpet-
shaped base, the neck of elongated funnel form, flanked by two
large wing-shaped handles perforated with circular holes. The
surface, except the mouldings, is entirely covered with a diaper-
pattern of ivory or briony leaves, tendrils and small flowers in
brownish lustre, and blue on the white ground. Spanish. 14th
or 15th century. (See woodcut.)

No. 486-'64. Bowl, funnel-shaped, with representation of a
ship in full sail, with the royal arms of Portugal, 15th century.

The following are also especially worthy of mention :—

No. 7659-'62. Bowl and cover, painted with a scroll diaper
in alternate compartments of gold lustre and blue, the cover surmounted by a cupola-shaped ornament in gold lustre. 16th
century.

No. 489-'64. Plateau with lustred arabesque ornaments in

VASE DIAPERED WITH IVY OR BRYONY IN GOLDEN LUSTRE. HISPANO-
MORESCO, 14TH OR 15TH CENTURY. SOUTH KENSINGTON MUSEUM.

M

compartments. In the centre are two simulated Arabic inscriptions. 15th century.

PLATEAU, DIAPERED AND WITH RAISED RIBS AND STUDS, IN BLUE AND
GOLDEN LUSTRE. THE ARMS OF LEON, CASTILE, AND ARAGON.
HISPANO-MORESCO. 15TH OR 16TH CENTURY. SOUTH KENSINGTON
MUSEUM.

No. 1680-'55. Plateau, gold shield in the centre, with the
arms of Leon, Castille, and Aragon. The diapered ground is
curiously ribbed, and dotted with raised studs. (See woodcut.)

No. 243-'53. Plateau, in the centre an escutcheon of arms of Aragon, Leon, and Castile. (See woodcut.)

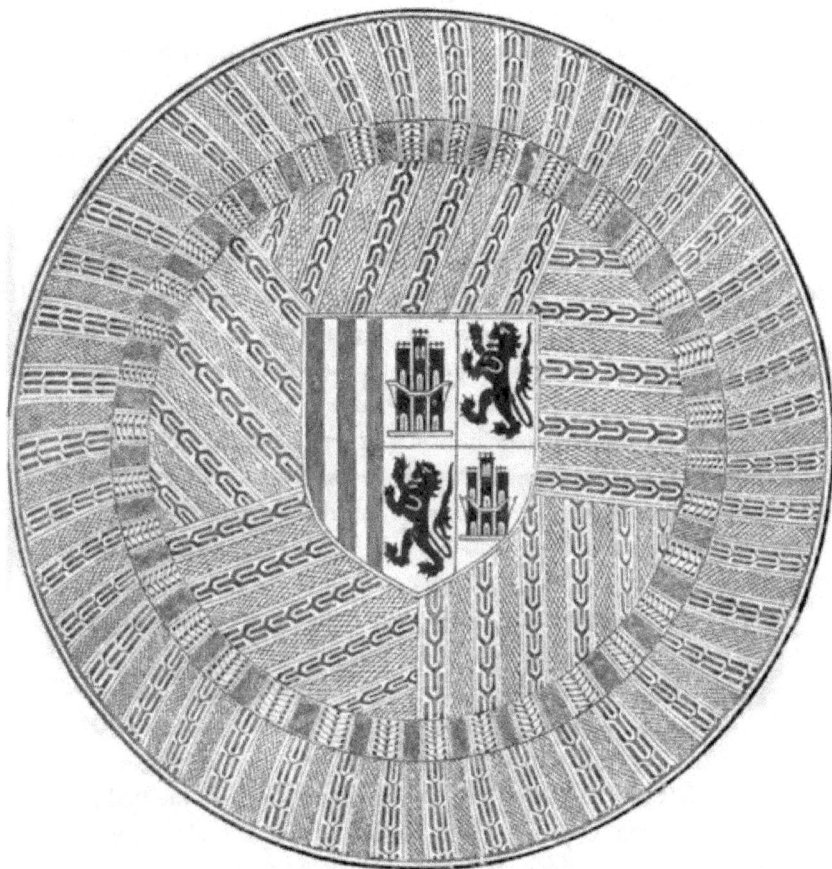

SALVER, DIAPERED IN GOLDEN LUSTRE, WITH THE SHIELD OF ARAGON, LEON, AND CASTILE. HISPANO-MORESCO. 15TH OR 16TH CENTURY. SOUTH KENSINGTON MUSEUM.

No. 104-'69. Vase, with shield of arms, seemingly of Sicily and Portugal.

Specimens of a later date are distinguished by the redness of

the lustre, such as No. 327–'66, a bowl, with feather-like ornament
in the centre; Nos. 326–'66 and 328–'66 are good examples of
this lustred ware of the last and early present century made at
Manises, Valencia.

It is almost impossible to classify the existing specimens of
Hispano-Moresque pottery. A few examples are marked with
the monogram of Manises, or possess some special sign, such as
the Eagle of St. John, which would make it appear they were made
in the province of Valencia, but as the texts from ancient authors
only praise this pottery and give no details of its general characteristics, it is very difficult to assign any given specimens to the
manufactories of Aragon and Valencia. The receipts which I
have given prove that the ingredients used were the same, the
modification in lustre was owing to the different combinations
of silver and copper. The system hitherto adopted of classifying
this ware by the localities in which it has been purchased is not
a safe one, unless borne out by further evidence. All that can be
done at the present time is to point out the oldest specimens, and
probable period of their manufacture. As a general rule the finest
specimens are also the oldest, for this industry decayed after the
Moors were expelled from Spain, and Italian pottery was imported
into that country in the 16th century.

The opinion which has been so generally accepted that gold
lustred pottery was made and exported from the Balearic Islands
has been contradicted by Dⁿ. Alvaro Campaner y Fuertes in a
letter addressed to Baron Davillier which appeared in the "Museo
Balear," Palma, 1875, in which he refutes the Baron's arguments
on the pottery which he supposes to have come from that
locality.

TERRA COTTAS.—*AZULEJOS*, OR WALL DECORATIONS OF
TILES.—EARTHENWARE.—BUCAROS AND UNGLAZED
POTTERY.

The earliest historical notice which I have met with of Terra-
cottas is in a grant made in A.D. 1222, by King Don Fernando el
Santo, in favour of the manufacturers of bricks or tiles at Talavera
(M. S. Bibl. Nacional Madrid, Dd. 114, p. 17), and another document of a similar kind by his son, King Don Alonso el Sabio
A.D. 1281, in favour of the Cathedral of Cordova, "that no
pottery works should be allowed inside the town, unless they were
established in the same manner as in the time of the Moors."
(Mem. Hist. Español, t. ii. p. 45). Although this information
is not of great importance, it enables us to infer that in the
13th century an industry existed in Spain which was closely
connected with pottery. Baron Davillier mentions a privilege
granted by King Dn. Jaime de Aragon to the inhabitants of Jativa,
province of Valencia, in which he commands, "that any master
potter who made jars, pots, pans, tiles, and bricks, should pay a
tribute of one *besant* yearly for each oven, and be permitted to
carry out his industry with no other obligation or service." (Col.
Doc. Ineditos, vol. xviii. p. 67.)

The details concerning this industry in Cataluña are more interesting ; especially on account of the references given to the marks
of the objects proceeding from this manufacture. The potters,
who were known by the generic name of *olleros* sent, in 1257, two
individuals to form part of the town council. They formed at that
time a guild ; in 1314 they agree in their regulations as to the
mark to be adopted for their pottery, and the actual spot is
mentioned on which every potter was to stamp his wares. This
stamp was ordered to be very visible, and instructions are given
as to the quality of the clay, and its manipulation, in order to

produce pottery of a first-class order. We find statutes in this sense up to 1355. But we cannot find in the "Libro de Orde-nanzas" of the potter's guild that any laws existed touching the technical details of this manufacture; most of the regulations refer

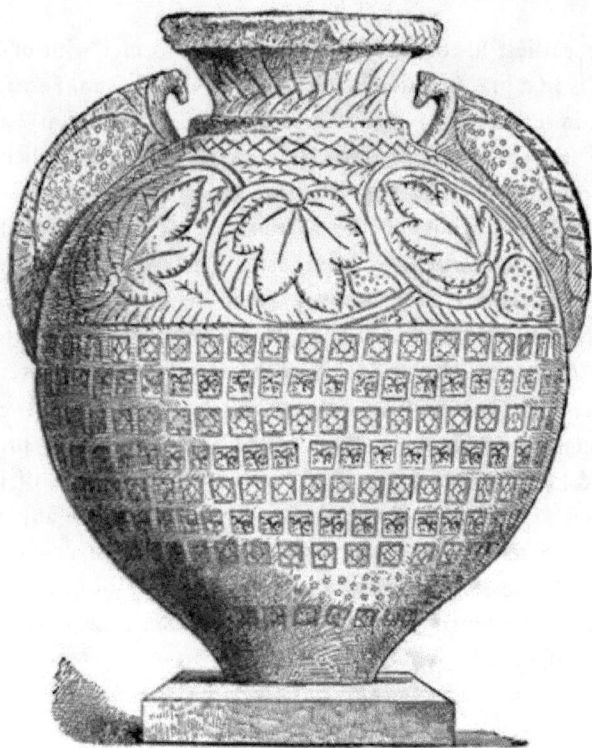

WINE JAR—"TINAJA." SOUTH KENSINGTON MUSEUM.

to the management of the guild from 1304, which was composed of potters, bricklayers, jar-makers, and manufacturers of pottery for domestic purposes of Barcelona. (Capmany, Memorias Historicas, 1779–92, vol. i. part 3, p. 69.)

These references are not, however, sufficient to identify the kind of pottery made at that time in Cataluña. It is highly probable that lustred ware was also made there to a great extent, not only because it was the most characteristic produce of the Peninsula, but also because this ware was exported to a great extent, and highly esteemed.

The most important examples of Spanish terra-cotta which have reached us are *tinajas*, large jars for holding wine and oil.

One of the best *tinajas* which I know is at the South Kensington Museum, No. 330-'66. (See woodcut.) It is a wine jar, amphora-shaped, and ornamented with incised pattern of vine leaves, and stamped diaper of a Gothic character. This and similar specimens have always been found in Andalusia and the province of Toledo, and hence we may infer that the chief centres of this industry existed at Toledo and Seville. They continue to be made there, and are used for the same purposes as in the Middle Ages, for keeping stores of wine, oil, meat, grain, etc.

Belonging to this section of objects of a large size, are some specimens of glazed earthenware made for brims of wells. I only know four or five examples in the local museums of Toledo and Cordova; the font of the church of San Salvador, Toledo, belongs also to the same pottery. The brim of a well, at the South Kensington Museum, No. 1763-'71, is of the same manufacture. It was bought at Toledo for three guineas at a shoemaker's shop. It is made of glazed white and green earthenware, with ornamental Cufic characters in high relief all round, which appear to be of the 14th century (see woodcut on next page). The inscription, which is repeated, is imperfect, and all that I can decipher are the words :

العزة المزة ,والسلامة

" The power, the excellence, and the peace."

There is no difficulty in affirming that this form of earthenware was made at Toledo, for Marineo Siculo, in his interesting volume treating of "De las Cosas Memorables de España," Alcala, 1539, says, "much coarse green and white pottery is made at Toledo."

The manufacture of tiles, as was the case with so many other industries in Spain, was imported by the Arabs.   In the Middle

BRIM OF WELL FROM TOLEDO.   SOUTH KENSINGTON MUSEUM.

Ages it attained great importance, and has never ceased in Spain up to the present day.   The earliest tiles (*azulejos*) made in Spain are composed of small pieces let into the wall, forming geometrical patterns.   The proceeding is similar to that employed by the workers of Byzantine mosaic,—tile decoration undoubtedly took the place of this mosaic work in Moorish buildings.   It is difficult to fix the precise period when they were first made, but it must have been posterior to the 10th century, when Moorish architecture underwent a radical change in its system of decoration.   The oldest tiles which exist in Spain are at the Palace of the Alhambra, Granada. They belong to the 14th century. The great variety of their design may be seen in Owen Jones' "Plans and elevations of the Alhambra," London, fol. 1842, and the fine work published by the Spanish government, "Monumentos Arquitectonicos." We can judge of the style adopted by two interesting fragments, both of which came from the Alhambra, No. 1104-'53, No. 324-'64, South Kensington Museum.

The earliest mention which I have found of this manufacture occurs in a letter from Doña Juana de Mendoza, the wife of the Almirante de Castilla, which is addressed to the lady abbess of the nunnery of Santo Domingo at Toledo. She begs that a large number of "azulejos" of different colours, black, white, yellow, and green should be sent to her. She alludes, in the same letter, to painted tiles, and says she was expecting a master potter from Seville to place these tiles in their proper places. This shows us that it was only in the province of Andalusia that the art was known of cutting these tiles into geometrical sections and mosaic patterns. This letter is not dated, but it is bound up with other documents of 1422, and evidence exists to prove that both the Almirante and his wife were dead in 1431. The locality for which the tiles were required was probably Palencia; the convent of Santa Clara was built by them at that time, and they both were buried there. It was extremely difficult to cut and join together these tiles; the workmen who did so had to pass through a regular examination in compliance with the municipal ordinances drawn up in the 15th century; without this requisite they were not allowed to exercise their trade.

We know, from documents existing at the Archives of the Alhambra, at Granada, that tiles were made there at the end of the 16th and beginning of the 17th century. We find the names of Antonio Tenorio, Gaspar Hernandez, and Pedro Tenorio working there at that time as master potters.

The use of these *azulejos* was not restricted to Moorish buildings; they were largely employed to decorate the walls of Christian churches, convents, palaces, and private houses. The style of work, however, soon changed, for instead of being made of mosaic work, they were formed of a single piece like the ordinary tiles, but imitating the Moorish colours. In the 16th century designs of the Renaissance style alternated with these, although the system and colouring continued the same. This style continued in vogue until the expulsion of the Moriscos in 1610. A fine collection may be seen at the South Kensington Museum of 200 tiles, in which upwards of 150 varieties of design will be found, Nos. 308-'66 and 367-'66. Their chief characteristic is that only pure colours are used without gradations or half tints. Lustred reflets are very seldom met with in tiles; the only examples I know are two beautiful plaques of the 14th century of a pale lustre which are on either side of the entrance door of the Moorish saloon called Cuarto Real de S^{to}. Domingo, at Granada; some small polygons of copper-coloured lustre at the Tower of la Cautiva, Granada: some few details in the coats of arms which are let into the tiles which adorn the walls of the Chapel at the Alhambra, and some few tiles with the arms of the Mendozas at the Casa de Pilatos, Seville.

A few dishes belong also to the 15th century, ornamented with the same colouring as the tiles without metallic lustre, and generally decorated with fantastic animals. They are very scarce. Two examples exist at the South Kensington Museum, Nos. 1459 and 1461-'70. They probably were made at Seville; all those I have seen come from there, and we know that the pottery from Seville was much esteemed. In Pedro de Medina's " Libro de Grandezas y Cosas Memorables de España," Sevilla, 1549, fol. lii., he says, " In this town of Triana much excellent pottery of Malaga is made, coloured white and yellow, and of different sorts and kinds. This pottery is made in about fifty houses, and it is exported from here to many localities. In the same manner excellent *azulejos* are made, of great variety of colour and design. And likewise fine reliefs of men and other things. Great quantities of these *azulejos* are taken to different localities."

At the introduction of Italian forms of art in Spain, at the beginning of the 16th century, artistic pottery divided itself into two schools—one kept to the traditional designs and strong tones of colour, the other used shaded colours, and especially yellow and blue tints, at times imitating Italian maiolica, but always following the decoration characteristic of the Renaissance style.

The Italian influence, and its finest results in Spain may be favourably studied in Seville, in the tile decorations of the chapel at the Alcazar, the doorway of the convent of Santa Paula, and a remarkable sepulchre decorated with tiles at the church of St. Anne at Triana. All these tile decorations are signed by the same person, and it would be difficult to find any more remarkable.

The *azulejos* at the Alcazar represent a picture in the manner and style of Pietro Perugino ; they are admirable in colour and design. Those which decorate the sepulchre at the church of St. Anne have the following inscription, *" Niculoso Francesco italiano me fecit, en el agno del mil cccciii."* Some very interesting tiles also may be seen in one of the rooms in the lower part of the Alcazar; they are marked in the following manner: A.V.S.T.A.— A.V.G.W.S.T.A. 1577–1578. On the floor of the pavilion of the Emperor Charles V. in the garden there are also some fine tiles which are signed Juan Hernandez, 1540.

We find mention in Cean Bermudez of a painter of *azulejos* named Juan Flores, a native of Flanders ; he painted tiles for the royal palaces of Madrid, the Pardo and Segovia ; he was appointed Maestro Azulejero by Philip II. in 1565.

Returning to other examples of earthenware we meet with the ancient manufactures of the Balearic Islands, although it is not easy to determine the kind of pottery which was really made there. Bernardo da Uzzano, in 1442, made a commercial treaty, (vide Davillier, "Faïences Hispano Moresques," p. 26), in which he mentions the "faïence" made at Mallorca and Minorca, which "was ex-

ported to a very large extent." The royal Ordinances for the island
of Iviza, which have not been mentioned by either of these authors,
state that the principal traffic and the greatest industry of ancient
times of the island of Iviza consisted in some vessels of the finest
earthenware, well baked and curiously worked, of which an innumerable quantity were sent off to Africa and other places, not
only on account of the excellence of their worth, which was admirable, but the speciality of the clay, which preserved from poison.
("Reales Ordinaciones de Iviza," Palma, 1751).

Manufactures of pottery also existed in a great number of
localities in Spain ; the most important centres were at Talavera,
Valencia, and Triana. Judging by the manner in which different authors praise the earthenware of Talavera, its productions
were evidently the most esteemed. The earliest mention we
find of Talavera pottery occurs in a MS. volume dated 1560
—a history of this town, in which mention is made of "white,
green, blue and other coloured Talavera ware." In the inventory
of the effects of Dᵐᵃ. Juana, a sister of Philip II., 1573,
several objects of "white earthenware of Talavera" are mentioned. In a report drawn up by order of Philip II. 1576, it is
stated that Talavera "produced fine white glazed earthenware-
tiles, and other pottery, which supplied the country, part of
Portugal and India." Father Ramon de la Higuera in his
"Republicas del Mundo," 1595, mentions the ware of Talavera
in terms of the highest praise. In a MS. history of Talavera
written in 1651, (Bib. Nac. Madrid, G. 112,) the author,
Father Alfonso de Ajofrin, says that "the pottery is as good
as that of Pisa, a large number of *azulejos* are also made to
adorn the front of altars, churches, gardens, alcoves, saloons,
and bowers, and large and small specimens of every kind.
Two hundred workmen work at eight different kilns. Four
other kilns are kept to make common earthenware. Red porous
clay vases and drinking cups are baked in two other kilns, in a
thousand different shapes in imitation of birds and other animals,

also *brinquiños* for the use of ladies, so deliciously flavoured that after drinking the water they contained, they eat the cup in which it was brought them." In another MS. history of Talavera (Bibl. Nac. G. 187) we find mention of "perfect imitations of oriental china," and that the pottery made there, "was used all over Spain, and sent to India, France, Flanders, Italy and other countries, and was esteemed everywhere for the perfection of the colouring and brilliancy of the glaze."

This information may be increased by quoting another interesting MS. on the history of this town (Bib. Nac. F. 142) in which the writer, Fr. Andres de Torrejon, who professed in the convent of Santa Catalina in 1568, says:—"The earthenware pottery made here has reached to a great height of perfection; it is formed of white and red clay. Vases, cups, *bucaros* and *brinquiños* are made of different kinds, dishes and table centres, and imitations of snails, owls, dogs and every kind of fruits, olives, and almonds. These objects are painted with great perfection, and the imitations of porcelain brought from the Portuguese Indies are most excellent. Every one wonders that in so small a town such excellent things should be made. The varnish used for the white pottery is made with tin and sand, it is now found to be more acceptable than coloured earthenware, so much so, that persons of importance who pass by this town although they have in their houses dinner services of silver, buy earthenware made at Talavera, on account of its excellence. The sand which was used to make the white varnish was brought from Hita, it is now found at Mejorada, near Talavera. This sand is as fine and soft as silk."

"The red pottery made at Talavera is much to be commended, for besides the great variety of objects which they make, the different medals which they place upon them, they have invented some small *brinquiños* of so small and delicate a kind, that the ladies wear them. Rosaries are also made of the same material. A certain scent is added in the manufacture of this pottery which excites the appetite and taste of the women, who eat the pottery so frequently that it gives great trouble to their confessors to check this custom."

In a volume of "Relaciones Topograficas de los Pueblos de España hechas en 1576," (MS. in fol. t. ii.) we find, in speaking of Talavera, that the author says : "What is most excellent there is the white pottery, and tiles and other objects of this earthenware with which the kingdom and part of Portugal are provided."

In Larruga's "Memorias Politicas y Economicas," (vol. x. Madrid, 1741,) we find, p. 22, that "the manufactory of fine earthenware of Talavera de la Reyna continued to make much pottery of importance until 1720 : eight kilns existed then, which employed more than 400 persons, men, women and children. These manufactories possessed at that time large sums of money. From that time this industry decayed to such an extent, that in 1730 only four kilns existed where pottery of a very inferior kind was produced."

The industry was revived later on in the century, but the finest specimens are of an earlier date. Larruga adds, in p. 17, vol. x., of his "Memorias," that "Talavera ware is of a lighter clay than the imitations of this earthenware which were made in other localities."

Pottery of a similar kind was also made in different other localities of Spain. Mendez Silva says that at Puente del Arzobispo, near Toledo, "fine pottery is manufactured in about 8 kilns, which produce more than 40,000 ducats yearly." ("Relacion General de España," Madrid, 1645, fol. 32.) Paton likewise in his "Historia de Jaen," 1628, writes that "the white unglazed earthenware made at these towns, is very remarkable for the curious manner in which they imitate different figures of animals, such as porcupines, fish, syrens, tortoises, &c." Objects of a similar kind are still made in Spain.

The English traveller Clarke, in his "Letters concerning the Spanish Nation during the years 1760-1761," London, 1763, p. 263, says, "the pottery fabrics are very numerous and excellent, particularly Talavera." And in "Annales de l'Espagne," by Alvarez de Colmenares, Amsterdam, 1741, we find, p. 187, in speaking of Talavera, that "On y fait des ouvrages vernissés d'une façon ingénieuse, avec des peintures de bon goût ; on estime ces ouvrages autant que ceux de Pise et des Indes Orientales ; on en fournit plusieurs provinces. Ce négoce rend plus de 50,000 ducats par an."

Udal ap Rhys in his "An Account of the Most Remarkable Places and Curiosities in Spain and Portugal," London, 1749, in speaking of Talavera says, "It is noted also for a very curious kind of earthenware that is made in imitation of China."

Although we find by the remarks we have quoted from contemporary authors that earthenware of every description was made at Talavera, the specimens which are more generally met with may be divided into two groups, which are painted on a white ground, either in blue, or in colours in the manner of Italian maiolica. The most important examples which have reached us consist of bowls of different sizes, dishes, vases, tinajas, holy-water vessels, medicine jars, and wall decorations. Blue oriental china was imitated to a vast extent, the colouring was successful but the design was an imitation of the baroque school of the time, and the figures, landscapes, and decoration follow the bad taste so general in Spain in the 18th century. The imitations of Italian maiolica are effective. The colours most commonly used are manganese, orange, blue and green.

Several specimens of this manufacture are in the South Kensington Museum ; among these may be noted—

No. 327-'76. A large vase painted in blue with cavaliers and men on foot in a hilly landscape, on the shoulder are the words "Silva Coronel."

No. 1282-'71. Holy-water vessel, with raised flowers and scrolls of foliage with polychrome decoration.

No. 1281-'71. Soup tureen and cover, white, with raised scrolls and groups of painted flowers.

No. 351–'76. Another soup tureen with cover and stand, painted with garlands and the arms of Portugal. On the cover is a group of fishes and shells in relief.

No. 1279–'71. A bowl decorated within with a bull-fight; out-

EARTHENWARE BOWL. TALÁVERA WARE. SOUTH KENSINGTON MUSEUM.

side are storks and trees in green, orange, and manganese. (See woodcut.)

Several pottery works were established in Spain in the 18th century, all of them, in the same manner as the earlier fabriques, modified the system of decorating their wares. In some instances the colours and designs of Italian maiolica were imitated, others copy the blue faïences of Pisa, Genoa, and Savona, while others adopted the styles of Moustiers, Nevers, and Rouen, or English earthenwares.

Ten or twelve manufactories existed at Toledo in the 17th century which imitated Talavera ware; in the 18th they hardly produced anything of importance. Ignacio de Velasco in 1735 founded one at great expense at Toledo in which imitations of Genoese pottery were chiefly made. At the death of Ignacio in 1738, these works passed to his son George; in 1742 Francisco Hernandez directed them, and in 1747 imitated Japanese models. Several specimens proceeding from Toledo, at the South Kensington Museum, painted blue on a white ground, in the style of Savona and Japan, belong to this period.

In 1755 thirteen pottery kilns existed at Puente del Arzobispo near Toledo; they still worked in 1791, but their productions were very inferior in artistic merit.

Earthenware pottery was made at Segovia from a very early period, chiefly for domestic use, until a manufactory was founded by two brothers—Manuel and Tomás Ledesma in 1752—they had seen some specimens which were made at Bolonia for Isabel Farnesio, the widow of King Philip V., and they endeavoured to imitate them. In 1774 they tried with a most unsatisfactory result to imitate English wares. This industry fell into decay towards the end of the century, and only ware of a very common description was made there.

Talavera ware was also imitated at Zamora. At the middle of the 18th century works existed there where pottery was made in the manner adopted at Alcora with few results, for soon after it was established the master potter, who was at the head of these works, left the locality. ["Memorias," Larruga, Vols. 13 and 34.]

The further we advance into the 18th century, the more we find the tendency in Spanish ceramic art to imitate the pottery most in vogue in other countries. Francisco Cavalli, a potter of Ruidoms, won a prize at Tarragona in 1787, for his excellent

N

imitations of brown and white Genoese ware. [MS. fol. Bibl. de S. Magestad el Rey, S. 2, E. B. pt. 8.]

The efforts made by King Charles III. towards increasing industrial arts in Spain, contributed to the reproductions and efforts made to imitate foreign wares. When the king founded in 1768 the villages of La Carolina and La Carlota in Andalucia, he ordered that pottery works should be set up there. At the same time that he established at Madrid the important porcelain manufactory of Buen Retiro, he wished that earthenware works should exist in the same locality, where specimens should be made in imitation of the best work produced elsewhere. The king was most anxious to revive to a great extent the almost extinct industry of metallic lustred pottery, and thanks to this we are able to know most accurately the receipt and manner in which this lustre was applied. In the same volume in which I found these documents, [Brit. Mus. MS. Egerton, 507], are two reports addressed to Count Florida Blanca in 1786, by Iriarte and Vargas, who were instructed to facilitate the development of this industry. The first report contains information relating to the pottery works of the county of Stafford; the second tells us that in the building of San Isidro el Real, essays had been made to reproduce English wares, and the lustred productions of Manises, with an idea of establishing inside or outside of Madrid pottery works on a large scale, under the protection of Count Florida Blanca. Iriarte and Vargas were of opinion that these works should be established far from Madrid, suggesting as the best spot El Viso in La Mancha, owing to the excellent quality of the clay. Don Sebastian Schepers, a son or brother of Cayetano Schepers, was at the head of these works. Cayetano was the chief modeller at the Retiro manufactory. Their imitations of English earthenware did not succeed; the varnish turned out badly, and they determined to bring out English workmen. Their imitations of gold lustred ware were eminently successful, so much so that competent judges declared it was equal to what was made at Manises. Pottery works where earthenwares of different descriptions were made existed also at this time in Madrid; the best were those of Rodriguez and Reato, mentioned in Larruga's " Memorias Economicas."

At the end of the 18th, and beginning of the 19th century, Valencia and Aragon supplied the country with painted tiles. One of the finest examples of this class which have reached us is the pavement of the chapter house of the cathedral of Saragossa, on which landscapes, medallions, and animals are finely designed in the Italian renaissance style. In a shield may be read the following inscription :

Real^s Fb^{cas}

D E

Dª Maria Salb

adora

Disdier

Bru   f^t

Año 1808.

Valencia has been much renowned for its manufacture of painted tiles, *azulejos*, which continue to be made there in a very creditable manner at the present time. J. Townsend, in his "Journey through Spain in the Years 1786–1787, London," 1792, says : " I was most delighted with the manufacture of painted tiles. In Valencia their best apartments are floored with these, and are remarkable for their neatness and elegance. They are stronger and more beautiful than those brought from Holland." In a "Nouveau Voyage en Espagne," Paris, 1789, p. 56, the author says : " L'industrie des Valenciens tire d'ailleurs parti de toutes les productions de leur sol. Il contient une espèce de terre, dont ils font ces carreaux de faïence colorée connus sous le nom de azulejos, et qu'on ne fabrique qu'à Valence. On en pave les appartements, et on en revêt leurs lambris; on y peint les sujets les plus compliqués, tels par exemple qu'un bal masqué, une fête de taureaux. La couleur rouge est la seule qui ne puisse être fixée sur cette espèce de faïence. Elle s'altère par la cuisson." In "Voyage en Espagne, 1797–1798," Paris 1801, the author says, p. 245 : "Les plats sont faits de faïence bleuâtre ou toute autre couleur orné de figures d'oies."

Before we pass to describe another most important branch of Spanish pottery the unglazed earthenware must be mentioned, which from a very early period has constituted and still constitutes a most important branch of its industry. This pottery, generally used for cooling water, consists of white porous vessels of which a large modern collection may be seen at the South Kensington Museum proceeding from Andujar and La Rambla (Andalusia). This industry remains in precisely the same state as in the time of the Arabs.

The earthenware vessels called *Bucaros* are similar to these. This porous pottery was made to a very large extent at Talavera. It was imported originally from America ; the great centre existed at Mejico. The paste of this ware is unglazed and whitish, black or red—when painted the colours chosen are generally red, black, and gold. It was made in Spain as early as the 16th century, and we constantly find *Bucaros* alluded to in documents of this period. In the inventory of the effects belonging to D^{ma} Juana, the sister of Philip the Second, drawn up in 1573, *bucaros* made at Lisbon, Estremoz, and Montemayor in Portugal, and those of Ciudad Rodrigo and Castille, are also mentioned. Madame d'Aunoy in her "Voyage d'Espagne," Lyon, [MDCXCIII.], mentions the habit of Spanish ladies of eating this porous clay. At the South Kensington Museum there are several good specimens of red pottery of this kind, Nos. 285 to 318-'72, which, as we have remarked were made at Talavera and Toledo.

ALCORA POTTERY AND PORCELAIN.

Don Buenaventura Pedro de Alcantara inherited in 1725 the estates belonging to the title of Aranda in the province of Valencia. Count Aranda found that the inhabitants of the village of Alcora made coarse earthenware of every description, and that their vicinity to the sea coast favoured exportation ; he determined, therefore, upon establishing in 1726 a manufacture of pottery there, in which fine wares might be made in imitation of those imported from Italy, Germany, France and England. The count's efforts were so successful that in less than two years specimens of different kinds of Alcora pottery were exported to a very large extent.

No account has hitherto been published which gives any idea of the importance of this manufactory, nor have the names of the artists who worked there been known, or the works which they executed. Wishing to ascertain this, I applied to the Duchess of Hijar, the present representative of the house of Aranda, and permission was granted me, thanks to the kindness of the Duchess's *Apoderado general*, Sr. Robles, to look through the Archives, where the accounts, contracts, and details of the manufactory are kept. This has enabled me to give an idea of the importance of this industry, and the names of the artists who worked there, which have been ignored until the present time by writers on ceramic art.

Count Aranda spent in 1726 about £10,000 in establishing the manufactory of Alcora, and in May, 1727, the first specimens appeared, consisting of pottery made "in the manner of China, Holland, and other localities." The manufactory was at that time under the superintendence of Dn. Joaquin Joseph de Sayas and Joseph Ollery, a Frenchman, chief draughtsman and

carver, who was engaged at a good salary in 1726, and brought
to Alcora from Moustiers by the painter, Edward Roux. In
1728 Count Aranda increased his salary owing to the "excellent
manner in which Ollery has worked at Alcora, the fine and
numerous models which he constructed, which have contributed
to make my manufacture the first in Spain."

Five painters and two modellers from Cataluña and six
Valencian painters and two modellers joined these French
artists. The personnel of the fabrique was completed with eleven
potters from the locality. The French painters, M. Pierre
Maurissy and M. Gras, and the master of the modellers, M.
Sebastian Carvonel, were engaged in 1728 for two years to work
at the manufactory. Ollery only appears in the lists up to 1737.
The Count granted him a yearly pension of 500 francs besides
his salary, "for his especial zeal in the improvement of the manufactory, and his great skill in directing the construction of every
kind of work." From this date until the manufacture of porcelain
in 1764, only Spanish artists worked at Alcora.

The Count was able from the year 1729 to circulate the pottery
made at Alcora through the Spanish dominions, free of custom-
house duties. The government granted him several other
privileges and the manufactory continued to improve, and spared
no pains to import the foreign shapes and designs which were
most acceptable. No Spanish pottery manufactory could compare
with Alcora in the excellence and beauty of its work.

Among the obligations of the artists engaged, whether Spaniards
or Frenchmen, was that of teaching drawing and modelling to a
certain number of pupils. A special Academy was created for this
purpose, which at one time held more than one hundred pupils,
who were constantly renewed and increased with those who
appear henceforward in the works at Alcora. In 1736 there were
fifty-six painters, eleven masters, twenty workers at the wheel,
and twenty-five apprentices. In this same year, 1736, specimens
of pottery made at Alcora were sent "to all the dominions of

Spain, Rome, Naples, Malta, many Italian cities, Portugal, and some provinces of France."

The manufactory produced yearly about 300,000 specimens of different kinds. The ordinances are interesting which in 1732–1733 prescribe, "that in our manufactory only pottery of the most excellent kind should be made, similar to the Chinese, to be equally fine as to the earths employed, that the models and wheels should be perfect, the drawing of a first-rate kind, and the varnish and colours excellent, and the pottery light and of good quality, for it is our express wish that the best pottery should only be distinguished from that of an inferior kind by the greater or less amount of painting which covers it."

Miguel Soliva, Christobal Cros, Francisco Grangel, Miguel Vilar, Christobal Rocafort, Vicente Serrania, and Joseph Pastor were the best painters at Alcora in 1743; they decorated a fine dinner service made for the Tribunal of Commerce, and the large slabs for the Convent of Las Descalzas Reales at Madrid, representing the Virgin as the Divine Shepherdess.

Pottery painted with metallic lustre was made in 1749. We find among the receipts used in that year one brought from Manises for this object.

We find it also stated in the communications which passed between the Tribunal of Commerce and the count in 1746, that "the perfection of the earthenware of Alcora consisted in the excellent models which had been made by competent foreign artists, the quality of the earth and receipts brought at great expense from abroad." Joseph Ochando is mentioned in that year as an excellent painter, and Juan Lopez as the best carver and modeller. This document tells us "that from the earliest period of the manufacture pyramids with figures of children, holding garlands of flowers and baskets of fruits on their heads, were made with great perfection, likewise brackets, centre and three-cornered tables, large objects, some as large as five feet high, to be placed upon them, chandeliers, cornucopias, statues of different kinds, and animals of different sorts and sizes. The entire ornamentation of a room has also been made here ; the work is so perfect that nothing in Spain, France, Italy or Holland could equal it in merit."

The objects which were made to a great extent at this time consisted in :

> Vases of different shapes.
> Small pots, Chinese fashion.
> Teapots and covers, Chinese fashion.
> Teapots and covers, Dutch fashion.
> Cruets, complete sets, Chinese style.
> Entrée dishes.
> Salt-cellars, Chinese style.
> Escudillas (bowls) of Constantinople.
> Barquillos (sauce bowls), Chinese style.
> Bottles, in the Chinese manner.
> Cups, plates, and saucers of different kinds with good painted borders in imitation of lace-work (*puntilla*); some were designed in the Chinese manner, and especial care was taken with fruit-stands, salad-bowls and dishes.
> Trays and refrigerators.

In 1750 Count Aranda passed the pottery works on to a private company, in whose hands they remained until 1766. We know the pottery continued to be excellent. Unfortunately almost all the details of this period are missing from the Archives. One of the few documents remaining is a contract drawn up in October, 1741, with François Haly (the name of this artist is given by Baron Davillier), a Frenchman, in which he agreed to work at the manufactory during a period of ten years with a yearly salary of over 1000 francs, under the following conditions :

"That the travelling expenses of his wife and children should be given him, and that his salary should be paid as soon as he made before the Director and two competent judges the different kinds of porcelain which he had undertaken to make." He agreed to give up his receipts, and it was promised him that he should have two modellers and one painter working by his side, and that if in one year Haly's porcelain was satisfactory the Count undertook to make him a present of 1000 livres (*tornoises*).

Towards the middle of the century, porcelain was made for the first time at Alcora. A contract was drawn up on 24th March, 1764, with a German, called John Christian Knipfer, who had already worked there in the pottery section. By the original agreement, which exists at the Archives, we find he was to prepare works of "porcelain and painting similar to those made at Dresden, during a period of six years, under the following conditions : "

" That the said Knipfer obliges himself to make and teach the apprentices the composition and perfection of porcelain paste, its varnishes, and colours, and whatever he may know at the present time, or discover during this period of six years ; he is not to prevent the Director of the Works from being present at all the essays made."

" The said Knipfer offers to make and varnish porcelain, and to employ gold and silver in its decoration, and in that of the ordinary wares ; likewise the colours of crimson, purple, violet, blues of different shades, yellow, greens, browns, reds, and black.

" That Knipfer will give up an account of his secrets, and the management and manner of using them, in order that in all times the truth of what he has asserted may be verified."

From the original documents which exist we gather that Knipfer was chiefly famed for his excellence in the painting and decoration of porcelain.

François Martin was engaged in 1774 for his skill in preparing different pastes for manufacturing porcelain and pipeclay. He agreed to make "hard paste porcelain, Japanese faïence, English paste (pipeclay), and likewise to mould and bake it. The necessary materials were to be provided by the Count of Aranda." His expenses were to be paid if the specimens he presented to the competent authorities gave a satisfactory result, and his salary was to be increased to 1200 francs a year.

Knipfer and Martin greatly added to the importance of the

works made at the manufactory.   Don Pedro Abadia, the Count's
steward, an intelligent man, possessing great scientific knowledge,
who had studied this subject in Paris and London, writes to the
Count that the presence of both these artists was of absolute
necessity at Alcora, "until the workmen who were near them
perfected themselves." For owing to the carelessness of the
managers of the porcelain works in 1776 Count Aranda wrote
from Paris, during his embassy there: "My pottery of Alcora,
notwithstanding every effort which has been made, the money
spent, and foreign masters which have been brought over, gets
worse every day instead of improving." Abadia repeats this in
his reports. Porcelain of other kinds decidedly improved. He
says also that the pipeclay which Martin had found at Alcora
was the best in Europe.

In my opinion, a large number of unmarked white biscuit and
demi-porcelain figures which are so constantly found in collections
belong to this period of the manufactory of Alcora.   They have
hitherto been classified with very great difficulty, and attributed
to the porcelain manufactory of Buen Retiro, without any reason
which justifies this opinion. For the help of collectors I will
mention the subjects which they represent, which I have found
in a document, dated 1777, of the figures and groups and other
objects made during that year.

FIGURES OF DEMI-PORCELAIN.

Figures of tritons.
      ,,   of soldiers, two sizes.
      ,,   ,,   one-third *palmos* high.
      ,,   of the four seasons (two sizes).
      ,,   of dancers.
      ,,   of tritons in form of children.
      ,,   with brackets.
      ,,   of different animals.
      ,,   of gardener and female companion in the Dresden style.
Dancing figures in the German style.
Figures of Neptune.

Figures of shepherd and shepherdess.
    ,,   of the Moorish king, Armenius.
    ,,   of the four parts of the world, two sizes.
    ,,   of peasant and his wife.
Small figures holding musical instruments.
Figures representing different monarchies.
    ,,   ,,   historical personages.
    ,,   ,,   the history of Alexander the Great, two sizes.
    ,,   ,,   Marius Curtius, two sizes.
    ,,   of elephants.
    ,,   of a man mounted on an elephant.
    ,,   representing Chinese figures.
    ,,   of Heliogabalus.
    ,,   of a general on horseback.
    ,,   of a grenadier supporting a candlestick.
Large figures representing Julius Cæsar.
Figures representing the different costumes worn in Spain, on brackets.
Groups of Chinese figures.
Snuff-boxes, sugar basins, inkstands.
Rabbits, horns, and pug dogs for holding scent.
Small scent bottles.
Needle cases.
Large vases with foot and cover.
Brackets.
Walking-stick handles.
Knife handles.
Tea-spoons.

FIGURES OF WHITE BISCUIT CHINA.

Figures representing Spanish costumes, two sizes.
Groups of two figures.
Large and small figures of the four parts of the world.
Figures of the four seasons, two sizes.

We find also the following figures of painted and glazed porcelain :

Four seasons, two sizes.
Groups of two figures.
Figure of a Moorish king.
    ,,   of musicians and huntsmen.

Figure of peasants.
„   of Chinese.
Small figures of a gardener and female companion.
Figures of soldiers in the German style.

In 1780 four rival pottery works were established in the neighbourhood which copied and imitated the pottery made at Alcora. The two most important were at Rivasalbes and Onda, the other two at Alcora itself. Many of the artists who belonged to the works established by Count Aranda worked at the rival factories; among them were Mariano Causada, Joaquin Ten, Francisco Marsal, Vicente Alvaro, Christoval Mascarós, Francisco and Miguel Badenas, and Nadal Nebot; some of these artists returned to the Count's manufactory. In order to distinguish the genuine pottery from imitations, orders were given, with the authorization of the Tribunal of Commerce, that the pottery made there should be marked henceforward with the letter A ; no special mark had hitherto been used at the manufactory, the artists very often signed the specimens they made with their monograms or signatures, of which those most frequently met with will be found accompanying the list of artists' names, for the help of collectors ; all of them have been copied from original documents. It is interesting for collectors to bear in mind, that all specimens which are marked with the letter A are *posterior* to 1784. The pottery works founded in imitation of the manufactory belonging to Count Aranda came to an end before 1790, some by special agreement with the owners themselves, and others by the express orders of the authorities, in virtue of the privileges granted to the Count.

Mr. Martin died at Alcora in the month of May, 1786. Knipfer left soon afterwards, and was succeeded by a French artist, M. Pierre Cloostermans, a skilful man, and well versed in the manufacture of porcelain pastes, as well as in painting and decorating them. According to his contract, which was drawn up in Paris in 1787, " Pierre Cloostermans, chemiste, natif de Paris, demeurant à Paris, Rue de Clery, au coin de celle Montmartre,"agreed to "live for thirty years at Alcora as director and workman, to make soft and hard porcelains, and all the necessary colours with which to paint and decorate it."

He also promised to make good pipeclay pottery and marbled wares which were to be as excellent as those of Strasburg. . The expenses of his journey were paid, his sons were to be employed in the works, and it was stipulated that if the works increased to a great extent, 500 pounds (Valencian money), was to be added to his yearly salary. It was against the Count's express desire that pottery of an exclusively artistic character should be produced at Alcora; his chief object was to improve the industry itself. In one of his letters to Abadia, written in October, 1789, he says: "I wish to export the porcelain of my manufactory, but chiefly in common objects, such as cups of different kinds, tea and coffee services, etc. These may be varied in form and colour, the principal point being that the paste should bear hot liquids, for we Spaniards above everything wish that nothing we buy should ever break. By no means let time be wasted in making anything that requires much loss of time. The chief object is that the pastes should be of first-rate excellence and durability."

Cloostermans suffered much discomfort and annoyance from other workmen at Alcora, who were envious of his merit: they put every difficulty in his path, insulted him daily with pasquins, accused him of not fulfilling his religious duties, and annoyed him incessantly. His letters are full of these complaints. Count Aranda treated him with every consideration. During Clooster-mans' stay at Alcora, the pottery made improved greatly in artistic merit. Figures and groups of many kinds were attempted, and even Wedgwood jasper ware was creditably imitated. In 1789, among other pottery that was sent to Madrid were "two hard paste porcelain cups, adorned with low relief in the English style." The most important one was moulded by Francisco Garcés, the garlands and low reliefs by Joaquin Ferrer, sculptor, the flowers on the covers by an apprentice, helped by Cloostermans. The composition of these objects was suggested by Abadia, who brought some specimens from Paris which came from England.

Cloostermans sent the Count in 1789 a number of objects of different kinds made of porcelain. Among them the most interesting were "a tea and coffee service painted and gilt of glazed porcelain, and ten unglazed figures. Those painted by Albaro are marked A, those by Escuder, E, and by Mas, M, and Cloostermans' son." A large and varied collection of marbled wares and toys were sent at the same time. Cloostermans' marbled wares are pronounced superb.

Count Aranda writes in July, 1790, to Diez Robles alluding to a large collection of pots for plants, which were made at Alcora for the King, decorated with the royal arms. Another series are still to be met with at the Royal Gardens; they are of pipeclay, and ornamented with rams' heads.

In 1784 the Count sent two potters, Christoval Pastor and Vicente Alvaro, to Paris to study the last improvements in porcelain. They returned in 1789, and the porcelain they made was much commended and highly approved. They write to the Count in September, 1789: "We know that Don Domingo has sent your Excellency 97 objects made by us, marked No. 3, 1, No. 4, No. 3, with a dot, and No. 3 with the letter 'P'; No. 4 with the letter 'H,' all made by me in clay, and varnished with the greatest care. Three flask-stands and two toothpick-stands were made by me, Pastor, before I went to Paris. The marble wares, Nos. 3 and 4, and other similar objects with gold lines, are also made by me."

In 1784, Mariano Garcia of Valencia made some experiments before the Directors of laying on gold, and different shades of purples. A number of specimens were sent to the Count, but Knipfer did not approve of the plan adopted, and it was afterwards abandoned.

Marbled wares of different colours were made at Alcora in vast quantities in 1790. A large depôt was established in 1791 of Alcora ware in the Calle de Luzon at Madrid. The printed prospectuses which were issued give a long and detailed list of the different productions of the manufactory, which chiefly consisted of dinner and tea services, and other objects of domestic use.

In 1792 nearly 100 painters and modellers existed at the manufactory; 45 were employed to work in porcelain and pipeclays, and 26 were apprentices.

Cloostermans was forced to leave Alcora in April, 1793, owing to certain disturbances which occurred at Valencia, when, owing to a proclamation of the Captain-Generals, he and other Frenchmen residing in the province of Valencia, were ordered to leave the country. The Count gives instructions that Cloostermans should want for nothing on his journey; he writes ordering that 3000 reales should be given him, and his yearly pension of 1200 pounds (*tornoises*). Cloostermans left with his three sons after giving up the receipts and other documents connected with the manufactory. In 1795 permission was given that Frenchmen might return to Spain, and he resumed his post in the manufactory.

The principal efforts at Alcora since Knipfer, Martin, and Cloostermans entered the manufactory, had been centred in making porcelain and pipeclay wares of different kinds. A great number of essays with foreign earths were made; and all those of a suitable kind which were known in Spain. Count Aranda was always most anxious that Spanish materials should be used in the manufactory; he says, in a letter written in 1790, "the Kaolin of Cataluña may be good or bad, but it is acknowledged to be Kaolin, and if not used these works must be closed." This Kaolin had been found by Christobal Pastor and Vicente Albaro on their return from Paris.

Baron Davillier has been good enough to inform me .that he

has found mention of some objects of Alcora wares which Count Aranda sent as a present to his friend Voltaire, at Ferney.

From 1789 to 1797 the following kinds of pottery were made at Alcora :—

Hard paste porcelain (French).
Porcelain of three different kinds called **Spanish**.
Porcelain of pipe-clay (English).
Blue pipe-clay porcelain.
Marbled pipe-clay porcelain.
Bucaro, painted and gilt.
Strasburg Ware.
Porcelain painted *en froid*.
Marbled and gilt wares, hitherto unknown.

PORCELAIN (FRITA).

Porcelain painted with gilt lines.
     ,,   ,,   without gold.
Porcelain (frita), canary colour.
Boxes in relief.
    ,, plain.
Porcelain (frita), painted with marble wares.
Plain boxes of the same kind.
Porcelain (frita), of blue and brown ground.
Cups and saucers of a similar kind.

BISCUIT PORCELAIN.

Figures.
Vases.
Pedestals.
White porcelain (frita) cups of different kinds.
    ,,   ,, ornamented and plain.
Boxes with busts.
Boxes with ornamentations in relief.
Figures.
Vases for holding flowers, plates, etc.
Large figures of the Four Seasons.
Flower vases with rams' heads.
Plain boxes.
Boxes with ornaments in relief.

WHITE PORCELAIN.

Plates, cups, etc.
Figures of different kinds.

PAINTED PORCELAIN.

Cups, saucers, plates, etc.
Cream pots.
Plain snuff boxes, or in the shape of a dog.
Fruit stands in relief.

In 1799 we find mention made of partridges modelled by Christoval Mas, and Clemente Aycart much commended for his dogs, ducks, tortoises and frogs.

Joseph Ferrer writes to the Duke of Hijar in the same year, that "he had just seen a bust of Dⁿ José Delgado, a trifle smaller than the one previously sent of your excellency." These busts and some medallion portraits were made of porcelain *frite*. Ferrer complains in the same letter that Delgado the manager had asked for a fine jug and basin of Sèvres, which had been given by the King of France to the late Count, and that he had been obliged to hide it away with some English specimens which were in the warehouse.

Count Aranda died in January, 1798, and was succeeded by his son the Duke of Hijar. Cloostermans died the same year; Vicente Prats is stated to be the best painter and decorator at Alcora at this date. In an extract drawn up of the state of the pottery works in 1798, it appears that 200 workmen were employed, and pottery of every description was made, common earthenware, pipeclays in imitation of the English ones, and porcelain in small quantities; common wares were made in large quantities; the pipeclays were pronounced superior to the English in brilliancy, but were so porous that they were easily stained, a large number of snuff-boxes and other small objects belong to this period.

In 1800, the Duke of Hijar, who succeeded the Count of Aranda in the management of the manufactory, writes to Dⁿ

o

Josef Ferrer, saying: "As I do not know the authors of the pipe-clay porcelain or that of other kinds which is sent here, I beg you to order the master workmen of porcelain and common pottery to engrave, in making it, the initials of their names, as it will enable me to distinguish the good from the bad."

Twelve porcelain baths with the arms of Spain in blue were made at Alcora for Queen Maria Louisa in 1800.

The Duke of Hijar ordered in 1800 that a dinner-service should be made there for his use. He sent instructions that it should be of the same kind as a tea-service previously sent to his son the Duke of Aliaga. The painter chosen to decorate it was Mariano Alvaro, and the designs selected by Ferrer were taken from the Loggie of Raphael.

In the same year some cases of pottery were sent to the Duke ; in one of them was a fine soup tureen modelled by Josef Ferrer, Cloostermans' son, Pierre, writes at this time, asking to be appointed to the post left vacant by his father's death; his petition however was not granted.

We have already seen that pottery and porcelain continued to be manufactured in the present century at Alcora in the same manner as in the 18th century, but owing to the French invasion of 1808 this industry suffered the consequences of war, and the work done there greatly diminished in excellence and quantity. Even before this the Director, D^n José Delgado complains in several documents of the bad state of the manufactory, the Directors who replaced him, D^n Juan Bautista Cabot and D^n Pedro Bezarco, write continually repeating the same thing. After the French were turned out of Spain, the industry was revived and strengthened by fresh artists from the porcelain manufactory of Madrid. D^n Luis Poggetti was appointed drawing master there in 1815, and D^n Domingo Palmera master of ornamental art, both these artists had worked at Buen Retiro, Poggetti as Director of pietre dure, and Palmera as second-class sculptor. After this time the manufactory of pottery at Alcora ceased to produce artistic works, and limited itself to send out common wares for domestic purposes ; this system continued until 1858, when the Duke of Hijar sold the manufactory to Dⁿ Ramon Girona, who brought over English workmen from Staffordshire in order to improve the wares. Many imitations of the older styles have also been made at Alcora of late years.

One of the most important results of the present study is the necessity of changing the classifications of a great number of specimens which have been believed to be manufactured at Moustiers and other localities in France, but which in fact were made at Alcora. It is sufficient to mention the names of Grangel, Cros, Soliva, and Vilar, which one of the best informed writers on Ceramic industry, Baron Davillier, has discovered on different specimens of pottery, and which, in his "Hist. des faïences et porcelaines de Moustiers, etc., Paris, 1863," he considers to be the names of artists who worked in France, although all of them belonged exclusively to Alcora, as will be seen in the subjoined list of artists' names. I am in hopes, also, that many errors may be corrected in future, touching French and English pottery, which was imitated to a great extent, and with much success at Alcora.

We gather also by this information that an immense number of objects were made of pipeclay porcelain, in imitation of English wares; and, in my opinion, a great quantity of objects of white pipeclay porcelain which have been found of late years in Spain are of Alcora manufacture. They have been hitherto classified by amateurs as Leeds pottery. We find, in papers relating to Alcora, that a decided distinction is made between white and straw-coloured pottery This indication may be sufficient to distinguish it from English wares.

Townsend, in "A Journey to Spain in the years 1786-1787," London, 1792, p. 255, says: "At Alcora, in the neighbourhood of Valencia, a manufacture of porcelain has been successfully

established by Count Aranda, and deserves encouragement. I
was much pleased with their imitations of gilding. It is very
natural, and the manager informed me that after many years'
trial it was found to be durable."

EARTHENWARE PLAQUE, ALCORA WARE.   SOUTH KENSINGTON MUSEUM.

Specimens exist of Alcora ware and porcelain at the South Kensington Museum.

Nos. 1051, 1052-'71.   Two fine plaques, painted with mythological subjects of Pomona and Galatea, the borders raised in
form of a frame, with scroll ornaments [see woodcut of No. 1052].

No. 341-'76. A porcelain cup and saucer, blue ground, gilt; painted with flowers in white medallions.

No. 333-'76. A plate painted with sprigs, and containing models of fruit in full relief.

A LIST OF THE DIRECTORS AND ARTISTS WHO WERE EMPLOYED IN THE MANUFACTORY OF POTTERY AND PORCELAIN OF ALCORA FROM ITS FOUNDATION, 1726, UNTIL THE BEGINNING OF THE PRESENT CENTURY.

DIRECTORS.

Dr. Joaquin Joseph de Sayas, 1727.
Joseph Ollery, 1727 to 1733.
Manuel de Molina, 1727 to 1735.
Cayetano Allue, 1727 to 1750.
Marcial Guirandeta, 1778 to 1783.
Juan Villalonga, 1789.
Pierre Cloostermans, 1789.
Domingo Abadia, 1789.
Gabriel Berenguer y Cebrian, 1789.
Josef Ferrer, 1799.
Josef Delgado, 1800.

ARTISTS.

Abella, Francisco, 1750, at Alcora.
Alvaro, Cristobal, 1750.
Alvaro, Joseph, paints pottery in 1743, 1750.
Alvaro, Vicente, el mayor, works at the wheel in 1750.
Alvaro, Vicente, painted with Knipfer in 1783; he was sent by Count Aranda in 1784 to Paris to learn the making of porcelain; he returned to Spain in 1789, and continued to work at Alcora.
Alvaro, Tiburcio, painted with Knipfer in 1783.
Andrés, Cristoval, modeller and carver in 1783.
Andrés, Francisco, modeller in 1783.
Andrés, Francisco, modeller, 1743 to 1750.
Andrés, Gabriel, painter, 1743 to 1750.
Andrés, Gabriel, figures as one of the leading painters in 1794.
Andrés, Jaime, painter, from 1728 to 1737.
Andrés, Mariano, paints from 1739 to 1750.

Andrés, Mariano, works in 1789.

Andrés, Miguel, painter, 1743 to 1750.

Aparicio, Manuel, painter, 1750.

Arqua, Vicente, 1750.

Aycart, Clemente, sculptor, worked at the porcelain works in 1789.

Aycart, Roque, worked at the wheel in 1783.

Aycart, Ventura, worked at the wheel in 1783.

Bachero, Vicente, painted porcelain in 1789.

Badenas, Cristoval, painter, 1727 to 1750.

Badenes, Francisco, establishes with Miguel Badenas pottery works, where pottery was made in imitation of Alcora : it was put a stop to by agreement in 1789.

Badenes, Miguel ; see Francisco.

Beltran, Pedro, retouched painting on porcelain in 1783 to 1789.

Berenguer, Cristoval, painter, painted from 1727 to 1750.

Blasco, Bautista, painted from 1727 to 1750.

Blasco, Francisco, painted from 1731 to 1738.

Blasco, Joaquin, painted in 1750.

Blasco, Joseph, modeller, 1731 to 1735 ; he painted in 1750.

Blasco, Manuel, painter, 1728 to 1750.

Blasco, Vicente, painted 1727 to 1750.

Buxadós, Ildefonso, painted 1727 to 1750.

Buxadós, Manuel, painted common pottery in 1783.

Calvo Perales, Joseph, painter from 1727 to 1750.

Calvo, Manuel, painter of common pottery in 1783.

Calvo, Ramon, painted common earthenware from 1750 to 1783.

Campion, Juan, a Frenchman, worked at the wheel in 1743.

Carnicer, Juan, worked at pipe-clay porcelain in 1789.

Carnicer, Vicente, modeller from 1783 to 1789.

Carbonel, Sebastian, a Frenchman ; he modelled in 1728.

Catalá, Cristoval, modelled in 1783.

Catalá, Juan, 1750.

Catalá, Manuel, 1750.

Catalá, Pascual, painter from 1729 to 1750.

Catalá, Pedro Juan, painted common pottery in 1783.

Caussada, mayor, Jacinto, painted from 1727 to 1750.

Caussada, menor, Jacinto, from 1727.

Caussada, Joseph, a son of Jacinto, painted from 1743 to 1750. He ran away from the manufactory and went to work at Talavera, and was brought back to Alcora.

Caussada, Mariano. It was proposed that he should be turned out of the manufactory, owing to his having gone over to the works established at Onda, where he gave them the receipts of the colours and varnishes used at Alcora ; he returned to Alcora in 1789.

Caveta, Pascual, painter, 1743.

Chiva, Cristoval de, painted porcelain in 1789.

Chiva, Joseph, painted from 1727 to 1738.

Chiva, Manuel, painted in 1789.

Cloostermans, Pierre, a French artist ; he entered the manufactory in 1787, and continued to work there until his death in 1798.

Cloostermans, a son of Pierre's, was an excellent painter on porcelain in 1789.

Corrás, Ignacio, a native of Cataluña, painted from 1727 to 1728.

Coll, Jaime, a native of Cataluña, painted from 1727 to 1736.

Cros, Cristoval, painted from May, 1727 to 1743 ; he was one of the best artists who painted at Alcora.

Cros, Manuel, worked at the wheel in 1783.

Cros, Manuel, 1750.

Cros, Pascual, painted from 1727 to 1736.

Cros, menor, Vicente, painted porcelain from 1750 to 1789.

Cros, Vicente, 1735 to 1750.

Datos, Gaspar, modeller, 1731 to 1750.

Datos, Julian, modeller, in 1783.

Datos, Ramon, painted in 1750.

Datos, Vicente, 1750.

Escuder, Vicente, painted with Knipfer from 1783 to 1789.

Fabra, Francisco, painted from 1730 to 1743.

Fabra, Vicente, painter, 1727 to 1735.

Falco, Joseph, painter, 1727 to 1743.

Falco, Pedro, painter, 1727 to 1735

Feliu, Vicente Tomas, painter, from 1727 to 1750.

Feliu y Thomas, Vicente, painted common pottery in 1783.

Ferrer, Joaquin, a carver, who worked with Mr. Martin from 1783 to 1789.

Ferrer, Esteban, painted porcelain in 1789.

Ferrer y Carnicer, Vicente, worked at the wheel in 1783. In December, 1789, he had an oven on his own account at Alcora, the only one which remained out of four which had been established four years previously there.

Ferrer, menor, Vicente, 1750.

Ferrer, Vicente, painted from 1727 to 1743.

Flor, Antonio, painted common pottery from 1750 to 1783.

Fores, Joseph, painter, 1727.

Fornench, Joseph, painted in 1739.

Fornench, Phelipe, painted common pottery in 1783.

Fornench, Francisco, worked at the wheel in 1783.

Fornench, Phelipe, painter, 1727 to 1750.

Fuste, Salvador, painter, 1727.

Galvez, Juan, modeller, 1731 to 1735.

Garcés, Joaquin, painter. He worked with Joaquin Ter at the manufactory which he established at Alcora, and returned to the Counts in 1789.

Garcés, Francisco, worked at the wheel with Mr. Martin in 1783, and was considered by Cloostermans, in 1789, his most able workman.

Garcés, Joseph, painter, 1727.

Garcés, Pedro, 1743.

Garcia, Mariano, a native of Valencia. He went to Alcora to try a system of gilding and purple which he had invented, which produced an unsatisfactory result.

Gasch, Agustin, painter from 1728 to 1750, although he was absent from the works from 1735 to 1741.

Gasch, Bruno, a son of Juan's, worked at the wheel from 1743 to 1750.

Gasch, Cristoval, worked with the turners, 1731 to 1741, and joined the painters until 1750.

Gasch, Francisco, worked at the wheel from 1729 to 1750.

Gasch, mayor, Joaquin, worked at the wheel in 1783.

Gasch, Joseph, painter, 1731 to 1735.

Gasch, Juan, worked at the wheel from 1728 to 1750.

Gasch, Manuel, worked at the wheel in 1783.

Gasch, Miguel, the son of Juan, painted in 1743.

Gasch, Vicente, 1750.

Gasch, Correo Vicente, worked at the wheel in 1783.

Gardo, Juan, painter and modeller, 1731 to 1735.

Gil, Francisco, modeller, 1783.

Giner, Manuel, painter, 1727.

Gomez, Cristoval, painter on common pottery, 1783.

Gomez, Francisco, modeller, 1731 to 1750.

Gomez, Vicente, painter, 1750, 1783.

Gomez, menor, Vicente, worked at the wheel and painted from 1783 to 1789.

Gorris, Joseph, 1750.

Granell, Cristoval, painter, 1729, 1750.

Granell, Joseph, modeller, 1731 to 1735.

Granell, Vicente, 1731 to 1750.

Grangel, Francisco, pintor, painted from 1727 to 1783. In 1743 the finest work was given to him.

Grangel, Juan, painted from 1727 to 1750.

Gras, Monsieur, painter, 1728.

Haly, François, 1751.

Herrando, Francisco, 1727.

Herrando, Joseph, painter, 1727 to 1736.

Herrando, Juan, painted from 1729 to 1735.

Herrando, Manuel, modeller, 1783.

Herrando, Pascual, worked at the wheel from 1728 to 1743.

Herrando, Thadeo, 1750.

Huguet, Cristobal, worked at the wheel in 1783.

Huguet, Francisco, worked at the wheel and modelled in porcelain from 1783 to 1789.

Huguet y Mascarós, Joseph, painter, 1783 to 1794.

Huguet, Vicente, painter. He worked at the manufactory established by Joaquin Ten at Alcora, and returned to Count Arandas in 1789, and continued there in 1794.

Huguet Serra, Joseph, modeller in 1783.

Ibañez, Juan, painter from 1727 to 1735.

Knipfer, Juan, a native of Saxony, 1783.

Lazaro, Joseph, painter, 1727.

Lopez, Julian, 1792.

Llorente, Francisco, 1750.

Lloscos, Joaquin, painter, 1783.

Llosca, menor, painter, 1783.

Malanco, Nicolas, painter, 1727.

Marin, Pedro, painter, 1727 to 1736.

Marques, Miguel, painter, 1794.

Marras, Francisco, painter and modeller in 1727.

Marsal, Bautista, painter from 1727 to 1743.

Marsal, Francisco. He worked at Alcora, and left it for the manufactory of Onda; in 1783 he returned to Count Aranda's works.

Marti, Miguel, worked at the wheel in 1783.

Martin, Francisco, modeller in 1783.

Martir, Pedro, worked at the wheel in 1739.

Mas, Cristoval, modeller from 1783 to 1789.

Mas, Francisco, painted common pottery in 1783.

Mas, Julian, a skilful painter on porcelain in 1789.

Mas, menor, Manuel, painted common pottery in 1783.

Mas, Manuel, painted from 1727 to 1750.

Mas, Pedro, painter in 1743.

Mascarós, Cristobal, painter from 1728 to 1750.

Mascarós y Thomas, Cristoval, painted on pottery from 1783 to 1794.

Mascarós, Francisco, 1743 to 1750.

Mascarós, Joseph, painted porcelain in 1789.

Mascarós, José, painter in 1735 to 1736.

Mascarós, Pedro Martin, painted from 1729 to 1736.

Mascarós, Vicente, worked at the wheel from 1750 to 1780.

Masso y Fabra, Vicente, painted in 1727.

Massó, Joseph, 1750.

Massó y Fabra, Francisco, painter, 1739, 1750.

Massó Nadal, Vicente, painter from 1727 to 1750.

Mallol, Joaquin, modeller, 1783.

Mallol, Cristoval, modeller in 1783.

Mallol, Vicente, modeller, 1783.

Maurisi, Pedro, a Frenchman, began to work in 1728.

Mezquita y Chiva, Francisco, worked at the wheel in 1783.

Mezquita, Francisco, painted in 1750.

Mezquita, Jaime, painter, 1731 to 1750.

Mezquita, Pascual, painter from 1727 to 1735.

Miguel, Vicente, 1750.

Miralles, Vicente, worked in clay from 1731 to 1743.

Moliner, Cristoval, worked at the wheel in 1783.

Moliner, Miguel, painted from 1728 to 1750.

Moliner, Vicente, modeller in 1783.

Monfort, Agustin, modeller in 1783.

Monfort, Pablo, modeller in 1783.

Montemenor, Joseph, modeller in 1783.

Montolin, Jacinto, painter, from 1731 to 1750.

Montolin, Juan, painter, the son of Jacinto, from 1735 to 1750.

Montolin, Juan, varnisher and painter in 1783.

Montolin, Joseph, painter on porcelain in 1789.

Montolin, Vicente, painter of common pottery in 1783.

Montolin, Vicente, painter, from 1727 to 1750.

Moya, Crisostomo, retouched porcelain in 1789.

Nadal, Felix, 1727 to 1735.

Nadal, Juan, master at the wheel, painter and carver from 1727 to 1737.

Nadal, Miguel, 1783.

Nadal, Nebot, works from 1743 to 1783.

Navarro, Cristoval, worked at the wheel in 1783, and painted porcelain in 1789.

Nebot, Bautista, painter, 1794.

Nebot, Cristoval, modeller, 1750.

Nebot, Cristoval, menor, 1794.

Nebot, Francisco, 1750.

Nebot, Francisco, painter in 1794.

Nebot, Joseph, worked at the wheel from 1728 to 1740.

Nebot, Joaquin, worked at the wheel in 1794.

Nebot, Juan, painter, 1750 to 1783.

Nebot, Miguel, painter, 1783 to 1794.

Nebot, Narciso, painter, 1794.

Negre, Deodato, painter, 1727.

Negre, Francisco, worked at the wheel from 1783 to 1794.

Negre, Julian, worked at the wheel in 1794.

Negre, Manuel, modeller, 1783 to 1794.

Negre, Ramon, painter, 1783 to 1794.

Negre, Vicente, modeller, 1727.

Nondedeu, Cristoval, modeller, 1729.

Nondedeu, Miguel, turner, 1731 to 1743.

Ochando, Joseph, draughtsman and carver, from 1727 to 1742.

Olery, Joseph, director of the works from 1735 to 1737. In August, 1729, he was appointed principal draughtsman.

Pacor, Bartolomé, painter, 1728 to 1735.

Palau, Francisco, painter, from 1727 to 1750.

Palmera, Domingo, master of ornamental art, 1815.

Pardo, Cristoval, turner, from 1727 to 1750.

Pardo, Francisco, 1750.

Pardo, Joseph, turner, from 1731 to 1750.

Pardo, Vicente, master at the wheel in 1728.

Pastor Bartolo, Antonio, painter, 1750.

Pastor Butoni, Antonio, painter, 1750.

Pastor, Bartolomé, a brother of Vicente's, from 1729 to 1750.

Pastor, Bautista, varnisher, 1783.

Pastor, Cristoval, worked at the wheel with Mr. Martin from 1783 to 1789.

Pastor, Gaspar, 1750.

Pastor, Joseph, painted in common pottery and porcelain from 1783 to 1789.

Pastor, Joseph, painter, from 1728 to 1750; his name appears in 1743 among the best artists of Alcora.

Pastor, Vicente, painter, from 1728 to 1743.

Pastor, Vicente, painter, was pensioned in Paris by Count Aranda in 1784; he returned to the works in 1789, and continued there for several years afterwards.

Peña, Vicente, modeller, 1783.

Perales, Ramon de, painter, 1750.

Periz, Joseph, modeller, from 1727 to 1731.

Periz, Joseph, mayor, painter, from 1750 to 1783.

Periz, Joseph, menor, modeller, 1783.

Perpiñan, Cristoval, a son of Vicente, painter, from 1727 to 1740.

Perpiñan, Vicente, modeller, from 1731 to 1743.

Pinazo, Andres, draughtsman and carver, 1727.

Poggetti, Luis, drawing master, 1815.

Porcar, Cristoval, painter, from 1727 to 1735.

Porcar, Pascual, modeller, from 1729 to 1735.

Prast, Antonio, painter of common pottery in 1783.

Prats, Cristoval, modeller, 1783.

Prats, Cristoval, turner, from 1731 to 1750.

Prats, Francisco, modeller, from 1750 to 1783.

Prats, Fulgencio, painter, 1783.

Prats, Vicente, painter, from 1750 to 1794. In 1789 he ranked among the first artists at Alcora.

Querol, Vicente, 1743.

Querol, Joseph, a son of Vicente, painter, from 1727 to 1750.

Querol, Manuel, painter, from 1750 to 1783.

Rech, Joseph, a native of Cataluña, painter, in 1727.

Redolat, Joseph, painter on porcelain in 1789.

Ribot, Joseph, turner, from 1731 to 1735.

Ricart, Antonio, turner, from 1729 to 1735.

Ricart, Clemente, modeller, in 1783.

Ricart, Joaquin, modeller, in 1783.

Robert, a Frenchman, painted in 1729.

Rocafort, Cristoval, painted from 1727 to 1750; he was one of the best artists at the manufactory in 1743.

Roman, Juan, painted from 1731 to 1735.

Roman, Manuel, painted from 1735 to 1750.

Romualdo, Joseph, painter, from 1728 to 1750.

Roux, Edouard, a French painter, who worked at Alcora, where he had been brought by Ollery in 1728 until 1735.

Rules, Joseph de, turner, from 1731 to 1735.

Saborit, Cristoval, modeller, in 1783.

Saborit, Cristoval, painted from 1727 to 1736.

Saborit, Joaquin, painter, 1783.

Saborit, Joaquin, painted from 1728 to 1750.

Saborit, Manuel, modeller, in 1783.

Sagao, Rafael, draughtsman and carver, 1727.

Salvada, Joseph, 1789.

Sancho, Joaquin, painted in 1783.

Serrania, Cristoval, 1750.

Serrania, Vicente, painted from 1728 to 1743.

Soliva, Joaquin, painted pottery in 1783, and retouched porcelain in 1789.

Soliva, Miguel, painted from 1727 to 1750. In 1743 he was considered the best artist at Alcora.

Soriano, Joseph, turner from 1731 to 1735.

Soriano, Nicasio, turner from 1731 to 1735.

Sorolla, Manuel, worked at the wheel in 1783.

Tarazona, menor, Cristoval, modeller, 1783.

Tarazona, Cristoval, painted from 1727 to 1750.

Tarazona, Ramon, retouched porcelain in 1783.

Tarragó, Joseph, painter from 1728 to 1735.

Tarragó, Vicente, painter from 1727 to 1750.

Ten, Francisco, modeller in 1783.

Ten, Joaquin, painter from 1732 to 1750. In 1789 he closes the pottery works which he had established in imitation of those of Alcora.

Ten, Joseph, 1750.

Ten, Jaime, painter from 1735 to 1750.

Terra, Cristobal, modeller, 1783.

Terra, Vicente, varnisher, 1783.

Thomas, Antonio, modeller, 1783.

Thomas, Gaspar, 1750.
Thomas, Joaquin, modeller in 1783.
Thomas, José, 1750.
Thomas, José, worked at the wheel in 1783.
Thomas, Juan, 1743, 1750.
Thomas, Mateo, 1750.
Thomas Feliu, Vicente, painter from 1729 to 1740.
Thomas, Vicente, 1783.
Torres, Cristoval, painter from 1728 to 1750.
Torres, Juan, from 1731 to 1735.
Vadenes, Cristobal, 1770.
Valentin, Pedro, painter from 1727 to 1743.
Vilar, Cristobal, painter from 1727 to 1750.
Vilar, Cristobal, sculptor, works in porcelain in 1789.
Vilar, Francisco, 1750.
Vilar, Joseph, modeller in 1783.
Vilar, Miguel, painter from 1727 to 1743.
Vilar, Pedro, worked in the ovens from 1735 to 1750.
Vilar, Ramon, retouched porcelain in 1789.
Vilar y Bordoñan, Cristobal, modeller in 1783.
Vilar y Bordoñan, Mariano, worked at pipe-clay porcelain in 1789.
Vilar Perpiñan, Cristobal, painted from 1739 to 1743.
Vilar Ricart, Cristobal, painter from 1727 to 1735.
Vilar Porcar, Cristobal, painter, 1727.
Vilar Ricart, Joseph, painter from January, 1731, to 1735.
Vilar Porcar, Joaquin, painter from 1727 to 1735.
Vilar Saboret, Joaquin, painter in 1729.
Yguet, Vicente, painted common pottery in 1783.
Zaragoza, Friar, worker in porcelain, 1799.

MARKS AND SIGNATURES OF THE PAINTERS WHO WORKED AT ALCORA.

From 1727 to 1784 no special mark was used at Alcora. In several instances specimens were signed with the painter's name or initials.

In order to distinguish the qualities or sizes, coloured numbers were frequently added.

From 1784 the letter A in gold or colours was used to mark the pottery and porcelain made at Alcora.

The following marks were used after 1784. The a underlined,
A, sometimes in blue.

A number and letter, No. 4 A, G 8; No. 3 P. In 1799 the
pottery made by Friar Joseph de Zaragoza was marked M. O. X.

Joseph calbo

Mariano Causado

Pedro Cloostermans. 1

Manuel Cros

Joseph Falio

Joaquin Ferrer

Josef Ferrer

Fran^{co} Gazces

Joaqⁿ Gameto

Pedro Gaxces

Christoual Casc.

Francisco Granget

Vuente Grande

Juan Christian Knüpffene

Knüpffene

Julian Lopez

François Martin

Fransisco Mas.

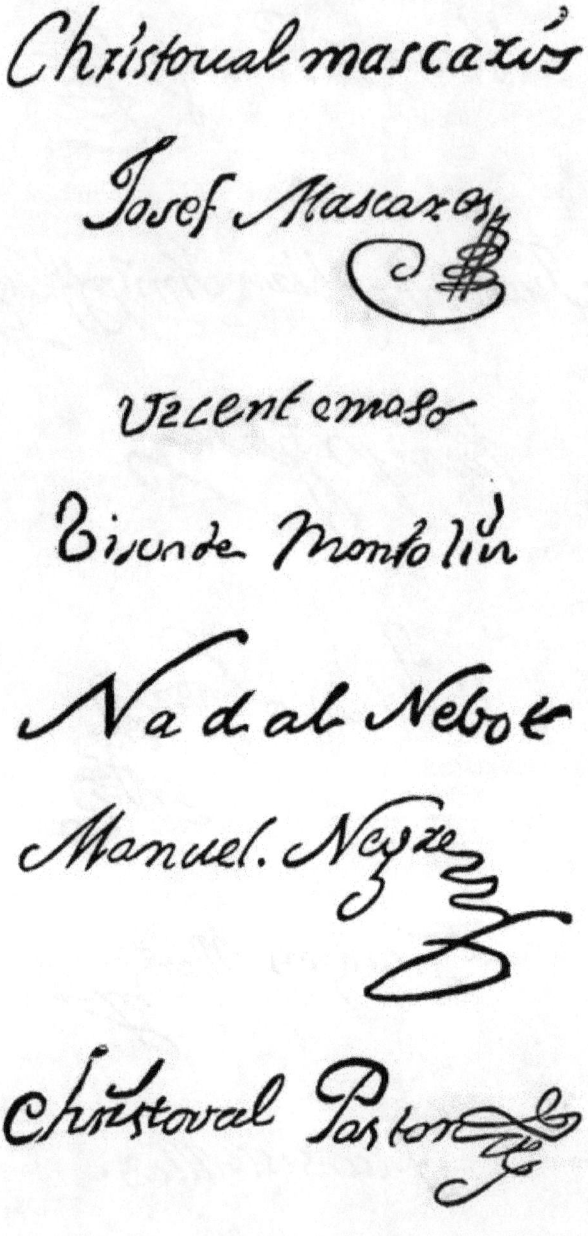

Christoual mascarós

Iosef Mascaros

Vicent emaso

Bisende Montoliu

Nadal Nebot

Manuel. Neyze

Christoual Pastor

Alnso Bats

Vicente Prats

Josef quarol
 Feliu

Chxistoval Rocafort

Christoval Parron

Joaquin ten

miguel Vilar

MADRID.—BUEN RETIRO PORCELAIN.

In 1759 King Charles III. came from Naples, having inherited the Spanish crown on the death of his brother Ferdinand VI. Soon after his arrival he determined to establish a porcelain manufactory at Madrid in the same style as one which in 1736 he had founded at Naples. The documents which exist relating to this manufactory at the archives of the Royal Palace, Madrid, Alcala, Ministry of Finance, etc., state that before the King left Naples, he ordered the following letter to be written to the Secretary of State, Richard Wall, on September 11, 1759: " Likewise the workmen and utensils used at the royal manufactory of porcelain of Capo di Monte must be embarked from Naples to Alicant, in the vessels prepared for that purpose, in order to continue from there the journey to Madrid. The necessary conveyances are to be provided, and the expenses to be charged to his Majesty's account."

Charles III. landed at Barcelona on the 17th of October, 1759, and we find a letter written by order of the King, by the Marquis of Esquilace to Secretary Wall, in November of the same year, in which he says that the King had heard of the arrival in Spain of the workmen from Capo di Monte, and gives orders that money should be supplied to the Director, Don Juan Thomas Bonicelli. Wall answers that he " will give orders and help the workmen who are to establish the manufactory, and let them have every facility to examine different sorts of earths and localities which may suit them, and that the Director, Bonicelli, should have the money he might require."

It appears also that 300 gold ducats were given to Giuseppe Gricci, " modeller," in absence of Bonicelli. The King ordered Wall to be informed that he understood that a place had been found near Madrid to establish these works, and that he was

anxious to see a plan of the exact locality.   Giuseppe Gricci drew
the plan of the spot chosen, and was paid 100 gold doubloons for
works connected with the manufactory.   Bonicelli sends the
following list of workmen who had arrived from Naples to the
King.

Cayetano Schepers, chief composer.	Joseph Santorum, modeller.
Pablo Forni.	Juan Bescia, ,,
Joseph Gricci, principal modeller.	Bautista de Bautista, ,,
Carlos Gricci.	Antonio Morelly, ,,
Esteban Gricci, modeller.	Salvador Nofri, ,,
Cayetano Fumo, ,,	Phelipe Esplores, ,,
Basilio Fumo, ,,	Ambrosio de Giorgi, ,,
Joseph Fumo, ,,	Pedro Antonio de Giorgi, ,,
Carlos Fumo, ,,	Pablo Frate, ,,
Macedonio Fumo, ,,	

WORKMEN EMPLOYED IN THE KILNS.

Jenaro Bonincosa.	Vincenzio Frate.
Nicolas Rocio.	Matheo Mayni.
Pasqual Rocco.	Giorchino Amable.
Juan Frate.	Joseph Esclavo.
Baldo de Beneditis.	Antonio Aquaviva Esclavo.

WORKMEN WHO FOUNDED THE COLOURS.

Francisco Conte.	Joseph Caramello.
Nicolas Conte.	Joachim Pataroti, carver in pietri
Angelo Lionelli.	dure.

WORKMEN EMPLOYED AT THE WHEEL.

Joseph Grossi.	Juan Remini, gold beater.
Nicolas Botino.	Pedro Chevalier, mounter.

PAINTERS.

José de la Torre.	Antonio Provinciale.
Juan Bautista de la Torre.	Joseph del Coco.
Nicolas de la Torre.	Carlos Remissi.
Fernando Sorrentini.	Francesco Simini.
Mariano Nani.	Xavier Brancacio.
Jenaro Boltri.	Joseph Esclavo.
Nicolas Donadio.	Francisco Esclavo.

On the 19th of December, 1759, Don Carlos de Borbon, the King's architect, presented him with the plans of the porcelain manufactory. The spot selected was inside the gardens of the Royal Palace of Buen Retiro. Ponz tells us in his "Viage," Vol. VI. p. 108, that the building was large and of regular architecture. We know it cost 179,130 reals.

Don Carlos de Borbon was a black slave who had been captured with other blacks during the reign of Ferdinand VI. The Queen-mother sent them to Naples, and Charles III. gave them an artistic education.

Don Carlos Antonio became the King's architect. On the 22nd of May, 1760, the building was finished, the money then spent amounted to upwards of 145,000 reals, and Larruga tells us, in his Memorias, "The King spent in establishing this manufactory £115,000, with a yearly cost to keep it up of £20,000."

William Clarke, in his "Letters concerning the Spanish Nation during the years 1760-1761," London, 1763, says, p. 262 : "At Madrid is lately set up a manufacture of porcelain in the gardens of the King's palace at the Retiro, wrought by artificers brought from Saxony." Documents exist proving that in 1760-1761, they were already working there. Townsend, in his "Journey through Spain in 1786 and 1787," London, 1792, says, Vol. II., p. 278 :—

"I tried to obtain admission to the china manufacture, which is likewise administered on the King's account, but His Majesty's injunctions are so severe that I could neither get introduced to see it, nor meet with any one who had ever been able to procure that favour for himself. I was the less mortified upon this occasion because, from the specimens which I have seen, both in the palace at Madrid, and in the provinces, it resembles the manufacture of Sèvres which I had formerly visited in a tour through France."

In the "Nouveau voyage en Espagne, ou Tableau de l'état

actuel de cette monarchie," Paris, 1789, Vol. I. p. 233, the author
tells us, how "Le monarque actuel à établi dans leur interieur une
fabrique de porcelaine, dont l'entrée est jusquà present interdite
à tout le monde.   On veut sans doute que ses essais se perfec-
tionnment dans le silence, avant de les exposer aux yeux des curieux.
Ses productions ne peuvent encore se voir que dans les Palais des
Souverains, ou dans quelques Cours d'Italie, auxquelles il les
envoie en presens."

We find in a "Nouveau voyage en Espagne," Paris, 1805, p. 34,
in describing this porcelain manufactory that the author says;
"Cet établissement tres couteux ne travaille que pour le Roi et a
son compte ; il en sort des vases d'une beaute et d'un fini qui ne
le cedent point à ceux de Sévres."

Citoyen Alquier, in 1800, the envoy of the French Republic, was
allowed to visit the manufactory.

We do not know the precise date when porcelain began to be
manufactured at the Retiro.   Clarke, writing in 1761, says the
works had begun, and in 1764 pupils attended the classes at the
Academy of Sⁿ Fernando.   Larruga, in his "Memorias," says that
as soon as the building was finished, china was made under the
superintendence of Don Cayetano Schepers ; the works, during his
superintendence, proved very unsatisfactory, to his great astonish-
ment, as the same process and workmen were employed as at
Naples.   Schepers attributes it to squabbles between the Spanish
and Italian workmen.   Sebastian Schepers, from 1783, a son of
Cayetano's, tried various experiments with different clays of the
country.

The porcelain made at Buen Retiro was kept for the first thirty
years for the exclusive use of the royal family, or to be sent as
presents to foreign courts.   Nothing was offered for sale until
January, 1789, after Charles III.'s death, 1788, when Charles IV.
determined that the china manufactured at Buen Retiro might be
sold.   Even in Spain the specimens of this china are very scarce ;
it is only at the palaces of Madrid, Aranjuez, the Escorial and La

Granja that an idea can be formed of the perfection of this manufacture.

The director at that time was Don Domingo Bonicelli, a son of Don Juan Bonicelli. Don Domingo chose a room within the Retiro, which was arranged at a cost of £350, in which to exhibit the objects for sale. Another room was taken in the Calle del Turco, which is mentioned in "Noticias varias y curiosas de Madrid," Valero Chicarro, 1762-1793, which we find was closed in 1800, as the "objects manufactured at the Retiro were simply for ornament, and could only be bought by very rich persons." Southey in his "Letters from Spain," London, 1797, p. 118, says, "The old palace of Buen Retiro is converted into a royal porcelain manufactory; the prices are extravagantly high, but they have arrived at great excellence in the manufacture. The false taste of the people is displayed in all the vases I saw there, which though made from Roman models, are all terminated by porcelain flowers."

Every kind of porcelain was made at Buen Retiro, hard and soft paste, white china, glazed or unglazed, or painted and modelled in the style of Capo di Monte. A great many existed imitating the blue jasper ware of Wedgwood, and they also made flowers, coloured and biscuit, groups, and single figures, and painted porcelain of different kinds. Great quantities of tiles for pavements were also made there, which may still be seen at the Casa del Labrador at Aranjuez; they are mentioned in the accounts which exist at the Ministry of Finance for 1807 and 1808. We find in these same accounts interesting details of the objects made monthly. In January, 1808, a large number of figures were made, including 151 heads for the table centre which was made for the king, 306 objects ornamented with paintings, 2,056 tiles, 577 objects of less artistic importance, such as dishes, plates, etc. The finest specimens which exist are in the Neapolitan style, and are two rooms at the Palaces of Madrid and Aranjuez of which the walls are completely covered with china plaques and looking-glasses, modelled in the most admirable manner with figures, fruits, and flowers. The room at Aranjuez is covered with a bold ornamentation of figures in the Japanese style, in high relief, painted with colours and gold with the most exquisite details. The figures unite the fine Italian modelling with the Japanese decoration. The chandelier is in the same style. Upon a vase on the wainscot to the right of the entrance door is the following inscription :

JOSEPH

GRICC\

DELINEAV^{it}

ET

SCUL^{it}

1763.

This same date is repeated in the angles, and in some shields near the roof we find,

AÑO

1765 ;

probably the year the work was terminated. Antonio Conca, in his " Descrizione Odeporica della Spagna in cui spezialmente si da notizia delle cose spettanti alle Belle Arti," Parma, 1793, Vol. III., p. 310, says, " Il Gabineto abbelitto di porcellana della Fabbricca del Retiro ha meritato le bodi de curiozi viaggiatori." We also find in p. 119, " Un altro Gabinetto vien chiamato della Cina pel sud principal ornata di bei putti, di bassi relievi, e di altre opere di porcellana della nuova Real Fabbricca del Ritiro." Ponz, in his " Viage de España," Madrid, 1782, describes the room at the Palace of Madrid, saying, " it is covered with large plaques of porcelain made at Buen Retiro. In some are represented figures of children copied from models, and between each compartment looking-glasses are let in." (See woodcut.)

From the establishment of the manufactory in 1759 by

ROOM DECORATED WITH BUEN RETIRO PORCELAIN, IN THE PALACE AT
MADRID.

Charles III. until 1803 the styles adopted at Capo di Monte had been followed. At the beginning of this century Dn. Bartolomé Sureda went to Paris to learn the manner in which Sèvres porcelain was made. On his return in 1803 he was appointed director of the works at Buen Retiro and endeavoured to imitate the paste and brilliancy of decoration of Sèvres. Two workmen came over from Paris—Victor Perche, and Vivien.

Among the finest specimens of this period of the manufactory are a splendid clock and four vases, two mètres high, with porcelain flowers, which exist in one of the state rooms of the Palace of Madrid. The vases are placed in the four corners of the room. The clock is ornamented with large biscuit figures. A large number of vases exist at the royal Palaces of Madrid, Aranjuez, and Escorial, of Retiro china. They are often finely mounted in gilt bronze with muslin or porcelain flowers. The blue of the imitations of Wedgwood is not so pure, nor is the biscuit work so fine as the English. Gold is often added to these specimens.

We find at the archives of the Ministry of Finance interesting details of a dinner service made in 1798 for Charles IV., and a centre-piece, which probably is that now in the Casa del Labrador at Aranjuez.

When the French made their entry into Madrid in the spring of 1808 they took possession of the position occupied by the royal manufactory. In July of the same year it continued in the hands of the French, who forced open the doors of the laboratory. Porcelain continued, however, to be made there during the reign of Joseph I.; we find in "Travels through Spain and part of Portugal," London, 1808, p. 23, that, the author says, "the gardens of the Buen Retiro are open to the public. In the neighbourhood of these the royal porcelain manufacture is carried on in a large white building." Lord Blayney, in his "Narrative of a Journey through Spain and France in 1810–1814," London, 1814, says that "the royal manufactures of tapestry and porcelain have declined since the death of Charles III. and have now entirely ceased."

We find in "Paseos por Madrid," Madrid, 1815-8, p. 87, it stated that " The English, at the second entry of our troops in Madrid, ruined this building in order that it should not be used as a fortress by the French troops."

Richard Ford, in his "Handbook for Travellers in Spain," London, 1845, says, "Everything was destroyed by the invaders, who turned the manufactory into a fortification, which surrendered with 200 cannon, Aug. 14th, 1812, to the Duke of Wellington. Ferdinand VII., on his restoration, re-created La China, removing the workshops and ware rooms to the Moneloa."

The South Kensington Museum contains an interesting collection of Buen Retiro porcelain of different kinds, of which may be named :

No. 344-'66. A vase of biscuit porcelain, two-handled, with frieze of classic dancing figures and flowers.

Nos. 333, 4-'66. Two small vases for tea, white porcelain, covered with flowers in relief.

No. 892-'75. A pair of vases painted with young bacchanals in rose camaïeu, and gilt.

No. 893-'75. A pair of draped female figures, each holding a cornucopia, standing on an altar-shaped plinth.

No. 894-'75. A clock case, white porcelain, of rock and scroll work, with flowers and groups of amorini.

No. 332-'76. A group of Ariadne and the panther.

No. 1068-'73. A pair of tall vases, with gilt serpent handles, the necks fluted with gold, the upper part of the body painted with classic groups, and with coloured scroll foliage in relief, the lower part painted with leaves and scrolls on white ground. (See woodcut on next page.)

BUEN RETIRO VASE. SOUTH KENSINGTON MUSEUM.

MARKS USED AT THE PORCELAIN MANUFACTORY OF BUEN RETIRO.

The usual mark in blue.

In blue, and sometimes in violet and gold.

Cayetano or Carlos Fumo. The initials and date are graved in the clay under the glaze; the fleur-de-lis is pencilled in blue. On a fine group of children playing with a goat.

This mark is graved in the clay, under the glaze, on a fine group modelled by Salvador Nofri.

Ochogavia? graved in the soft clay on a figure.

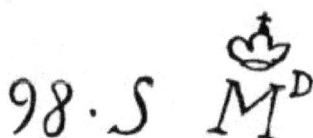

1798, Sorrentini? These marks are pencilled in red on a pink cup and saucer, with landscapes painted *en grisaille.*

Pedro Antonio Georgi? The initials P. G. are gilt; the M crowned in red; the V and M graved in the clay; on a cup and saucer buff coloured.

Po ✳

X° ✳

R · F · Œ · PORCELANA

Œ · S · M · C ·

R MADRID S

JOSEPH
GRICCĬ
DELINEA ᶦᵗ
ET
SCUL ᶦᵗ
1763

Provinciale? The letters
Po are graved in the clay, the
fleur-de-lis in blue; on two
saucers, beautifully painted
with children.

Probably the initial of the
king. On two jardinières; the
interlaced C's graved in the
clay, the fleur-de-lis in blue.

On two large vases imi-
tating Wedgwood's blue and
white jasper, with white
biscuit flowers.

On a group of biscuit Re-
tiro porcelain of two figures
representing Painting. The
same mark appears on a
figure of Apollo, about one
foot high. This mark is
stamped on the porcelain;
the letters are in relief tinted
rose colour.

At the room decorated
with Buen Retiro plaques at
Aranjuez. It appears on a
vase in relief, which is placed
on the basement to the right
on entering. The date 1765
appears on the ceiling, probably the year when the
work was finished.

Graven on the clay on a
white soft paste bracket
painted with coloured flowers
belonging to Count Valencia
de Dⁿ Juan.

On a cup at the Museo Arqueologico, Mad., painted with landscapes. The initials are of Pedro Antonio Giorgi, who painted from 1802 to 1808.

Engraved on the clay on a plaque of blue biscuit porcelain imitating Wedgwood jasper ware, representing a mythological subject.

On a dessert plate representing a vine leaf at the Museo Arqueologico. The initials appear to be those of Felipe Gricci, a son of the first modeller José, who came with Charles III. from Naples.

Fleur-de-lis graven in the clay on a fine group of three figures.

List of Directors and Artists who were employed in
the Royal Manufactory of the Buen Retiro from
its foundation, in 1759, until 1808 :

DIRECTORS.

Bonicelli, Juan Thomas, principal Director at the establishment of the manu-
factory in 1759.
Bonicelli, Domingo. In 1786 he was Director; in 1796 he solicits his retire-
ment, and died soon after.
Cristobal de Torrijos, appointed Director in 1797, after the death of Don
Domingo Bonicelli.
Sureda, Bartolomé, Director in 1804, and continues in 1808.

PRINCIPAL MODELLERS AND SUPERINTENDENTS, POSSESSING THE SECRETS OF THE FABRICATION (SECRETISTAS).

Schepers, Cayetano, first Modeller in 1759.
Gricci, Carlos, son of Joseph Gricci, came to Spain, 1759.   He appears in a
list of artists employed in 1764 : he died 1795.
Gricci, Felipe, 1785. In 1802 he was first Modeller.
Forni, Antonio, second Modeller in 1802.

SCULPTORS.

Agreda, Esteban, born at Logroño, 1759. He obtained several prizes at the
Academy of San Fernando; employed in 1797, and continued to work
there in 1808.
Avila, Ceferino de, employed 1799, and continued there in 1808.
Avila, Juan de, 1771, and continued there in 1808.
Bautista, Bautista de, 1759.
Bautista, Cayetano, 1785.
Bautista, Juan Lopez, employed from 1799 to 1808.
Benedictis, Cayetano, 1785, 1802.
Benincasa, Miguel, 1778, and continues to work in 1808.
Benincasa, Vicente, 1785.
Bergaz, Alonso, 1764.
Bescia, Juan, 1759.
Borbon, Geronimo, 1802
Borbon, Genaro, 1784 and 1808.

Caravielo, Miguel, 1785.

Chaves, Alonso, born at Madrid in 1741. In 1760 was appointed Modeller, and in 1763 obtained a Second Prize at the Academy, and a First Prize in 1766.

Chaves, Justo, 1785.

Esplores, Felipe, 1759.

Estebe, Antonio, 1778 and 1808.

Flores, Josef, 1785.

Forni, Pablo, 1759.

Francholy, Angel, 1776 to 1808.

Francholy, José, 1804 to 1808.

Francholy, Luis, 1785.

Frate, Carlos, 1785 to 1802.

Frate, Josef, 1785.

Frates, Juan, 1794 to 1808.

Frate, Pablo, from 1759 to 1785.

Frates, Mateo, 1797 to 1808.

Frates, Mateo, born at Madrid in 1788. First Prize of the Academy in 1805 ; in 1829 was appointed Director of the China establishment at the Moncloa.

Frates, Francisco, 1764 to 1808.

Fumo, Basilio, in 1759 was Director of the China manufactory ; in 1779 he was appointed a Member of the Academy of San Fernando ; died in 1797.

Fumo, Carlos, 1759.

Fumo, Cayetano, 1759.

Fumo, Joseph, 1759 ; died in 1799.

Fumo, Macedonio, 1759, and continues in 1802.

Fumo, Bernabé, 1802.

Giorgi, Pedro Antonio de, 1759, and continues in 1785.

Giorgi, Carlos, 1785 to 1808.

Giorgi, Ambrosio de, 1759.

Giorgi, Antonio, 1795 to 1808.

Gricchi, Joseph, 1759. In 1766 was appointed Honorary Director of the Academy of San Fernando ; died in 1769.

Gricci, Esteban, 1759.

Guijarro, Dionisio, 1798 to 1808.

Llorente, Manuel, 1764 to 1785.

Morelly, Antonio, 1759 to 1785.

Nofri, Salvador, 1759 to 1785.

Nofri, Justo, 1778 to 1808.

Nofri, or Noferi, Juan, 1802.

Ochogavia, Manuel, 1764. Born in Galicia in 1744 ; in 1760 won a Second Prize of Sculpture at the Academy, and in 1763 a First Prize.

Palmerani, Domingo, 1795, 1808.

Palmerani, Angel, 1799 to 1808.

Penaba, Joseph, 1793 to 1808.

Rodriguez, Antonio, 1797 to 1808.

Sancho, Dionisio, 1788. Born at Cienpozuelos in 1762 ; won a Prize at the Academy in 1793 ; was appointed a Member of the Academy, 1796 ; in 1810 he went to Mexico, where he died, 1829.

Santorum, Joseph, 1759.

Sorrentini, Fernando, 1785 to 1808.

Sorrentini, Rafael, 1785.

Sorrentini, Francisco, 1802.

Valentin, José, 1779 to 1808.

Valentin, Miguel, 1785.

PAINTERS.

Alonso, Francisco, 1764.

Boltri, Genaro, 1756. Born in Naples in 1730; in 1759 he came to Madrid with Charles III.'s household, and worked at the Retiro ; died in Madrid in 1788.

Brancasio, Xavier, 1759.

Brancacho, Domingo, 1762 to 1803.

Branga, Ignacio de, 1800, painter of figures ; he continues there in 1808.

Camaron, Josef, 1802. Born at Segorbe in 1760 ; in 1776 he won a prize of painting at Valencia ; he was pensioned to Rome, and appointed Painter in Ordinary to the King.

Castillo, Fernando del, born at Madrid in 1740. He was appointed Painter at the manufactory, and worked there until his death in 1777.

Coco, Joseph del, 1759.

Cruz, Mariano de la, 1807, 1808.

Domeu, Carlos, 1785.

Donadio, Nicolas, 1759.

Giorgi, Pedro Antonio, 1802.

Martinez, Antonio, 1764.

Martinez, Pedro, 1796 to 1808.

Nani, Mariano, 1759. His wife received a pension from 1804, probably the year of his death.

Peshorn, Jorge, 1788, and continues working in 1802.

Provinciale, Antonio, 1759 and 1785.

Quirós, Juan José, 1802.

Quirós, Juan José, 1802.

Rimini, Carlos, 1759.

Romero, Juan Bautista, 1800. Flowers and fruit ; appears in lists of 1802.

Rubio, Joseph, 1799 to 1808.

Semini, Francisco, 1759.

Soriano, Joaquin, 1799. Landscape painter in 1800; continues in 1808.

Sorrentini, Josef, 1756, probably from Capo di Monte. In 1802 he asks for a retiring pension.

Sorrentini, Fernando, 1759.

Sorrentini, Pablo, 1764 to 1808.

Sorrentini, Gabriel, 1769 to 1808.

Sorrentini, Manuel, 1785 to 1802.

Torre, Joseph de la, 1759.

Torre, Nicolas de la, 1759. In 1802 asks for a retiring pension.

Torre, Raphael de la, 1759.

Torre, Juan Bautista de la, 1759 and 1808.

Torre, Josef de la, 1785 and 1802.

Torre, Francisco de la, 1796 to 1808.

Torre, Julian de la, 1802.

Velasquez, Castor, 1807, and continued in 1808. Born in Madrid in 1768 and obtained a prize at the Academy in 1787.

VARIOUS ARTISTS EMPLOYED IN THE MANUFACTORY.

Agreda, Manuel, Sculptor, a brother of Esteban Agreda; he superintended the making of biscuit china; born at Haro in 1773; won prizes at the Academy; and was employed at the Manufactory from 1805 to 1808.

Bautista, Juan, employed to make porcelain flowers from 1785 to 1808.

Bautista, Francisco, appears in 1802 as maker of porcelain flowers.

Bautista, Sebastian, appears in 1802 as a maker of porcelain flowers.

Chevalier, Pedro, mounter of snuff-boxes from 1759, and continued to work at the Manufactory in 1763.

Escalera, Josef, mounter of snuff-boxes from 1781, and continued to work at the Manufactory in 1808.

Perche, Jaime Victor, French workman brought from Paris to prepare porcelain, from 1803 to 1809.

Vivien, French workman, brought from Paris to prepare porcelain, from 1803 to 1809.

At the same time that porcelain was made at Retiro and Alcora, other manufactories of a similar kind were established in Spain; but none of them could compete with these. The most important was established at Sargadelos, Galicia, in 1804. One of the finest specimens which have reached us of this manufactory is a large bas relief representing the massacres of the Spaniards by the French in Madrid on the 2nd of May, 1808.

GLASS.

SINCE the South Kensington Museum purchased the largest collection of old and modern Spanish glass in Europe, the taste for and study of this branch of industry has increased to a very great extent. It is evident that this manufacture attained great importance during the three last centuries, and possibly existed at an earlier period ; and that glass objects made in Spain possess a special and distinct character, different to those made in other countries. Before the objects at the Kensington Museum were collected, the existence of this industry in Spain was comparatively unknown.

The earliest mention of glass works in Spain will be found in Pliny, who, while explaining the proceedings which were employed in this industry, says that glass was made in a similar manner in France and Spain: "Jam vero et per Gallias Hispaniasque simili modo harenae temperantur."—L. XXXVI. cap. 66.

The next allusion to this industry will be found in the works of San Isidoro. This eminent man lived in the 7th century, and after quoting the observations of the Roman author, gives us to understand that this industry existed before his time in Italy, France, and Spain : "Olim fiebat et in Italia, et per Gallias, et Hispaniam arena alba mollissima pila mola que terebatur." [Divi. Isid. Hisp. Etymologiarum, I. XVI. cap. 16.] It is evident, therefore, from this passage, that glass was made to a large extent in the Spanish Peninsula during the Roman period. This is confirmed by the number of specimens which are constantly found in ruins. We learn also that the manufacture had ceased to exist in the seventh century.

Glass vessels of the Roman period found in Spain are similar in form and manufacture to those which we know were made in France and Italy. This is not to be wondered at, if we remember that the Romans imposed their artistic forms on the countries they conquered. It is impossible to classify the specimens of this industry into determined localities. The study of the glass paste may, at some future period, give materials for such a classification.

One special characteristic of Roman glass may be taken into account to be applied to Spanish glass of a later period. We find ancient specimens constantly ornamented with a sort of thread or line which runs all over the vase. These lines are sometimes made of transparent glass, and sometimes of white opaque glass, termed in Italy *latticinio* from its milky whiteness. When the industry of glass making was revived in Europe during the fifteenth and sixteenth centuries, classical forms were copied in this as in other industries ; this line ornamentation was copied on a much smaller scale in Italy than in Spain, where it constituted the chief and constant characteristic of glass making. It is an interesting fact that objects of a traditional Moorish form have the greatest amount of lines of this style of ornamentation. We cannot, until this subject is more thoroughly investigated, do otherwise than infer either that the tradition of this industry was preserved in Spain, or that the Arabs imported this style of decoration from the same localities from which it had been copied by the Romans centuries before.

The comparison of these different styles of glass making can be carried out in a most satisfactory manner in London by examining the fine specimens of glass in the British Museum (Slade collection), and the old Spanish glass at South Kensington.

We have no specimens of glass of the Visigothic period. If, as is most probable, glass was used by the Visigoths, they may have imported it from the East, for the text I have quoted from the works of St. Isidore seems to prove that this industry had ceased to exist in his time. The glass paste of different colours must, however, be mentioned, which is set in gold in the Visigothic crowns found at Guarrazar, near Toledo. It imitates precious stones, and was very generally used during the Byzantine period ; its occurrence here makes it appear probable that at any rate the tradition of this industry existed in Spain.

From the 8th to the end of the 15th century, during the Mahomedan domination, I infer that the industry of glass making became as important in Spain as that of pottery. No specimens, however, of the earlier period have reached us, and we must judge of what it was from the glass vessels in the Kensington Museum, belonging to the Renaissance period, which preserve their Oriental form, and are of a different style to that of Venice and other localities in Europe.

A most interesting fact, which confirms this theory, will be found in a translation made from Hebrew to Arabic of a work which treats of the virtues of precious stones, *Lapidario* [MS. Biblioteca del Escorial], quoted by Rico y Sinobas in " Almanaque de la Industria," 1873. We do not know exactly when the author Abolais lived, but in the prologue to this MS. it is mentioned that D^n. Alfonso el Sabio found this book at Toledo, and gave orders to a Jew called Juda Mosca, and a priest, Garci Perez, to translate it into Spanish. The translation was terminated in 1250. Technical details are given in this volume concerning the substances which are employed in glass making, and some of the minerals found in Spain which are used in painting or enamelling it, but as this work was written to explain the properties of minerals, as they were understood in the author's time, he does not enter into any interesting details, or describe the forms of these objects. Another allusion to glass making in Spain will be found in Al Makkari, the Arabian author of " Mohamedan Dynasties in Spain," [London, 1840, 2 vols. 4to], who quotes an Oriental writer of the 13th century, who says, "Almeria was also famous for the fabrication of all sorts of vases and utensils, whether of iron, copper, or glass." (Vol. I. p. 51.)

The tradition of this industry has been undoubtedly preserved at Almeria until the present day, for in this province, and in the adjoining villages of the province of Granada, we find that specimens are to be met with, which possess a marked Oriental form, and are completely free from the influence of Italian models which existed in other localities. The most characteristic specimens consist of jars of two, four and eight handles, bowls with ribs and handles, pilgrim's bottles, etc., of which interesting examples exist at the South Kensington Museum. Woodcuts of several of these are given.

All these objects are decorated with a serrated ornamentation of buttons, trellis-work, and the lines to which I have already alluded which were placed there after the object was made, in the Roman style. The paste is generally of a dark green colour, and when we find these same features in vessels of white clear glass, we may affirm that they are contemporary imitations made at Cadalso or elsewhere, for they are very seldom to be met with in the provinces of Almeria and Granada, and are generally found at Toledo and other localities; it is, moreover, a common condition of Oriental art that its general form complies with a geometrical tracery, and we never find as in Italian works of art, forms and capricious ornamentations which interfere with the symmetry of the general lines, and sacrifice them to the beauty of the whole.

I have been unable to find the glass industries of this period mentioned by any contemporary author, but I owe to the courtesy of Sʳ. Romero Ortiz some interesting details which have been taken from the archives of certain villages, which although of a more modern date prove that this industry existed in these localities. At about 14 miles from the Puebla de Dⁿ. Fadrique, there is a locality called Pinar de la Vidriera, where traces of ovens and scoriæ exist belonging to an ancient glass manufactory, which is likewise mentioned in documents of the municipality as continuing to work in 1620.   At Castril de la Peña, a manufactory yet exists where glass is still made, and which has existed from time immemorial in the village.   The

GLASS VASE.—SPANISH, 16TH CENTURY.

building itself is decorated with the escutcheon of the family of Hernando de Zafra, one of the secretaries of Queen Isabel, late in the 15th century, who must have purchased it with other lands which he possessed there, towards the year 1492.   A gallery, one mile long, which exists at the entrance of the town from whence the sand has been extracted for this manufacture, gives an idea of the antiquity of this industry in this particular locality. It has been calculated that about two tons of sand were used at these glass works every month. At Royo Molino, in the province of Jaen, a very ancient building still exists, now half in ruins, which has been used until very lately as a glass factory. At Maria, in the province of Almeria, several glass manufactories have existed.

PILGRIMS' GLASS BOTTLE.—SPANISH, 17TH CENTURY.

The oldest, it is believed, was about two miles from the town, and is called traditionally "del Campo," but I have not found mention of it in any document. Three glass ovens existed inside the town : one was established by Vicente Botia, towards the year 1750, which lasted until 1790. Juan Martinez established at about this period an industry of a similar kind near the former one, which continued to work until 1854. The same green glass has been constantly made in these localities, the same forms have been copied, the only difference between the older and more modern specimens consisting in the coarser and heavier quality of the glass.

In treating of the glass manufactures in Spain, where Italian models were imitated to a very great extent, we find very few allusions in contemporary authors of the Middle Ages; it may be because glass vessels were chiefly used with wooden and pottery utensils by the poorer classes, and metal utensils of all kinds by those who were able to afford them. At any rate, it is only towards the end of the Middle Ages that we meet with information concerning this industry, which continues uninterrupted until the present day.

Barcelona is one of the towns distinguished for the antiquity and excellence of its glass. In a municipal edict of 1324, we find a special prohibition that the glass ovens shoud not be inside the city, owing to the danger they might cause to the rest of the population. In 1455, permission was granted to the *vidrieros*, glassmakers, to form a guild under the patronage of St. Bernardino, and from this period some of its members figure as holding municipal charges. Capmany, "Memorias," Vol. I. p. 134. According to this author, the special Ordinances of this corporation are not known, but only those which were given by the municipality in 1659. He adds that the master *vidrieros* required six years of apprenticeship and practice to be admitted to work.

From the 15th century several authors praise the glass made at Barcelona. In a MS. by Jeronimo Paulo, who writes in 1491, a description in Latin of the most remarkable things at Barcelona, he says, "they also send to Rome and other places many glass vessels of different sorts and kinds which may well compete with those of Venice." In the account of Philip le Bel's journey to Spain on his marriage with Queen Joanna we find the following mention of the town of Barcelona : "Et sont là faicts les plus beauls ouvrages de voires (verres) et de cire qui soient faicts au monde. Le Jordi (19 Janvier, 1503) Monsigneur alla au dehors de la ville vioir ung jour où on faict voires (verres) de cristallin très beaus." ["Collection des Voyages," Bruxelles, 1876, Vol. I., p. 257.] Marineus Siculus, who writes early in the 16th century says, "the best glass made in Spain is that of Barcelona," and Gaspar Barreiros in his " Chorographia," [Coimbra, 1569,] tells us, "they made excellent glass at Barcelona, almost equal to the Venetian." At the beginning of the 17th century the authors, Jaime Rebullosa, in his " Descripcion del mundo," [Barcelona, 1603, 8vo,] and Luis Nuñez in " Hispania," [Antverpiæ. 1607, 8vo, p. 279,] continue to praise the glass made at Barcelona, and from that period we find its merit and the vast quantity which was exported constantly alluded to. The fame of Spanish glass must have been justified, for in the "Viage del Cardinal Infante," by Aedo, printed in 1639, we find it stated that when the Infant Cardinal was at Barcelona, in 1632, he went with his galleys to Mataró, four leagues from Barcelona, to see the " glass made there which was so abundantly sold all over the country." The Spanish translator of "La Piazza universale di tutte le professioni," [Madrid, 1615,] adds the name of Barcelona to the Italian author's mention of glass objects made in Venice, saying, " This industry has reached such a degree of excellence at Murano and Barcelona that nothing can be compared to it ; there is nothing now which cannot be made of glass and crystal, even cabinets have been made, and castles with their towers, battlements, artillery, and fortifications." Mendez Silva in his " Poblacion de España, [Madrid, 1654, p. 243,] repeats the same idea when he says they made at Barcelona, "fine glass which might compete with the Venetian." This industry continued in Cataluña to a great extent in the last century, and was praised by the following writers. The author of the " Atlante Español," [Vol. IV., Madrid, 1778—1795,] tells us that "they continued to make excellent glass at Barcelona, in imitation of the Venetian, with which it might compete," and that this industry was carried out to a great extent at Mataró, Cervelló, and Almatret, all three towns of Cataluña ; he says that in this

last mentioned town the glass made was "so excellent, and
the number of workmen employed was so large, that an oratory
had been built in order that the workmen should hear mass
there."

The constant comparisons which we find between the glass
made at Barcelona with that of Murano suggests two things—that
Spanish glass must have been of a first-rate order, and that the
form of the glass vessels was similar to those made at Venice.
It is highly probable that a great part of the specimens of glass
of different kinds which are classified as Italian in several collections, are really Spanish, although it is extremely difficult to point
out the difference. In this, as in other branches of industry, the
mania for classifying has gone too far, and comparative studies of
a more concrete order are necessary ; until these are made, the
principal fact to be borne in mind in classifying glass vessels is
to compare them with objects of a similar manufacture which
have been made until very lately in Cataluña, and of which an
extremely interesting collection exists at the South Kensington
Museum, proceeding from Barcelona, Mataró and Cervelló, (Nos.
149 to 193) which will enable the amateur to see how the industry
of glass-making has continued traditionally to be preserved in that
province. See woodcut opposite representing a glass bottle, also
the central vessel in woodcut on p. 238.

Among the specimens of old Spanish glass we may consider to
have proceeded from Cataluña the following examples, forming part
of the collection acquired in 1873. Bottles, Nos. 249 to 262, cups,
Nos. 336 to 339, and tumblers, Nos. 303 to 305, 312 to 314, and
328, '29. Among these, there are some which are undoubtedly still
made n the locality. The most characteristic are the *arruxiadós*,
or *borracha*, a vessel spirally ribbed with several narrow spouts, used
by the peasant girls of the villages to sprinkle rose water in the
festival of the patron saint of the district ; the *porrones*, a bottle
with a long spout, used by the peasantry for drinking wine ; the
cantaro, a jug, funnel shaped with wide mouth, handle and curved

spout, and the *pilas de agua bendita,* a holy water vessel of different shapes.

Very few details have reached us of the famous glass works which existed at Cadalso, in the province of Toledo; we know,

GLASS BOTTLE.—MODERN SPANISH.

however, that the glass made there was as excellent as that made at Cataluña, and was compared in a similar manner to the Venetian. The unknown author of "El Crotalon," published by the Spanish Bibliophiles from a rare MS., in 1871, writing in the time of the Emperor Charles V., mentions "the fine glass made at Cadalso." Marineus Siculus also writes in 1517 in his "De las Cosas Memorables de España," [Alcala de Henares, 1539, fol., Vol. I.,] that "Glass was made in several towns of Castile, the most important of them being Cadalso, which supplied the whole kingdom." It would appear therefore that this glass manufactory was already established in that locality in the 16th century, and we frequently meet with allusions to the excellence of its productions in contemporary authors. The town itself has continually been called "Cadalso de los vidrios." Mendez Silva in his "Poblacion general de España," [Madrid, 1645, p. 40,] says: "They make in three glass ovens fine glass of beautiful colours and forms, which can compete with the Venetian." At the South

GLASS VESSELS FROM SPAIN, IN THE SOUTH KENSINGTON MUSEUM.

Kensington Museum, there are two fine specimens of glass made at Cadalso—No. 1068, '73, a drinking vessel of white glass, the upper part in form of the Spanish vessel called "bucaro," ribbed and streaked with colours; the stem pineapple shape, with remains of gilding (this is represented in the woodcut); and No. 1082, '73, a bowl of plain glass, the lower part spirally waved, and decorated with scale pattern in gold and coloured dots. Both these objects proceed from a nunnery in a village near Cadalso.

Larruga says in his " Memorias," [Madrid, 1791, Vol. X., p. 53,] that "two glass ovens existed at Cadalso, which belonged to the Marchioness of Villena ; they are worked by the inhabitants of this town. One of the ovens has fallen into disuse from the beginning of the present (18th) century, and the fame of the glass made there, formerly so renowned for its clearness and variety of the objects made, has declined. In examining the state of this

GLASS VASE.—SPANISH (CADALSO), 17TH CENTURY.

industry during the reign of Charles II. we find how much it had fallen off, for Dn. Antonio de Obando in 1692, undertook to re-establish it, and to make glass vessels, and window glasses as had been made there formerly. It appears that 200 dozens of objects of different kinds were sent out from there yearly." The vase, No. 333, '73 represented in the woodcut is an example of the coloured glass of Cadalso.

Glass ovens existed from a very early period in the central

provinces of Spain, which probably imitated from the 16th century
the productions of Cadalso. We know from papers at the
Archives of the Convent, of two of these which paid a yearly rent
to the monastery of San Jeronimo de Guisando, from 1478 to
1480. One of these glass works was situated at the Venta del
Cojo on the borders of Escalona, and the other at the Venta de
los Toros de Guisando.

It is evident that a glass manufactory existed at Toledo, from
some accounts which I have found in the Archives of the
Cathedral, in which Bartolomé Lopez, vidriero, is mentioned in
1546—Pedro Fernandez in 1590, and Tomas Nuñez in 1660;
as furnishing glass vessels, principally lamps for the cathedral.
Tomas Nuñez is also paid for "three crosses of crystalline glass."
In a letter written in 1690 to Count Gondomar, the celebrated
ambassador to James I., (Archives of the Palace at Madrid), I
find a glass manufactory mentioned which existed at Cebreros in
the province of Segovia. The writer says, "Your lordship knows
we have a glass oven here; this week we have made the glass
called crystalline, of which I send in a basket sixteen specimens
for my lady Dna. Costanza."

Larruga tells us in his "Memorias," [Madrid, 1792, Vol. XVI.,
p. 222,] "That in 1680 a glass manufactory was established at San
Martin de Valdeiglesias, where glass in the Venetian style was
made—the glass was excellent. This manufactory was under the
direction of Diodonet Lambot a native of Namur. He was succeeded by Santiago Bandoleto, who was by no means as skilful.
Glass ovens were also established at the Torre de Estevan,
Hambroz, under the direction of Guillermo Torcada." At
Recuenco, in the province of Cuenca, glass works existed at the
beginning of the 16th century; but in 1722 Don Fernando Lopez
de Aragon established a manufactory on a large scale. The glass
made there was used by the king and the greater part of the rich
people at Madrid. In 1739 two other glass works existed there,
which continued their operations during the rest of the century.

In the same province several glass ovens existed towards the middle of the last century. The principal ones were established in the villages of Arbetota, Vindel and Armallones; only coarse specimens were made there, but at an earlier period their productions had been, Larruga tells us in the nineteenth volume of his "Memorias," very important. The glass works which we find mentioned in the "Atlante Español," [Madrid, 1795,] were also of a very inferior quality; they were established at the end of the last century at Busot, in the province of Alicante, Hinojares and Carolina, province of Jaen. The "Correo de España," [Vol. I. Madrid, 1771,] mentions an important glass manufactory which existed at Andorra near Alcañiz, and one where glass of an inferior quality was made at Cabra, in the province of Cordova. Cabanilles, "Historia y descripcion del reino de Valencia," Barcelona, mentions the existence from a very early period of glass works at Olleria, a village of the kingdom of Valencia.

The only mention which I have found in which Seville appears as a centre of this industry, is an interesting allusion to the village of Cala, which was represented in a festival which was given to Philip II. in 1578, "with a crystal glass in its hand, and several others at its feet, because a famous glass oven existed there." ["Recibimiento que hizo Sevilla al Rey Don Phelipe." Por Juan de Mallara, Sevilla, 1570, p. 89.]

In the 17th century, during the reign of Philip IV., the glass made at Valdemaqueda in the province of Avila was very celebrated. In a royal schedule, dated 1680, which states the price at which things were sold at Madrid, "the glass made at Barcelona, Valdemaqueda, and Villafranca" are mentioned. We find the glass of Valdemaqueda was sold for a higher price than that made at the other localities.

The principal value of these extracts is to prove that the industry of glass-making existed in these localities; none of the authors mentions the principal characteristics by which the vessels made may be classified. Those made at Almeria and Barcelona are more easily known, for they have kept until very recently their general character; while at Cadalso and other localities of the centre of Spain, the tradition of the Italian models has quite disappeared. In one fact every author agrees, namely, that the glass made in those provinces closely resembled the Venetian, and was completely different to the system followed by the Arabs. It is, therefore, highly probable, as I have already stated, that a

VASE OF GREEN GLASS, WITH BLACK HANDLES AND RIBS.—SPANISH, 17TH CENTURY.

large number of objects of glass of different kinds, which have been hitherto considered Italian, were made in Spain.

The following observations may serve as a guide in the difficult task of classifying this group. The specimens of glass vessels most generally met with in the neighbourhood of Cadalso are :—

Objects of white transparent glass, sweetmeat dishes ornamented with ribs, buttons, and reticulated rims with touches of gold.

Objects of clear greenish glass of a paler hue than is made in the province of Almeria, decorated with blue, or some opaque colour (see woodcut); in some instances part of the object is decorated with a rough crackled surface.

Objects of opaque glass with different colours, vases, glasses, cups and saucers, of thin milk-white texture with blue spots, or imitations in the Japanese style of different colours. Vases for holding flowers, and other objects, of dark blue glass, milk-white cups, glass and other objects ornamented with lines of red or blue of a thicker paste than the preceding ones.

Although these objects are copied from Venetian models, they are coarser in every detail, they are heavier and thicker, and the delicate and elegant ornamentation which we find on Italian specimens is almost always wanting, we seldom find examples of the beautiful *millefiori* chalcedony or tortoise-shell paste, and the outline of these objects is symmetrical and Oriental in style.

The royal glass manufactory at La Granja de San Ildefonso, was founded on the remains of an important one which had been established some years before, under the protection of Philip the 5th, at the Nuevo Bastan, in the province of Madrid.

Towards the years 1712 to 1718, this king commissioned D⁹. Tomas del Burgo and D⁹. Juan B. Pomerague to establish glass-works at the Bastan ; twenty foreign workmen were brought over with this purpose, with their families, and the necessary implements. These gentlemen did not carry out the undertaking to the king's satisfaction, and in 1720 his majesty gave D⁹. Juan de Goyeneche special privileges that he might "make every kind of glass manufacture up to the height of twenty inches, and have these glasses worked and polished, embroidered and covered with metal ; to make looking-glass and similar decorations, and every kind of glass vessels, and white glass for window-panes, and every sort of glass vessel of different kinds and forms which have been invented in the present time, or likely to be invented in this art."

In order to carry this out, the king allowed them to have as many foreign masters and workmen as they might require, with the sole condition that a fourth part of the workmen employed should be Spaniards. It was prohibited that any industry of a similar kind should be established in Spain for thirty years, or that glass made abroad should be imported into the country.

After a long series of annoyances of every kind, Goyeneche succeeded in meeting with the king's approbation, but as fuel was very scarce at the Bastan, he removed the glass works to Villanueva de Alcorcon, in the province of Cuenca. From the ruins of this glass manufactory, Larruga says in his "Memorias," [vol. xiii., p. 274], "was founded the splendid glass manufactory of San Ildefonso."

Ventura Sit, a native of Catalonia, constructed an oven there, which worked from 1728 to 1736 with great success. Queen Doña Isabel encouraged Sit, and the king ordered him to make some glasses which might serve for mirrors. Those he made at first were small, but Sit began by making them 30 inches long and ended by making them as large as 145 inches. The machine for polishing them was invented by a Catalan called Pedro Fronvila.

The section of glass vessels of a superior quality began to work in 1771. Glasses, bottles, and objects of all kinds were made there under the direction of a glass worker called Eder, a Swede, and Sivert, a Frenchman. Another section where the same quality of glass was made was directed by Don Segismundo Brun, a native of Hanover, but who had been brought up from a very early age at La Granja. It was this artist who invented gilded glass *a feu*. A large number of foreign artists worked at this manufacture; they impressed their special style on the objects they made, which were similar to those of the same kind manufactured in France, England, and Germany.

From the time of Ventura Sit, towards the year 1734, the manufactory of glass at La Granja belonged to the crown, and

continued under the protection of the Spanish kings, who spareo
no expense to obtain its development. Early in the present
century this industry began to decay. Towards 1828 it passed
into private hands, and continued to work until 1849. The manufactory is now closed, although there is some talk of reviving this
industry.

The glass objects made at La Granja possess a very marked

GLASS VESSELS FROM SPAIN, IN THE SOUTH KENSINGTON MUSEUM.

French style, which renders them liable to be mistaken for
French and German productions of a similar kind. The greater
part of the objects which were made were of white clear transparent glass, richly cut and engraved, or ornamented with gold
(see woodcut). The cut glass is generally engraved with inscriptions, views, flowers, and devices, and until very lately has been
made there in a rougher style. Coloured and enamelled glass

has also been made there, but not to so great an extent. Glass for window panes and mirrors were ordered for the Royal palaces. Lustres of all kinds of white and coloured glass were also made there in the Venetian style, richly ornamented with coloured flowers. A small chandelier of this kind is in the South Kensington Museum (No. 998, '73), the only example I have seen of a lustre of latticinio glass. In the collection of old Spanish glass at the Museum will be found a sufficient variety of specimens of this manufacture to give an idea of the different styles made at La Granja. A fac-simile of one of the engraved mirrors and a fine cut glass will be found in "Museo Español de Antiguedades, vol. IX."

Besides glass vessels and objects of a similar kind, painted glass windows have been made in Spain from a very early time, of which most important specimens exist at Toledo, Leon, and other Spanish cathedrals. The proceedings employed in this industry are too well known to require repetition in this volume. The industry was undoubtedly imported by foreign workmen from France and the north of Europe, and as was the case with other industries it took root in the country, and a large number of Spanish artists followed and took part in this industry.

In order to convey an idea of the height of this industry in Spain, I give a list of the painters who worked on glass which I have collected from the following works, to which I refer the student who may wish for further details on the subject. Cean Bermudez, "Dicc. Hist. de los mas ilustres Profesores de las Bellas Artes en España. Madrid, 1800." Villanueva, "Viage á las Iglesias de España." Piferrer, "Recuerdos y Bellezas. Mallorca." "Documentos Ineditos." Zarco del Valle.

GLASS PAINTERS IN SPAIN.

Years in which they worked.	Artists.	Residence.
1682.	Alcalde, Francisco.	Burgos.
1504.	Aleman, Cristoval	Toledo.
1458.	Aleman, Pedro	Toledo.
1645.	Alonso, Francisco	Burgos.
1544.	Arce, Juan de	Burgos.
1581.	Arce.	Burgos.
1613.	Argete, Luis de	Leon.
1424.	Aragan, Maestro Joan	Leon.
	Arfian, Antonio	Sevilla.
	Arteaga, Matias	Sevilla.
1516.	Ayala, Francisco	Palencia.
1605.	Babel, Jorge	Madrid.
1442.	Baldovin, Maestro.	Leon.
1519.	Bernal, Juan	Sevilla.
1533.	Borgoña, Jorge	Palencia.
1439.	Bonifacio, Pedro	Toledo.
1562.	Bruges, Carlos	Cuenca.
1602.	Campo, Diego del	Madrid.
1522.	Campa, Juan	Toledo.
1674.	Chilberri, Pierres de.	Segovia.
1509.	Cuesta, Juan de	Toledo.
1513.	Cordova, Gonzalo de	Toledo.
1538.	Cotin, Gaspar de	Burgos.
1459.	Cristoval, El Maestro	Toledo.
1566 to 1573.	Dangles, Sebastian	Mallorca.
1676.	Danis, Juan	Segovia.
1565.	Diaz, Diego	Escorial.
1418.	Dolfin, El Maestro	Toledo.
1485.	Enrique, Maestro	Toledo.
1566.	Estaenheyl, Ulrrique.	Madrid.
1565.	Espinosa, Francisco de	Escorial.
1565.	Espinosa, Hernando de	Escorial.
1551.	Ferrera, Rodrigo de	Leon.
1526.	Fernandez, Pedro	Sevilla.
1557.	Flandes, Arnao de	Sevilla.
1494.	Fontanet, Gil	Barcelona.
1459.	Frances, Pedro	Toledo.

Years in which they worked.	Artists.	Residence.
1571.	Galceran, Il Maestro	Escorial.
1518.	Gelandia, Bernardino de	Sevilla.
1608.	Guillermo, Maestro	Leon.
1571.	Guasch, Juan	Tarragona.
1674.	Herranz, Francisco	Segovia.
1520.	Holanda, Alberto de	Burgos.
1548.	Holanda, Geraldo de	Cuenca.
1535.	Holanda, Nicolas de	Burgos.
1509.	Jacques, Juan	Sevilla.
1427.	Juan, Maestro	Burgos.
1510.	Juan, Hijo de Jacobo	Sevilla.
1458.	Juanico	Toledo.
1428.	Loys, Maestro	Toledo.
1600.	Ludeque, Diego de	Madrid.
1569.	Menandro, Vicente	Sevilla.
1538.	Ortega, Alonso de	Toledo.
1534.	Ortega, Juan de	Toledo.
1458.	Pablo, Fray	Toledo.
1459.	Pedro, Maestro	Toledo.
1639.	Perez, Sebastian	Leon.
1553.	Pesquera, Sebastian de	Sevilla.
1600.	Pierres, Antonio	Madrid.
	Resen, Pelegrin	
1565.	Resen, Renerio	Madrid.
1500.	Rolando, Alberto de	Avila.
1500.	Rolando, Nicolas de	Avila.
1624.	Ruiz, Valentin	Burgos.
1625.	Ruiz, Simon	Burgos.
1368—1369.	Sacoma, Francisco	Mallorca.
1420 to 1447.	Sala, Antonio	Mallorca.
1542.	Salcedo, Diego de	Palencia.
1512.	Santillana, Diego	Palencia.
1498.	Santillana, Juan de	Burgos.
1392.	San Amat, Juan	Lerida.
1503.	Troya, Vasco de	Toledo.
1579.	Valerio, Octavio	Malaga.
1562.	Valdivieso, Diego de	Cuenca.
1497.	Valdivieso, Juan	Burgos.
1538.	Vergara, Arnao de	Sevilla.
1521.	Vergara, Nicolas de	Burgos.
1606.	Vergara, Nicolas de, El Mozo	Toledo.

Years in which they worked.	Artists.	Residence.
1574.	Vergara, Nicolas de, el Viejo	Toledo.
1590.	Vegara, Juan de	Toledo.
1518.	Vivan, Juan	Sevilla.
1605.	Volui, Gil	Leon.
1509.	Ximenez, Alexo	Toledo.
1458.	Ximeno	Toledo.

TEXTILE FABRICS.

THE silence of San Isidoro on the subject of textile fabrics in Spain would lead us to suppose that this industry only became important during the Arab domination; the Moors probably imported this industry into Spain from the earliest times of their conquest. A great number of provinces were famed then for the excellence of their textile fabrics; the most important of them, according to the testimony of Moorish and Christian writers, was Almeria. The Cordovese historian, Ash Shakandi, who wrote at the beginning of the 13th century, says: "Almeria is an opulent and magnificent city, whose fame has spread far and wide; the inhabitants are very elegant in their dress. Almeria is the greatest mart in Andalus, Christians of all nations came to its port to buy and sell, and they had factories established in it. From thence the Christian merchants who came to its port travelled to other parts in the interior of the country, where they loaded their vessels with such goods as they wanted. Costly silken robes of the brightest colours are manufactured in Almeria," [Moh. Dyn. in Spain, I. 52]. Almakkari adds, [p. 51]: "But what made Almeria superior to any other city in the world was its various manufactures of silks and other articles of dress, such as the *dibaj* [silken stuff of many colours], a sort of silken cloth surpassing in quality and durability anything else manufactured in other countries; the *tiraz* or costly stuff on which the names of sultans, princes, and other wealthy individuals are inscribed, and of which no less than 800 looms existed at one time; of more inferior

articles such as the *holol* (striped silks) and brocades, there were
1000 looms, the same number were continually employed in
weaving the stuffs called *iskalátón* (scarlet). There were also 1000
for weaving robes called Al jorjáni (Georgian), and another 1000 for
weaving robes called Isbahani, from Isfahan, and a similar number
for Atabi. The manufacture of damask for curtains and turbans
for the women, of gay and dazzling colours, employed a number of
hands equal to that of those engaged in the manufacture of the
above mentioned articles."

An oriental author asserts that Abd-ul-Rahman II. A.D. 825—
852 was the first sultan of his race who introduced into Spain the
use of the *tiraz* [*ib.* Vol. II. 434]. Another explains that Atabi
took the name of a suburb of Bagdad "where were made the stuffs
called *otabi*, composed of cotton and silk of different colours."
[Consult Dozy, ' Dict. des vêtements.']

Ash Shakandi also mentions Malaga as famous for its textile
fabrics; he says—" Malaga is also famous for its manufactures of
silks of all colours and patterns, some of which are so rich that a
suit made out of them will cost many thousands; such are the
brocades with beautiful drawings, and the names of khalifs, amirs,
and other wealthy people, woven in them." [Moham. Dynast. Vol. I.
49.] Further on the same writer adds, "As at Malaga and Almeria,
there are at Murcia several manufactures of silken cloth called *al
washiu thalathat*, [variegated, of many colours.] It is likewise
famous for the fabric of carpets called *tantili*, which are exported
to all countries of the east and west; as also a sort of mat, of the
brightest colours, with which the Murcians cover the walls of their
houses." [*ib.* p. 69.]

Arabic texts are frequently met with which allude to the manufactures of textile fabrics of Granada, Seville, and other towns,
in which their productions are praised, and there is no doubt that
they were very remarkable; for Christian authors of the middle
ages refer to them so continually. Students who wish for a
more extensive idea of this subject must remember the quotations

and information given by Francisque Michel concerning Spanish
stuffs, [Recherches sur le Comm., la Fabric. etc., des Etoffes, etc.
Paris, 1852.] He tells us—"Nous trouverons tout d'abord les pailles
d'Almérie, ville de la côte meridionale d'Espagne, qui jouissait
d'une réputation proverbiale pour la beauté et la finesse de ses
tissus de soie, vantés dans mille endroits de nos vieilles chansons de
geste, de nos anciens poëmes" [Vol. I. p. 284]. Further on he
continues [Vol. I. p. 286], "à l'époque à laquelle appartiennent
les textes, et même auparavant, la culture et la fabrication de la
soie étaient des plus prospères à Almérie et en général dans le
royaume de Grenade. ' Du royaume de Grenade vient cire, soie,
figues, etc.' . . . . ce qu'il y a de bien certain, c'est que les étoffes
d'Espagne étaient célèbres dès le 9e siècle. Anastase le Biblio-
thécaire en parle en quatre endroits sous le nom de *spaniscum ;*
et en plaçant ce tissu à la suite de *fundatum* et du *stauracin* il
nous donne suffisamment à entendre qu'il était de grand prix, et
de soie comme eux. Un biographe de Saint Ansegise, mort en
835, placé de même une couverture d'Espagne, *stragulum, His-
panicum unum,* à la suite de tapis ou teintures.

"Il est malaise de déterminer la matière des étoffes qu'un écri-
vain byzantin du 12e siècle nous dit fabriquées en Espagne et aux
colonnes d'Hercule—tout nous permet de croire qu'elles étaient
de soie de tout ou en partie, ou du moins qu'elles étaient comptées
parmi les tissus précieux . . . Saragosse produisait aussi des draps
d'or—et nous trouvons au 13e siècle que le géographe Edrisi
pouvait dire qu'il y avait dans le seul territoire de Jaen 3000
villages où l'on élevait des vers de soie. Nous savons qu'à
Seville, sous la domination des Maures, elle comptait 6000 métiers
pour ces étoffes de soie. Les règlements municipaux dont les
royaumes de Grenade et de Seville ont été l'objet suffisaient pour
nous apprendre que l'industrie de la soie fut florissante durant le
moyen âge. Nous signalerons les draps d'or et de soie que
D. Pedro de Luna en 1327 apporta à l'infante Léonore, sœur
d'Alphonse XI., à l'occasion de son mariage, et nous savons

qu'un ministre de Pedro le cruel possédait à Toledo 125 coffres de drap d'or et de soie."

Edrisi in his "Déscrip. de l'Afrique et de l'Espagne," [Leyde, 1866,] writing in the 12th century, says p. 239: "Almérie était la ville principale des Musulmans à l'Espagne des moravides. Elle était alors très industrieuse, et on y comptait entre autres 800 métiers à tisser la soie, où l'on fabriquait des étoffes connus sous le nom de *holla*, de *debady*, de *siglaton*, d'*espahani*, de *djordjani*: des rideaux ornés de fleurs, des étoffes ornés de clous, de petits tapis, des étoffes connus sous les noms de *attabi*, de *mi djar*."

To complete this historical information, and especially in order to add details as to the technical character of this manufacture, the Rev. Daniel Rock's interesting introduction to "Textile Fabrics, a Descriptive Catalogue, London, 1870," must be consulted; although, notwithstanding the learned author's remarks, it is extremely difficult, in my opinion, to classify textile fabrics proceeding from Syria, Sicily, or the Spanish Arabs, as all, whether imitations or originals, are similar in manufacture.

M. Michel and Dr. Rock enter into numerous details concerning the ancient names of stuffs, and in order further to illustrate this subject I venture to propose a different etymology than the one given by these writers of the word Samit, Samitum, or Xamet, which, although slightly different in orthography, is met with everywhere in Europe. My opinion is that it means stuff made at Damascus, for the word Sham شام is applied to the name of this town as well as to that of Syria, and the appellative Shami and Shamit شامى شامية appears in the lexicon to express what comes from Damascus or Syria.

The oldest specimen which I know of Spanish Arab textile fabric, is a woollen fragment of very fine quality embroidered in colours, which is at the Real Academia de la Historia, Madrid. It is about 1½ yards long, by 18 inches wide. In medallions embroidered in silks are represented seated figures which appear to be a king, a lady, lions, birds, and quadrupeds. In two borders

occurs the following inscription, repeated in cufic characters : " In
the name of God, clement and merciful : The blessing of God
and happiness for the caliph Iman Abdallah Hixem, favoured of
God, prince of believers."

بسم الله الرحمن الرحيم البركة من الله واليمن والدوم للخلافة الامام عبد الله هشام
الموبد بالله امير المومنين

Hixem reigned from A.D. 979 until the first years of the 11th
century.   This fragment was found inside a small casket on
the altar of a church in the town of San Esteban de Gormaz,
province of Soria, where it was probably taken as a war trophy :
it may be classified as a stuff called *tiraz* طراز, the skirt of
a robe.   An oriental author tells us that among the customs
which contribute to give splendour to sovereignty is that of
putting the name, or some other sign belonging to kings on the
stuffs of their robes ; that these inscriptions are woven into the
material with gold or coloured thread of a different hue to
the ground, and that royal robes were always made of *tiraz*.
The caliphs of Cordova had a place set apart in their palaces
where this stuff was kept : this custom lasted until the 11th
century when it disappeared, and was re-established in the 13th
century with the kings of Granada.   (Moh. Dyn. vol. i., pp. 356
and 397 ; Mus. Esp. de Ant. vol. vi. pp. 464 and 465.)

Another most important object, although less ancient than the
former one, is an Arabian banner which is traditionally believed to
have been taken from the Almohades at the battle of Las Navas,
A.D. 1212.   This banner, which is preserved at the monastery of
Las Huelgas of Burgos, is ten feet high by seven feet three
inches wide.   It is made of a crimson stuff, covered with an
ornamentation woven and embroidered in gold and colours.   In
the centre is a large circle, placed within a square, which is enlarged
in parallel bands.   The four largest bands, which are also the last,
are covered with inscriptions in blue African characters.   The

upper part of this banner is prolonged with several bands, one of which has inscriptions of a similar kind to those already mentioned; other borders contain several sentences in small African letters. The lower part is also prolonged and is terminated by eight points cut in a semicircle, inside which there are discs with illegible inscriptions. Three violet coloured lions, similar in form to those which appear on the arms of Leon, may be seen on three of the sides of the square. In the large circle in the centre of this banner, appears eight times repeated the word "The Empire," الملك. This inscription is embroidered or woven in Cufic characters, in a similar style to those at the Alhambra; it is a strange circumstance that the letters appear on the wrong side, as if this was the back of the stuff; the word which seems to be required to complete this sentence, "God," is also wanting. The large inscriptions in blue of the five bands reproduce Suras of the Koran, and pious sentences in one of the small ones on the upper part. S͏ͬ Fernandez, who has published an article on this banner in Mus. Esp. [vol. vi., p. 469], thinks he finds a date which corresponds with the year A.D. 1140. I am not, however, satisfied with his interpretation of the inscription contained in the large centre circle, or the date he gives; for comparing the ornamentation of this specimen with other textiles, and the designs used in Moorish architecture, it appears to me that it must be considered as belonging to the 14th century. This may be easily accounted for by some historical mistake in the tradition respecting it at the convent of Las Huelgas. It is highly probable that King Alfonso XI. may have given this banner to the convent, and have been mistaken for King Alfonso VIII.; the conqueror of the battle of Las Navas.

The specimens of Spanish moresco stuffs in the Kensington Museum, will be found numbered 51, 121, 124, 125, 152, 160, 180, 241, 244. (V. Dr. Rock's Catalogue.)

The artistic industry of silk manufactures which was initiated in Spain by the Arabs, continued to flourish during the Middle Ages and a great part of the Renaissance. Malaga and Almeria were important centres, but later on this industry was chiefly centred at Granada. The silk fabrics made at Seville, Toledo, Murcia and Valencia were much esteemed. The Moorish style of ornamentation in embroideries and stuffs must soon have fallen into disuse. Owing to the materials of similar kinds imported from Italy, France, Flanders, and other countries, these manufactures were imitated to a great extent, as may be gathered by the immense number of specimens which are still to be met with in Spanish churches. The cathedral of Toledo is quite a museum of objects of this kind, but all the textiles there are woven in the European manner.

The Moorish style in stuffs was preserved at Granada longer than in any other town in Spain. In 1502, ten years after its conquest by the Christians, we find it stated in the " Voyage of Philip le Beau," the father of the Emperor Charles V. : " Grenade est fort marchande, principallement de soyes, car les marchans y achattent la pluspart des soyes que l'on maine en Italie, pour faires les draps de soyes. Le lieu où on les vendt est nommé le Sacquatin. Auprès de ce lieu est une place appellée l'Allecasserie, où on vendt les draps de soyes ouvrés à la Moresque, qui sont moult beaus pour la multitude des couleurs et la diversité des ouvrages, et en font une grande marchandise." [" Collect. de Voyages, par M. Gachard, Bruxelles," 1870, i. 205.] Navagiero, who visited Spain twenty years after, tells us in his "Viaggio fatto in Spagna " [Vinegia 1563, p. 21] : " One enters a place called Alcaiceria which is enclosed within two doors, and full of alleys where the Moors sell silks and embroideries of every kind " [p. 29] : " All sorts of cloths of silks are made there ; the silks made at Granada are much esteemed all over Spain ; they are not so good as those which come from Italy. There are several looms, but they do not yet know how to work them well ; they make good taffetas, sarcenet, and silk serges. The velvets are not bad, but those that are made at Valencia are better in quality."

Dr. Rock considers the following specimens in the Kensington Museum to have been made at Granada: Nos. 26, 27, 60, 65, 73, 128. 161, 166.

Larruga tells us in his "Memorias" [vol. vii. 205], that the silk manufactures established at Toledo consumed in 1480 about 450,000 pounds of silk : they decreased about forty years afterwards. In the ordinances issued from that town in 1494, which were confirmed by the Emperor Charles V. we find that the following stuffs were made at **Toledo** :

" Stuffs of gold and silver which are made in the same manner as satin.

" Satins woven with gold.

" Satins brocaded with silk and gold or silver flowers.

" Silver serges with double filigree.

" Silver and gold materials, which are made like *gorgoran* or serge.

" Silver and gold stuffs which are made like taffetas, spring silver with silk flowers.

" Embroidered stuffs.

" Embroidered stuffs called silver serge, or *berguilia*.

" *Lama*, cloth of silver, shaded with silver watering.

" Plain silk stuffs woven with silver or gold called *restaño*.

" Silk stuffs woven with gold or silver called *relampagos*.

" Serges woven with gold and silver for church vestments.

" Plain filigree serges.

" *Velillo* of silver.

" Satin woven with gold and silver.

" Brocades of different kinds.

" Church vestments.

" Silver *primaveras*.

" Serges for church vestments."

("Ord. Ant. de Toledo," Tol. 1858, p. 223).

Until the middle of the 17th century, Larruga tells us in vol. vii. p. 208 of his "Memorias," the silk manufacture of Toledo was one of those most highly esteemed in Spain; from this time it was superseded by the manufactures of Seville, Granada, Valencia, and others.   These cheapened their productions; but Toledo insisted on keeping to the old Spanish yard and weight in every kind of stuffs.   In 1651 fifty looms belonged to this manufacture, although most of them were established in the suburbs.   In this year there was a great decrease in the price of the coin, and the Genoese introduced a large quantity of silk stuffs, so much so that only twenty looms could be kept working at Toledo.   After this, in 1663, 2061 looms existed there.

The silk manufacture of Toledo continued to lose its import-ance in consequence of the vast importations of foreign silks, but the traditions of this industry have never disappeared from the city.   Larruga, who enters into this subject at great length in the seventh and eighth volumes of his "Memorias," mentions the silk manufacture of Dⁿ. Miguel Gregorio Molero, "who made from the year 1714, under his direction and that of Christoval de Morales, his father-in-law, a large quantity of silk fabrics of wide and narrow materials of every kind, and stuffs woven with silver and gold."   It is an interesting fact that the manufactory of Molero continues to work in the present day, and gold and silver stuffs are made there for ecclesiastical purposes similar in design and manufacture to the early established one of 1714; specimens exist at the South Kensington Museum of the silks made at Toledo by Molero.

Towards the middle of the 18th century the most important centre of artistic silks existed at Talavera, where it was established on a very large scale by King Fernando VI. and supported by the state.   It was founded in 1748 under the superintendence of a Frenchman called Jean Roulière, who was educated at Lyon, a great mechanician, who entered the manufactory with a yearly salary of £450, and 4 per cent. of the sale.   Fine church vestments were made there, and the richest stuffs woven with silver and gold for decorating apartments and furniture, of which a vast quantity remain in the palaces of Madrid, Aranjuez, the Escorial and La Granja. In 1762 the Spanish government handed over this manufactory to the firm of Uztariz and Company; it remained in their hands until 1780, and at this period it continued to be worked for five years by the state; in 1785 it passed to the superintendence of the Tribunal of Commerce entitled Cinco Gremios Mayores de Madrid. The French invasion of 1808 and general decay of the country contributed towards the extinction of this industry.

In a similar manner to the silk manufactures established at Toledo, silks of all kinds were made at Seville, Granada, Murcia, and other provinces, to a very great extent during the 16th and 17th centuries. This industry continues in the present day, and specimens exist at the South Kensington Museum, made in 1874, which recall the ancient style of these stuffs.

EMBROIDERIES.

It is probable that the history of embroidery in Spain followed the same steps as that of gold and silver stuffs, owing to the great similarity which exists between these industries, as may be seen by the banner called de las Navas, which is composed of both these materials. Ornamentation in the Oriental style must have fallen sooner into disuse than in woven fabrics owing to the fashion of introducing figures in ecclesiastical vestments, which much before the Renaissance period became so general in Europe. The first mention which I find of the existence of this artistic industry appears in the Ordenanzas de Sevilla, 1433; it refers to regulating this industry, and preventing certain frauds, by which we may infer its existence from an earlier period. Similar dispositions appear in one of the Ordinances of Toledo, dated 1496, and as sumptuary laws were continually issued we have constant references to the existence of this industry : [consult "Sempere, Hist. del Lujo," vol. ii. 8vo]. These legal prohibitions did not, however, reach church vestments; after the aggrandizement of the monarchy by the conquest of the New World such enormous sums were spent on these objects, that notwithstanding the ravages of time, wars, disturbances of all kinds, and vandalisms and neglect, the cathedrals of Toledo and Seville, and many other churches, are museums of this style of art.

The art of embroidery was imported by Italians and Germans early in the 16th century, in the same manner as wood carving, metal work, and other industries. The comparative study of embroideries of different kinds which are preserved in churches and museums in other countries confirms this theory; some have been made in the north and others in the south, while their historical origin may be traced to Italy. In Spain itself this comparison may be made, and the Germanic influence is most apparent. At the cathedral of Burgos there is a fine series of ecclesiastical vestments which Bishop Alonso de Cartagena gave to the cathedral on his return from the council of Bâle, 1431-43. Another series of most important specimens is at Toledo, a present to Cardinal Mendoza by the German emperor Frederic in 1489. In both these instances we find that the embroidery is identical with what was made in Spain at this period, until they changed the Gothic for the Italian Renaissance style.

I must mention two splendid altar frontals of foreign workmanship which exist in Spain, one of them is at the chapel of the Disputation of Barcelona ; it represents St. George slaying the dragon. This embroidery is in high relief, and is so perfect in every detail that it appears to be chiselled. Another altar frontal of the same style is at the Colegiata of Manresa, Cataluña ; on this one the Crucifixion is represented, with eighteen other subjects, taken from the Old and New Testaments. This frontal is signed—*Geri Lapi Rachamatore Me fecit in Florentia.*

Almost all Spanish towns of importance are distinguished for their embroidery, Toledo, Seville and Valencia are especially so; Ciudad Rodrigo figures as an important centre of this industry during the 16th century. We find the sentence, "obra de Ciudad Rodrigo" applied to embroidery of gold thread, [Acad. de la Historia, MS. C. 122.] Father Siguenza tells us in his "Hist. de la orden de San Jeronimo" that this style of embroidery was exclusively Spanish, and probably the remains of the Moorish influence. The principal localities where embroideries and artistic work of every kind can be studied are the cathedrals of the towns we have mentioned, which were great centres of artistic industries in other times, and the monastery of the Escorial. The collection at the cathedral of Toledo alone is sufficient to illustrate this subject.

About forty sets of splendid vestments exist at this cathedral which are embroidered with the most exquisite taste, belonging to the 15th and 16th centuries. Each set generally includes a chasuble, dalmatic, cope, altar frontal, covers for the gospel stands, and other smaller pieces. The embroideries on the orphreys, which are formed of figures of saints, are as perfect as the miniatures on illuminated MS. The *manga*, or case which hangs round the processional cross given by Cardinal Ximenez, is one of the most splendid specimens of this collection. As a fine specimen of embroidery on a large scale must be mentioned the *dosel* or canopy called the tent of Ferdinand and Isabel, also at the cathedral of Toledo, which is interesting as being the same which was used in the reception of the English envoys Thomas Salvaige and Richard Nanfan who were sent in 1488 to Spain to arrange the marriage of Prince Henry with the Infanta D⁻ Catalina. The ambassadors describe it in the following manner: "After the tilting was over, the kings returned to the palace, and took the ambassadors with them, and entered a large room : and there they sat under a rich cloth of state of rich crimson velvet, richly embroidered with the arms of Castile and Aragon, and covered with the device of the king, which is a . . .

(blank in original), and his motto, written at length, which is 'Tanto Monta.'" ("Memorials of King Henry the Seventh," Gairdner, Lon. 1858, p. 348.)

The most remarkable specimen of embroidery which exists in Spain, not so much on account of its artistic merit as for the enormous value of the materials employed, is the mantle of the Virgin del Sagrario at Toledo. It is completely covered with pearls and jewels forming a most effective ornamentation. This embroidery was made in the beginning of the 17th century, during the lifetime of Cardinal Sandoval, who presented it to the church. Sr. Parro in his exhaustive volume of "Toledo en la Mano," [vol. i., p. 574,] describes it in the following manner: "It is made of twelve yards of silver lama, or cloth of silver, which is entirely covered with gold and precious stones. In the centre there is a jewel of amethysts and diamonds. Eight other jewels appear on each side of enamelled gold, emeralds and large rubies; a variety of other jewels are placed at intervals round the mantle, and at the lower part are the arms of Cardinal Sandoval enamelled on gold and studded with sapphires and rubies. The centre of this mantle is covered with flowers and pomegranates embroidered in seed-pearls of different sizes. Round the borders are rows of large pearls. Besides the gems which were employed in this superb work of art, no less than 257 ounces of pearls of different sizes, 300 ounces of gold thread, 160 ounces of small pieces of enamelled gold, and eight ounces of emeralds were used."

A fine altar frontal of a similar kind embroidered in corals may be seen in the same room where this mantle of the Virgin is kept at the cathedral of Toledo.

We find in Madame de Villars' letters, [p. 39, Paris, 1823,] the description of a similar embroidery. Writing in 1680 she says, "Ce que j'ai vu de plus riche, de plus doré, de plus magnifique, est l'appartement de la reine. Il y a entre autres meubles dans sa chambre, une tapisserie, dont ce qu'on y voit de fond, est de perles. Ce ne sont pas des personnages, on ne peut dire que l'or y soit massif, mais il est employé d'une manière et d'une abondance extraordinaires. Il y a quelques fleurs : ce sont des bandes de compartimens ; mais il faudrait être plus habile que je ne suis pour représenter les choses, pour vous faire comprendre la beauté que compose le corail employé dans cet ouvrage. Ce n'est point une matière assez précieuse pour en vanter la quantité ; mais la couleur et l'or qui paraissent dans cette broderie, sont assurément ce qu'on aurait peine à décrire."

From the period when these embroideries were made until the middle of the 18th century, Spanish embroideries lost much of their artistic character, although the work itself continued equally excellent. During the whole of the 17th century, a style of embroidery became very general in Spain, which appears to have been copied from eastern importations by the Portuguese or the Spanish possessions in America. The specimens most generally met with in Spain are chiefly bed covers, the ground of which is either linen or satin, embroidered in chain stitch, with figures and exotic birds and animals. Their effect is very rich, and the ornamentation is arranged generally in circles. Specimens exist in England of this kind of work ; for example, a quilt, said to have been made for an Archbishop of Toledo, lent by Lady Cornelia Guest to the Special Exhibition of Embroidery held at South Kensington in 1873.

At the Mus. Arq., Madrid, is a fine quilt of this kind embroidered with maize-coloured silk on linen, with representations of figures and animals.

Embroideries were made in Spain to cover furniture. Sedan chairs, coffers, &c., were ornamented in this manner. At the Kensington Museum there is an interesting example of a trunk with silver lock, covered with embroidery, which was given towards 1680 by Count Olivares to the nuns at Loeches. Some fine embroidered tapestries belonging to the same collection are at the Museo Arquelogico, Madrid. A varied collection of ecclesiastical vestments of the kinds described may also be studied at the museum. (V. Nos. 78, 79, 84, 673, 1194, 1195, 1250, &c., in Dr. Rock's Catalogue.)

The sumptuary laws, and especially the Decrees issued by Philip IV. in 1622, prohibited any display or ostentation in costume, and embroideries were confined to ecclesiastical purposes. In the middle of the 18th century embroideries were introduced in the costumes of men and women when French fashions were imported into Spain. Although many of them came from France, they were imitated in Spain to a large extent. A guild of embroiderers was formed in 1779, who submitted their statutes to the Tribunal of Commerce. We find that Madrid was the principal centre of this industry, and that French designs were universally copied, as was the case in the whole of Europe. The splendid curtains and embroidered hangings for apartments which exist at the royal palaces of Madrid, the Escorial and Aranjuez, are admirable specimens of this industry.

The following list of Spanish embroiderers is taken from Cean's " Dic. de Prof de las Bellas Artes;" Martinez, " Hist. del Templo Cat. de Burgos;" Suarez de Figueroa, " Plaza Universal," etc.

Years in which they worked.	Artists.	Residence.
1603.	Alcala, Fr. Fernando de .	Escorial.
1526.	Alonso, Esteban	Toledo.
1688 to 1715.	Arroyo, Diego de .	Burgos.
1594.	Aspe, Simeon de	Burgos.
1646.	Ansin, Francisco de	Burgos.
1500.	Barcelona, Fr. Rafael de	Escorial.
1599.	Berrio, Francisco de	Burgos.
1452.	Bilbao, Juan	Burgos.
1514.	Burgos, Pedro	Toledo.
1574 to 1580.	Camiña, Alonso	Burgos.
1580 to 1593.	Camiña, Miguel, a son of Alonso	Burgos.
1580.	Castillo, Juan del	Madrid.
1571.	Cordova, Fr. Francisco .	Escorial.

Years in which they worked.	Artists.	Residence.
1616.	Corral, Felipe de.	Toledo.
1514.	Covarrubias, Marcos de	Toledo.
1422.	Fernandez, Garcia	Burgos.
1422.	Fernandez, Pedro	Burgos.
1645.	Garcia de Jalon, Juan	Burgos.
1500.	Gil Francisco	Madrid.
1688.	Gomez, Juan	Sevilla.
1514.	Hernandez, Alonso	Toledo.
1630.	Landa, Alonso de	Burgos.
1625.	Martinez de Manurga, Sebastian	Burgos.
1521.	Monte, Cornieles de	Burgos.
1576.	Montserrate, Fr. Lorenzo	Escorial.
1580 to 1593.	Ochandiano, Andrès	Burgos.
1595.	Ortiz de Zarate, Pedro	Burgos.
1565.	Palenzuela, Francisco de	Burgos.
1591.	Palenzuela, Jeronimo	Burgos.
1500.	Perez, Gabriel	Madrid.
1580.	Perez, Juan	Madrid.
1514.	Rica, Hernando de la	Toledo.
1500.	Rosales	Toledo.
1500.	Rosicler, Luis de	Madrid.
1514.	Ruiz, Martin	Toledo.
1716 to 1734.	Ruiz, Antonio	Burgos.
1585.	Rutinez, Diego	Escorial.
1563.	Salas, Juan de	Granada.
1718.	Santos Martires, Fr. Esteban de los	Cardeña. Burgos.
1561.	Sarabia	Burgos.
1514.	Talavera, Juan de	Toledo.
1500.	Toledo, Fr. Juan de	Escorial.
1752.	Transmontana, Fr. F. Javier de	Burgos.
1684.	Valle, Antonio del	Burgos.
1500.	Vega, Felicis de	Madrid.
1563.	Villegas, Nicolas de	Granada.
1502.	Xaques, el Maestro	Toledo.

TAPESTRIES.

The manufacture of tapestry or carpets was introduced into Spain by the Arabs.   The earliest historical information which I have been able to find relating to this industry occurs in Edrisi, an oriental author of the beginning of the 12th century, ["Descrip. de l'Afr. et de l'Esp., trad. de Dozy el Goeje,"] when speaking of Chinchilla in the province of Alicante, he says : "On y fabrique des tapis de laine qu'on ne saurait imiter ailleurs, circonstance qui dépend de la qualité de l'air et des eaux."   In mentioning Cuenca, he says : "Les tapis de laine qu'on y fait sont d'excellente qualité," p. 237.   Although we find very few descriptive details of this industry, it is undoubtedly the fact that in a wide zone which comprehends from the kingdom of Valencia until that of Granada, carpets have been constantly made ; for even in the present day this industry is alive in a number of towns, where not only the old technical proceedings are continued, but also much of the primitive character of the designs and colours.   In confirmation of this, I find frequent mention in books and MSS. of the 16th century of carpets of Letur, made in the kingdom of Murcia, Alcaraz, and Baeza.

The first time I find this industry mentioned by Christian authors is in Francisque Michel's work on "Étoffes de Soie," vol. i., p. 292 ; he says : "A une époque qu'il nous serait difficile de préciser un poète Latin vantait les teintures précieuses à sujets, et les tapis d'Espagne."

"Tunc preciosa suis surgunt aulaea figuris.

"Ac in se raptis ora tenent animis.

"Tunc operosa suis *Hispana tapetia* villis.

"Hinc rubras, virides inde ferunt species."

At the cathedral of Gerona an extremely interesting tapestry of the 12th century may be seen, which may have been made in the locality.

TAPESTRY AT THE

This tapestry is about 4½ yards wide by 4 yards high. The composition represents the Genesis. In the centre is a geometrical figure formed by two concentric circles. In the lesser circle is a figure of Christ holding an open book, on which appear the words, *Sanctus Deus*, and on each side *Rex fortis*, surrounded by the inscription, *Dixit quæque Deus, Fiat lux, Et facta est lux.* In the larger circle are the words, *In principio creavit Deus cœlum et terram, mare et omnia quæ in eis sunt, et vidit Deus cuncta quæ egerat et erant valde bona.*

The space between the two circles is divided by radiating lines into eight portions, in which are represented the Mystic Dove, the angels of light and darkness: the division of land from water, the creation of sun, moon, and stars, of birds, fishes, and beasts, and of Adam and Eve. In the angles outside the larger circle are the four winds, and the whole is surrounded by a border, imperfect in parts, containing representations of the months, and apparently of certain scriptural incidents, too much defaced to be clearly made out. The accompanying engraving, though imperfect and inaccurate in some of its details, gives a general idea of this work.

Although this tapestry is embroidered with crewels on linen, it appears advisable to include it in the description of Spanish tapestries, owing to its similarity and general aspect to other tapestries. It is easy for students of Spanish works of art of the Middle Ages to fix the period and style to which this example belongs. Several remarkable illuminations exist in Spain representing the Apocalypse which were painted in the X. XI. and XIIth. centuries, which have already been alluded to in other articles of this work. The figures of the tapestry of Gerona are disposed in a precisely similar manner to the miniatures of the 12th century. They are in the same style as the paintings on the ceiling of the chapel of St. Catalina, at St. Isidoro of Leon, which were painted at that period. There can be therefore no doubt that they belong to that period and style. Several MSS. may be

mentioned to further illustrate the subject. An excellent specimen
is at the cathedral of Gerona, those at the National Library,
Museo Arqueologico, and Academia de la Historia, Madrid,
Escorial, Bibliotheque Nationale, Paris—and especially the fine
MS. at the British Museum (Add. II. 695),—dated A. D. 1109,
referred to in the chaper on Arms, page 90. The illuminations
of this volume are extremely similar to the design of this tapestry.
Plate 83, twelve inches by eight, within a circle, representing
Christ holding a book in his hand, may be given as an example.

I do not find any information of a later date which suggests the
existence of the manufacture of tapestries in Spain during the
Middle Ages. There are constant allusions to the splendid
tapestries which were brought from Flanders, many of which are
at the Royal palace of Madrid. The earliest mention I find is a
memorial printed without date, in which Pedro Gutierrez, tapestry
maker of Salamanca, asks Philip II. to protect this industry. He
evidently gained his object, for in the documents published by
Sʳ. Cruzada in his "Tapices de Goya," [Madrid, 1870,] it appears
that in 1578 Queen Doña Ana appointed him to work in her
Camara as tapestry maker to make *reposteros*,* and Philip II. in
1582 confirms this appointment. Gutierrez worked at this
period. at Salamanca and Madrid. He was succeeded in his
charge in 1625 by Antonio Ceron, who established this industry
definitively in the Calle de Santa Isabel at Madrid. The fine
picture by Velasquez, at the Madrid Gallery, "The Weavers,"
which represents the interior of the tapestry manufactory, belongs
to this time. We find this industry soon fell into decay. In 1694
a Belgian named Juan Metler tried to revive it, but without suc-

---

* *Reposteros* is the ancient name given to the hangings which are placed
outside the balconies on state occasions in Spain. Several splendid examples
of the sixteenth and seventeenth centuries may still be seen at the houses of
Spanish grandees, of which those belonging to the Conde de Oñate and
Marques de Alcañices at Madrid are the most remarkable for their artistic
design.

cess; the same thing occurred with Nicolas Hernandez, a tapestry maker of Salamanca, in 1707.

The tapestry manufactory of Santa Barbara at Madrid was founded soon after; it was the most important of all, and continues to produce excellent work in the present day. It appears that Jacobo Vandergoten of Antwerp was engaged expressly by the king; he began to work in 1720, and continued there until his death in 1724. He was succeeded by his sons, Francisco, Jacobo, Cornelius, and Adrian, who worked in *basse lisse* looms until 1729, when a Frenchman, Antonio Lenger mounted a *haute lisse* one.

On the occasion of the temporary removal of the court to Seville, the king established a tapestry manufactory there in 1730; Jacobo Vandergoten was put at the head of it, and the painter, Andres Procaccini, helped him in the direction of the manufactory. It only lasted three years, at the end of which the artists returned with their implements to establish themselves in the old tapestry manufactory of the Calle de Santa Isabel: and continued to work there until 1744, at that time they again joined the works at Santa Barbara.

Three of the brothers Vandergoten were already dead in 1774. Cornelius alone was alive. In the same year the Spanish artists, Antonio Moreno, Domingo Galan, Tomas del Castillo, and Manuel Sanchez were placed at the head of these works, under the superintendence of Sanchez, who continued there until his death in 1786, when he was succeeded by his nephew, Livinio Stuck. This manufactory was much neglected at the end of the last century; it was destroyed by the French in 1808, and was rehabilitated in 1815 under the direction of a son of Stuck. This family continues to work there in the present day. The carpets made at the manufactory of S$^{ta.}$ Barbara are of the highest excellence and artistic order.

Very fine tapestries have been made at this manufactory during the last century, some after original cartoons of excellent painters

and others reproductions of ancient Flemish ones belonging to
the royal collections.   During the years 1721 to 1724 the tapestries
representing pastoral subjects after Teniers were woven there,
and a series of hunting subjects which still exist at the Pardo and
palace of Madrid.   The excellent copy of the series of tapestries
representing the conquest of Tunis, after cartoons by William
Pannemaker were made partly at Seville and partly at Santa
Isabel and Santa Barbara.   The tapestries representing scenes
from the life of Don Quixote, designed by the painter Procaccini,
were also made at the looms of Santa Barbara.

Fine carpets in the Turkish style were made there under the
superintendence of Cornelius Vandergoten, who excelled in this
special industry.   Carpets also in the French style of the Gobelin
manufactory were made at the same time.   The best specimens
of carpets and tapestries of the manufactory of Santa Barbara,
will be found at the palaces of the Escorial, the Pardo, and
Madrid.   The series made from cartoons of Teniers and the
Spanish painter Goya are extremely interesting.   A complete
collection of photographs of the foreign and Spanish tapestries at
the palace of Madrid will be found in the Art Library of the
South Kensington Museum.

LACE.

IT is not easy to give a clear idea of the history of the manufacture of ancient Spanish lace; the principal reason being that this industry was carried out by private persons, who never formed themselves into Guilds or corporations, as was the case during the middle ages and Renaissance period with those who devoted their time to other arts and industries. We find in the Royal Ordinances constant references to weavers, silver and goldsmiths, tailors, etc., but in none do we find the manufacture of lace mentioned. The most important Ordinances relating to Spanish industries are those published at Toledo and Seville in the 15th and 16th centuries, and at Granada in the 16th and 17th centuries, and in none of them do we find lace even alluded to. In the innumerable laws which appeared from the middle ages until the 18th century for the object of reforming costumes and checking their excessive luxury no mention is made of lace; when it is referred to, it is only when *puntas* or *entredoses*, edgings or insertions, are mentioned in which gold and silver are introduced. We never find any allusion in contemporary writers to the fine heavy thread lace, sometimes called Point d'Espagne or Point de Venise, the origin of which has been a source of so much doubt to collectors of the present day.

The only thing which we can do therefore at the present, until this subject is more fully investigated, is to assert that lace of different kinds has been made from the very earliest times in Spain, and do our best to classify the different kinds by the differences which we observe in those of other localities.

T

Father Fr. Marcos Antonio de Campos in his " Microcosmia y Gobierno Universal del Hombre Cristiano," [Barcelona, 1592, p. 225,] says : " I will not be silent and fail to mention the time lost these last years in the manufacture of *cadenetas*, a work of thread combined with gold and silver ; this extravagance and excess reached such a point that 100 and 1000 of ducats were spent in this work, which, besides destroying the eyesight, wasting away the lives, and rendering consumptive the women who worked it, and preventing them from spending their time with more advantage to their souls, a few ounces of thread and years of time, were wasted with so unsatisfactory a result.   I ask myself, after this fancy has passed away, will the lady or gentleman find that the chemises that cost them 50 ducats, or the *basquiña* (petticoats) that cost them 300, are worth half their price, which certainly is the case with other objects in which the material itself is worth more."   This quotation is interesting as proving that lace was made during the 16th century.   The friar, in following the prevalent fashion of preaching against luxury and extravagance, shows us that this industry must have reached to a great height in order to be an object of censure.

From the 16th century until the end of the 18th we find this manufacture continued in Spain, but that foreign lace of different kinds was likewise imported to a great extent, although we may affirm that black lace especially was made in Spain during the whole period.

We find lace mentioned by ancient Spanish authors under the following names : *punta, randa, cadeneta, entredos, red, deshilado, franja, blonda,* and *encaje,* which may be translated as edging, or points, réseuil, chain stitch, insertion, netting, ravelling, fringe, blonde, and lace.

M. H. de Cocheris in his introduction to "Patrons de Broderies," Paris, 1872, says that "gold and silver laces were made at Paris and Lyons."   The four books which are reproduced in this volume mention Lyons as being a great centre of this particular branch of industry. Gold and silver lace was, however, also made and copied in Spain during the 17th century. We find in the "Pragmatica y Nueva Orden cerca de los Vestidos y Trajes, asi de Hombres como de Mugeres," [fol. Madrid 1611, p. 5,] "May we be allowed to border or edge the said silken materials with thread lace, which are not to be made of chain stitch, or gold or silver, and when these laces are mentioned we should understand they are exclusively for women's use." We also find in an Ordinance of the time of Philip III., dated 1623, that gold and silver lace was prohibited, and that "simple edgings, and cuffs, and fraises for women were enjoined for women's use." In the " Fenix de Cataluña, compendio de sus Antiguas Grandezas y Medio para Renovarlas," Barcelona, 1683, by Narciso Feliu, the author states, p. 75, that "edgings of all sorts of gold, silver, silk, thread, and aloe, is made there with greater perfection than in Flanders."

Many interesting details have reached us of the costume of a Spanish lady in the 17th century. We will copy the description given by Madame d'Aunoy in her "Voyage d'Espagne," Lyon 1628. " Under the vertingale of black taffety they wear a dozen or more petticoats, one finer than the other, of rich stuffs trimmed with lace of gold and silver to the girdle. They wear at all times a white garment called sabenqua; it is made of the finest English lace, and four ells in compass. I have seen some worth 500 or 600 crowns, and so great is their vanity, they would rather have one of those lace subenquas than a dozen coarse ones, and either lie in bed till it is washed, or else dress themselves without any, which they frequently enough do." A number of portraits exist in the Spanish galleries, especially by Velasquez and Carreño, in which these extravagant costumes are fully portrayed, but in very few Spanish portraits of the seventeenth century does thread lace of the kind known as Point d'Espagne or de Venise ever appear. Mrs. Palliser, in her interesting " History of Lace," p. 80, quotes a vast number of descriptions of these gold and silver laces.

The celebrated bed at Versailles, the interior lacings of the carriages, the costumes of the gentlemen and ladies of court, and wedding dresses, were all trimmed with this silver and gold lace, either made in Spain, or called Point d'Espagne.

We copy again Madame d'Aunoy's description of a Spanish bed. "It is of gold and green damask lined with silver brocade and trimmed with point of Spain. Her sheets were laced round with an English lace half an ell deep. The young Princess of Monteleon bade her maids bring in her wedding clothes. They brought in thirty silver baskets so heavy four women could only carry one basket : the linen and lace were not inferior to the rest." Beckford, in describing the apartment of a Spanish lady, writes : " Her bed was of the richest blue velvet trimmed with point lace." Aarsens de Sommerdyck in his " Voyage d'Espagne," [Paris, 1665,] writes, in describing the costume worn by the men : " Leurs collets ou cravates sont de grandes pointes, qui sans doute coustent beaucoup, bien qu'elles ne paroissent pas belles. La mode en est presque la mesme qu'en France, l'ayant prise de la princesse de Carignan quand elle estoit à Madrid, dont elles les nomment Valonas à la Carignan." In the interesting " Journal du Voyage d'Espagne," Paris, 1669, l'Abbé Bertaut tells us that on the 15th of October, 1659, on the occasion of his embassy to Madrid, the king of Spain sent eight postilions, and forty post-horses, the saddles and bridles of eight of which were covered with gold and silver lace.

Notwithstanding the opinion of so competent an authority as Mrs. Palliser, I doubt the statement, finding no evidence to support it, that thread lace of a very fine or artistic kind was ever made in Spain, or exported as an article of commerce during early times. The lace alb, which is mentioned, to prove this, as existing at Granada, a gift of Ferdinand and Isabel, is of Flemish lace of the 17th century. The chasuble, etc., splendid ecclesiastical vestments embroidered on crimson velvet, were certainly the gift of these kings, and if Cardinal Wiseman officiated in this vestment, it is probable he may have made a mistake and not separated the alb from the chasuble, which certainly may be worth 10,000 crowns. J. Barretti, in his "Journey from London to Genoa, through Portugal and Spain," London, 1770, describing the fine church of Las Salesas, lately built, writes, "The nuns showed me in the sacristy some surplices for the mass priest, that are made of the finest Flanders lace. Each surplice has cost about 1000 doubloons." In "Tassa de los Precios a que se han de vender as Mercaderias," Madrid, 1628, we find that the "puntas or edgings made in Spain are to be sold at the same price as those imported from Paris." Puntas from Flanders are estimated in this tariff at a much higher rate than those which were brought from France; we may calculate they were sold for double the price. The "Ordenaciones" made at Barcelona to settle commercial tariffs state in 1704: "As experience has shown us that most of the edgings or puntas made in this principality are sent out of the country, and we do not find them mentioned in the financial accounts, to the great disadvantage of the community, it is determined—"

We find reference to lace brought from Flanders, Paris, and Lyon, in the first volume of "Apendice a la Educacion Popular," [p. 61.] [Madrid, 1775,] the author mentions the large sums of money which were taken out of the country by the importations of foreign lace, and he adds, [vol. ii., p. 61,] "Lace is employed to a very considerable extent; all the fine qualities come from foreign lands, and the greater varieties of the coarser ones. Spanish matrons, among other branches of their education, are taught to make lace of different kinds, and many respectable people live on this industry." Larruga, in his "Memorias," Madrid, 1788, mentions, vol. ii., p. 149, a manufacture of gold and silver lace which had been set up lately at Madrid; and in the 17th vol., p. 294, in mentioning lace made at La Mancha, "the industry of lace has existed at Almagro from time immemorial. Dⁿ. Manuel Fernandez and Dᵃ Rita Lambert, his wife, natives of Madrid, established in this town in 1766 a manufacture of silk and thread lace." This industry also existed at Granatula, Manzanares, and other villages of La Mancha. At Zamora "lace and blonde were made in private houses. The finest kinds are sold to lace merchants." In Sempere, "Historia del Lujo," [Madrid, 1788, 8vo,] we find that in the Ordinance issued in 1723, the "introduction of every sort of edgings or foreign laces was prohibited, the only kinds allowed were those made in the country."

Cabanillas writes in his "Observaciones sobre la Historia natural del Reino de Valencia," Madrid, 1797, that at Novelda a third part of the inhabitants made lace, "more than 2000 among women and children worked at this industry, and the natives themselves hawked these wares about the country." Swinburne, in his "Travels in Spain in 1775," also says, "The women of the hamlets were busy with their bobbins making lace." Laborde writes that in 1809 the manufacture of blonde was almost entirely confined to Cataluña. Barcelona is in the present day the great centre of this industry in Spain ; the black and white blondes which are made chiefly for mantillas are very fine. The white laces made there are in the style of Lille and Buckinghamshire laces, Brussels and Duchesse laces, and Chantilly is also made to a large extent. Gold and silver blondes were revived during the years 1830—40 ; and it may interest my readers to know that the late Queen Mercedes, in her wedding trousseaux, had a garniture de robe, mantilla included, of gold blonde.

Modern torchon laces are still made at Almagro to a very large extent. Bed linen, even in the poorest houses, is elaborately trimmed with lace or embroidery. Valances for beds of ravellings, point coupé and lace work are still constantly found to decorate beds at weddings in the provinces of Spain.

THE END.

RICHARD CLAY AND SONS, LIMITED, LONDON AND BUNGAY.